United States

1740–1919

Derrick Murphy ■ **Mark Waldron** ■ **Kathryn Cooper**

Collins

Published by Collins
An imprint of
HarperCollinsPublishers
77–85 Fulham Palace Road
Hammersmith
London W6 8JB

Browse the complete Collins catalogue
at www.collinseducation.com

ISBN-978 0 00 726874 0

British Library Cataloguing in
Publication Data
A Catalogue record for this
publication is available from the
British Library

Original series commissioned by
Graham Bradbury
This edition commissioned by
Michael Upchurch
Edited by Graham Bradbury
Design and typesetting by Derek Lee
Cover design by Joerg
Hartmannsgruber, White-card
Map Artwork by Tony Richardson
Picture research by Celia Dearing
and Michael Upchurch
Production by Simon Moore
Indexed by Malcolm Henley, Henley
Indexing
Printed and bound by CPI Group
(UK) Ltd, Croydon, CR0 4YY

ACKNOWLEDGEMENTS
Every effort had been made to
contact the holders of copyright
material, but if any have been
inadvertently overlooked the
publishers will be pleased to make
the necessary arrangements at the
first opportunity.

The publishers would like to thank
the following for permission to
reproduce pictures on these pages.
T=Top, B=Bottom, L=Left, R=Right,
C=Centre

Private Collection, Peter Newark
Military Pictures / The Bridgeman
Art Library 101, 106; Private
Collection, Peter Newark American
Pictures / The Bridgeman Art Library
137; Private Collection, The
Stapleton Collection / The
Bridgeman Art Library 121(T);
Private Collection, / The Bridgeman
Art Library 23; © Corbis 52, 63, 85,
89, 115, 133, 157, 158, 186;
© Stefano Bianchetti/Corbis 17;
© The Gallery Collection/Corbis 31;
© Bettmann/CORBIS 51, 76, 82 162;
© Christie's Images/CORBIS 68;
© Sunset Boulevard/Corbis 70;
© The Mariners' Museum/CORBIS
121 ©; © David Jay
Zimmerman/Corbis 121 (B); © The
Mariners' Museum/CORBIS 150;
© Lake County Museum/CORBIS
182 (T); © Minnesota Historical
Society/CORBIS 182 (B); Unknown
137, 171.

Contents

Study and examination skills

This section of the book is designed to aid Sixth Form students in their preparation for public examinations in History.

- Differences between GCSE and Sixth Form History
- Extended writing: the structured question and the essay
- How to handle sources in Sixth Form History
- Historical interpretation
- Progression in Sixth Form History
- Examination technique

Differences between GCSE and Sixth Form History

- The amount of factual knowledge required for answers to Sixth Form History questions is more detailed than at GCSE. Factual knowledge in the Sixth Form is used as supporting evidence to help answer historical questions. Knowing the facts is important, but not as important as knowing that factual knowledge supports historical analysis.

- Extended writing is more important in Sixth Form History. Students will be expected to answer either structured questions or essays.

Structured questions require students to answer more than one question on a given topic. For example:

(a) What were the reasons for westward expansion in the USA in the period 1800 to 1860?

(b) How did westward expansion affect the development of the USA in the period to 1860?

Each part of the structured question demands a different approach.

Essay questions require students to produce one answer to a given question. For example:

To what extent was Northern victory in the American Civil War due to economic reasons?

Similarities with GCSE

● **Source analysis and evaluation**
The skills in handling historical sources, which were acquired at GCSE, are developed in Sixth Form History. In the Sixth Form, sources have to be analysed in their historical context, so a good factual knowledge of the subject is important.

● **Historical interpretations**
Skills in historical interpretation at GCSE are also developed in Sixth Form

History. The ability to put forward different historical interpretations is important. Students will also be expected to explain why different historical interpretations have occurred.

Extended writing: the structured question and the essay

When faced with extended writing in Sixth Form History students can improve their performance by following a simple routine that attempts to ensure they achieve their best performance.

Answering the question

What are the command instructions?
Different questions require different types of response. For instance, 'In what ways' requires students to point out the various ways something took place in History; 'Why' questions expect students to deal with the causes or consequences of an historical event.

'How far' or 'To what extent' questions require students to produce a balanced, analytical answer. Usually, this will take the form of the case for and the case against an historical question.

Are there key words or phrases that require definition or explanation?
It is important for students to show that they understand the meaning of the question. To do this, certain historical terms or words require explanation. For instance, if a question asked 'how far' a politician was an 'innovator', an explanation of the word 'innovator' would be required.

Does the question have specific dates or issues that require coverage?
If the question mentions specific dates, these must be adhered to. For instance, if you are asked to answer a question on US domestic policy in the period 1865 to 1919.

Planning your answer

Once you have decided on what the question requires, write a brief plan. For structured questions this may be brief. This is a useful procedure to make sure that you have ordered the information you require for your answer in the most effective way. For instance, in a balanced, analytical answer this may take the form of jotting down the main points for and against an historical issue raised in the question.

Writing the answer

Communication skills
The quality of written English is important in Sixth Form History. The way you present your ideas on paper can affect the quality of your answer. Therefore, punctuation, spelling and grammar, which were awarded marks at GCSE, require close attention. Use a dictionary if you are unsure of a word's meaning or spelling. Use the glossary of terms you will find in this book to help you.

The quality of your written English will not determine the Level of Response you receive for answer. It may well determine what mark you receive within a level.

To help you understand this point ask your teacher to see a mark scheme published by your examination board. For instance, you may be awarded Level 2 (10–15 marks) by an examiner. The quality of written English may be a factor in deciding which mark you receive within that level. Will it be 10 or 15 or a mark in between?

The introduction

For structured questions you may wish to dispense with an introduction altogether and begin writing reasons to support an answer straight away. However, essay answers should begin with an introduction. These should be both concise and precise. Introductions help 'concentrate the mind' on the question you are about to answer. Remember, do not try to write a conclusion as your opening sentence. Instead, outline briefly the areas you intend to discuss in your answer.

Balancing analysis with factual evidence

It is important to remember that factual knowledge should be used to support analysis. Merely 'telling the story' of an historical event is not enough. A structured question or essay should contain separate paragraphs, each addressing an analytical point that helps to answer the question. If, for example, the question asks for reasons why the 13 Colonies won the American War of Independence, each paragraph should provide a reason why victory occurred. In order to support and sustain the analysis evidence is required. Therefore, your factual knowledge should be used to substantiate analysis. Good structured question and essay answers integrate analysis and factual knowledge.

Seeing connections between reasons

In dealing with 'why'-type questions it is important to remember that the reasons for an historical event might be interconnected. Therefore, it is important to mention the connections between reasons. Also, it might be important to identify a hierarchy of reasons – that is, are some reasons more important than others in explaining an historical event?

Using quotations and statistical data

One aspect of supporting evidence that sustains analysis is the use of quotations. These can be from either a historian or a contemporary. However, unless these quotations are linked with analysis and supporting evidence, they tend to be of little value.

It can also be useful to support analysis with statistical data. In questions that deal with social and economic change, precise statistics that support your argument can be very persuasive.

The conclusion

All structured questions and essays require conclusions. If, for example, a question requires a discussion of 'how far' you agree with a question, you should offer a judgement in your conclusion. Don't be afraid of this – say what you think. If you write an analytical answer, ably supported by factual evidence, you may under-perform because you have not provided a conclusion that deals directly with the question.

Source analysis

Source analysis forms an integral part of the study of History.

In dealing with sources you should be aware that historical sources must be used 'in historical context' in Sixth Form History. This means you must understand the historical topic to which the source refers. Therefore, in this book sources are used with the factual information in each chapter. Also, specific source analysis questions are included at the end of most chapters.

How to handle sources in Sixth Form History

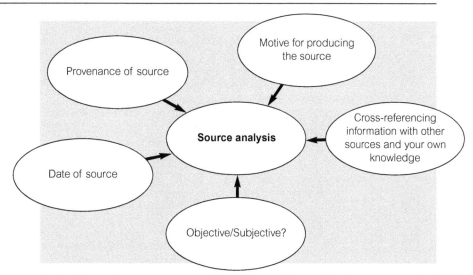

In dealing with sources, a number of basic hints will allow you to deal effectively with source-based questions and to build on your knowledge and skill in using sources at GCSE.

Written sources

Attribution or Provenance and date

It is important to identify who has written the source and when it was written. This information can be very important. If, for instance, a source was written by Abraham Lincoln in 1863, this information will be of considerable importance if you are asked about the usefulness (utility) or reliability of the source as evidence of Lincoln's actions in that year.

It is important to note that just because a source is a primary source does not mean it is more useful or less reliable than a secondary source. Both primary and secondary sources need to be analysed to decide how useful and reliable they are. This can be determined by studying other issues.

Is the content factual or opinionated?

Once you have identified the author and date of the source, it is important to study its content. The content may be factual, stating what has happened or what may happen. On the other hand, it may contain opinions that should be handled with caution. These may contain bias. Even if a source is mainly factual, there might be important and deliberate gaps in factual evidence that can make a source biased and unreliable. Usually, written sources contain elements of both opinion and factual evidence. It is important to judge the balance between these two parts.

Has the source been written for a particular audience?

To determine the reliability of a source it is important to know to whom it is directed. For instance, a public speech may be made to achieve a particular purpose and may not contain the author's true beliefs or feelings. In contrast, a private diary entry may be much more reliable in this respect.

Corroborative evidence

To test whether or not a source is reliable, the use of other evidence to support or corroborate the information it contains is important. Cross-referencing with other sources is a way of achieving this; so is cross-referencing with historical information contained within a chapter.

Visual sources

Cartoons

Cartoons are a popular form of source used at both GCSE and in Sixth Form History. However, analysing cartoons can be a demanding exercise. Not only will you be expected to understand the content of the cartoon, you may also have to explain a written caption – which appears usually at the bottom of the cartoon. In addition, cartoons will need placing in historical context. Therefore, a good knowledge of the subject matter of the topic of the cartoon will be important.

Photographs

'The camera never lies'! This phrase is not always true. When analysing photographs, study the attribution/provenance and date. Photographs can be changed so they are not always an accurate visual representation of events. Also, to test whether or not a photograph is a good representation of events you will need corroborative evidence.

Maps

Maps which appear in Sixth Form History are predominantly secondary sources. These are used to support factual coverage in the text by providing information in a different medium. Therefore, to assess whether or not information contained in maps is accurate or useful, reference should be made to other information. It is also important with written sources to check the attribution and date. These could be significant.

Statistical data and graphs

It is important when dealing with this type of source to check carefully the nature of the information contained in data or in a graph. It might state that the information is in tons (tonnes) or another measurement. Be careful to check if the information is in index numbers. These are a statistical device where a base year is chosen and given the figure 100. All other figures are based on a percentage difference from that base year. For instance, if 1800 is taken as a base year for cotton production in the USA it is given the figure of 100. If the index number for cotton production in 1860 is 333 it means that production has risen by 233% above the 1800 figure.

An important point to remember when dealing with data and graphs over a period of time is to identify trends and patterns in the information. Merely describing the information in written form is not enough.

Historical interpretation

An important feature of both GCSE and Sixth Form History is the issue of historical interpretation. In Sixth Form History it is important for students to be able to explain why historians differ, or have differed, in their interpretation of the past.

Availability of evidence

An important reason is the availability of evidence on which to base historical judgements. As new evidence comes to light, a historian today may have more information on which to base judgements than historians in the past.

'A philosophy of history?'

Many historians have a specific view of history that will affect the way they make their historical judgements. For instance, Marxist historians – who take the view from the writings of Karl Marx the founder of modern socialism – believe that society has been made up of competing economic and social classes. They also place considerable importance on economic reasons in human decision making. Therefore, a Marxist historian of fascism may take a completely different viewpoint to a non-Marxist historian.

The role of the individual

Some historians have seen past history as being moulded by the acts of specific individuals who have changed history. George Washington, Thomas Jefferson and Abraham Lincoln are seen as individuals whose personality and beliefs changed the course of American history. Other historians have tended to 'downplay' the role of individuals; instead, they highlight the importance of more general social, economic and political change.

Placing different emphasis on the same historical evidence

Even if historians do not possess different philosophies of history or place different emphasis on the role of the individual, it is still possible for them to disagree because they place different emphases on aspects of the same factual evidence. As a result, Sixth Form History should be seen as a subject that encourages debate about the past based on historical evidence.

Progression in Sixth Form History

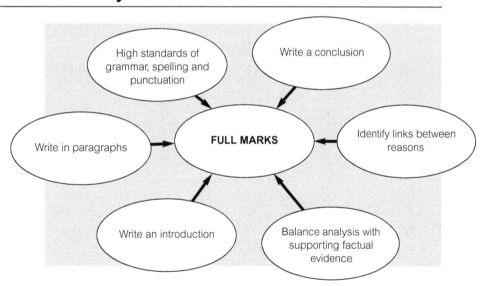

The ability to achieve high standards in Sixth Form History involves the acquisition of a number of skills:

● Good written communication skills

● Acquiring a sound factual knowledge

● Evaluating factual evidence and making historical conclusions based on that evidence

● Source analysis

● Understanding the nature of historical interpretation

● Understanding the causes and consequences of historical events

● Understanding themes in history which will involve a study of a specific topic over a long period of time

● Understanding the ideas of change and continuity associated with themes.

Students should be aware that the acquisition of these skills will take place gradually over the time spent in the Sixth Form. At the beginning of the course, the main emphasis may be on the acquisition of factual knowledge, particularly when the body of knowledge studied at GCSE was different.

When dealing with causation, students will have to build on their skills from GCSE. They will not only be expected to identify reasons for an historical event but also to provide a hierarchy of causes. They should identify the main causes and less important causes. They may also identify that causes may be interconnected and linked. Progression in Sixth Form History will come with answering the questions at the end of each sub-section in this book and practising the skills outlined through the use of the factual knowledge contained in the book.

Examination technique

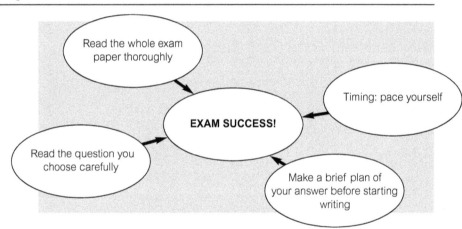

The ultimate challenge for any Sixth Form historian is the ability to produce quality work under examination conditions. Examinations will take the form of either modular examinations taken in January and June or an 'end of course' set of examinations.

Here is some advice on how to improve your performance in an examination.

● **Read the whole examination paper thoroughly**
Make sure that the questions you choose are those for which you can produce a good answer. Don't rush – allow time to decide which questions to choose. It is probably too late to change your mind half way through answering a question.

● **Read the question very carefully**
Once you have made the decision to answer a specific question, read it very carefully. Make sure you understand the precise demands of the question. Think about what is required in your answer. It is much better to think about this before you start writing, rather than trying to steer your essay in a different direction half way through.

Revision tips

Even before the examination begins make sure that you have revised thoroughly. Revision tips on the main topics in this book appear on the Collins website:

www.collinseducation.com

- **Make a brief plan**
  Sketch out what you intend to include in your answer. Order the points you want to make. Examiners are not impressed with additional information included at the end of the essay, with indicators such as arrows or asterisks.

- **Pace yourself as you write**
  Success in examinations has a lot to do with successful time management. If, for instance, you have to answer an essay question in approximately 45 minutes, then you should be one-third of the way through after 15 minutes. With 30 minutes gone, you should start writing the last third of your answer.

Where a question is divided into sub-questions, make sure you look at the mark tariff for each question. If in a 20-mark question a sub-question is worth a maximum of 5 marks, then you should spend approximately one-quarter of the time allocated for the whole question on this sub-question.

1 United States 1740–1919: A synoptic overview

Key Issues

- How did the government of America change between 1740 and 1919?

- How did the USA develop into a major power?

- What were the reasons for the changes in American society in the period 1740–1919?

1.1 How did the relationship between central and local governments change between 1740 and 1919?
1.2 How important was westward expansion?
1.3 What impact did immigration have on the development of America?
1.4 Why did America develop into a major economic power?

1.1 How did the relationship between central and local governments change between 1740 and 1919?

The move to independence

One of the key themes in American history has been the relationship between central government and the localities. Between 1740 and 1783 this was centred on the relationship between the British government and the individual governments of the 13 Colonies. Tensions over trade and taxation formed the basis of growing antagonism, and this became acute after the conclusion of the French and Indian War in 1763. British attempts to make the 13 Colonies pay their way led to colonial resistance, which took many forms. For instance, in response to the Stamp Tax of 1765, colonists engaged in mob violence against officials and boycotted British goods. Of greater significance was the growing support for the idea that the British government did not have the constitutional right to tax the 13 Colonies without their consent. 'No taxation without representation' became a political battle cry in the conflict with Britain, and by 1775 the position had deteriorated so much that fighting broke out between the British army and the Colonists. The American War of Independence had begun.

The Creation of the USA

In 1783 at the Treaty of Paris, the 13 Colonies gained independence from Britain as the newly independent 'United States'. However, the relationship between the now 13 'states' and the new central authority was weak and poorly defined in the 'Articles of Confederation'. It took the Constitutional Convention of 1787 to resolve these difficulties, and the Constitution formulated at that Convention has formed the basis of US government ever since. It established a strong central government – the **Federal Government** – comprising an elected president and Congress. From 1789 it also included a US Supreme Court. As a federal state, political power was divided between the federal government and the state

Federal government: The central government of a country (or group of states) which deals with things concerning the whole country, such as foreign policy. Each state within the Union has it own local powers and laws.

governments. Although the Constitution dealt effectively with many of the shortcomings of the Articles of Confederation it created new questions to be answered – in particular 'How independent were the individual states?'. Amendment 10 of the Constitution, passed in 1791, suggested that those powers that were not expressly given to the Federal Government in the Constitution were state responsibilities. This issue was a major contributory factor to the development of sectional conflict, which eventually erupted into civil war in the years 1861 to 1865.

The growth of sectional conflict

As the USA developed, it became apparent that it comprised two different types of economy and society. The states in the North were developing industry and manufacturing – indeed, by the mid-nineteenth century the Northern states were rivalling Britain as a centre of industrial power. The Southern states, on the other hand, developed differently. They became the centre for the production of cotton and goods such as tobacco, and a key feature of the Southern economy was the employment of African-American slaves to work in large plantations. By the early nineteenth century cotton was 'king' in the Southern states and the basis of its economic wealth. As a result of these differences, the USA was becoming a divided society. The South saw slavery as essential to its economy and way of life. The North saw free labour as the basis of its industrial and economic growth.

In 1819 the first of a series of conflicts occurred about the balance between the sections. Missouri wanted to be admitted to the USA as a slave state, but this would have resulted in slave states outnumbering 'free' states in the US Congress. In the Missouri Compromise of 1820, therefore, Maine was admitted as a free state to balance Missouri's admission. Political compromise on this important sectional issue continued from 1820 to the 1850s.

The 1850s saw a major deterioration in relations between North and South as the American frontier moved westward and new territories were admitted as states. A centre of conflict was Kansas, where both Northern and Southern settlers attempted to influence the territory's decision about whether to be admitted as a free state or a slave state.

Then, in 1860, a turning-point occurred, when Abraham Lincoln was elected president on a platform of not extending slavery westward. As a result, eleven Southern states seceded from the USA. They believed that they had the right, under the Constitution, to control their own affairs. Lincoln and the North believed the USA to be an indissoluble union where, once admitted, states could not leave. The Civil War of 1861 to 1865 resolved this issue in favour of the North, and in the process slavery was abolished.

The rise of segregation in the South

Northern victory in the Civil War did not resolve the sectional conflict between North and South. From 1863 to 1877 the North attempted to 'reconstruct' the South through the imposition of military occupation and the election of pro-Northern state governments. In 1877 the reconstruction came to an end and the Southern states were allowed to develop their own internal self-government. From 1877 to 1919 Southern governments were dominated by Whites who wanted to ensure their position of superiority, not just in politics but also in society. Southern governments began to introduce 'segregation' whereby Whites and African-Americans had separate facilities in education, transportation and housing. These policies were associated with a wave of terror against African-Americans, with the number of lynchings and murders increasing rapidly in the 1890s. The height of this terror came with the 'Red Summer' of 1919.

In 1919, therefore, the USA still seemed to be two different societies. In the North, the USA was free and a modern industrial society. In the South, the Whites and African-Americans lived separate lives in what was still a predominantly agricultural society.

1.2 How important was westward expansion?

Title: To have title over land is to rule or govern it effectively.

Ever since English colonists first settled in Virginia and Massachusetts, the history of America has been one of westward expansion. The 'frontier spirit' has been an important theme in American society. In 1783, when the 13 colonies won independence from Britain, the USA had **title** over territory as far west as the Mississippi river.

During the early history of the Republic, the North American continent was the scene of colonial competition between the USA and several European powers. Britain still controlled Canada and the Oregon territory. The French controlled the vast lands west of the Mississippi. The Russians controlled the Alaskan coast with outposts as far south as Fort Ross in northern California. In Florida and the South and West, a vast Spanish empire existed.

The history of the United States, from its creation until 1890, was to dominate much of the North American continent from the Atlantic to the Pacific. They were able to buy Louisiana from the French in 1803. The Spanish were forced out of Florida in 1819 and they defeated Mexico in a

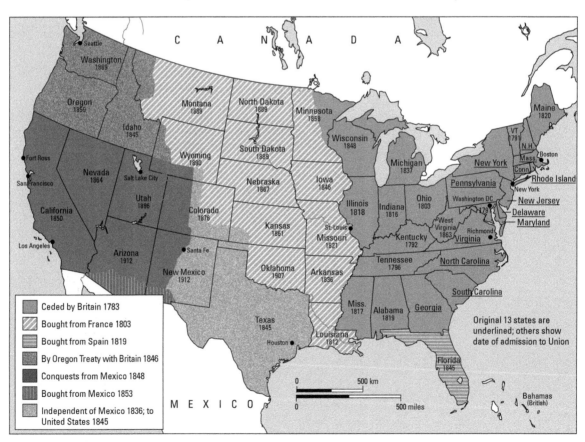

Growth of the United States of America

Admission of states into the Union

State	Date of admission		State	Date of admission
1 Delaware	12 December 1787	25	Arkansas	7 December 1836
2 Pennsylvania	18 December 1787	26	Michigan	26 January 1837
3 New Jersey	2 January 1788	27	Florida	3 March 1845
4 Georgia	9 January 1788	28	Texas	29 December 1845
5 Connecticut	6 February 1788	29	Iowa	28 December 1846
6 Massachusetts	28 April 1788	30	Wisconsin	29 May 1848
7 Maryland	23 May 1788	31	California	9 September 1850
8 South Carolina	21 June 1788	32	Minnesota	11 May 1858
9 New Hampshire	25 June 1788	33	Oregon	14 February 1859
10 Virginia	26 July 1788	34	Kansas	29 January 1861
11 New York	21 November 1789	35	West Virginia	20 June 1863
12 North Carolina	29 May 1790	36	Nevada	31 October 1864
13 Rhode Island	4 March 1791	37	Nebraska	1 March 1867
14 Vermont	1 June 1791	38	Colorado	1 August 1876
15 Kentucky	1 June 1792	39	North Dakota	2 November 1889
16 Tennessee	1 March 1796	40	South Dakota	2 November 1889
17 Ohio	30 April 1803	41	Montana	8 November 1889
18 Louisiana	11 December 1812	42	Washington	11 November 1889
19 Indiana	10 December 1816	43	Idaho	3 July 1890
20 Mississippi	3 December 1817	44	Wyoming	10 July 1890
21 Illinois	14 December 1818	45	Utah	4 January 1896
22 Alabama	15 March 1819	46	Oklahoma	16 November 1907
23 Maine	10 August 1820	47	New Mexico	6 January 1912
24 Missouri	15 June 1821	48	Arizona	14 February 1912

Prairies: The large, flat areas of grassy land in North America, with very few trees.

war (1846–48). They negotiated with the British over Maine and Oregon between 1842 and 1846, and they purchased Alaska from Russia in 1867.

Even though the USA had claim on these vast lands, they still had to be settled and the Native-American peoples defeated. A theme of US history is the conflict between the government and the 250 Indian tribes that inhabited the USA. Superior military technology and divisions amongst the Indian tribes were the main reasons for US success. However, successive governments from the 1830s onwards believed westward expansion was the God-given right to dominate the continent. As a result, Native Americans were treated as second class. In the early 1830s, in defiance of a Supreme Court ruling, President Jackson forced the five 'civilised' tribes of the South-East to move westward to Indian Territory, now the state of Oklahoma. During the course of westward expansion, the US government made and then broke virtually every treaty it ever had with Indian tribes.

It is clear that the westward movement of population, and the settlement and cultivation of the **prairies** were one of the greatest achievements of the 19th century. However, they were achieved at a cost. The vast herds of North-American bison (buffalo) were wiped out and Native-American society was destroyed.

The move westward also had a major impact on the East. With every new admission of a state to the Union (see map opposite and chart above), the issue of whether it should be a free state or a slave state was raised. The uneasy compromises of 1820 and 1850 prevented conflict between the 'free North' and the 'slave South'. However, it was the Kansas–Nebraska Act of 1854 – which created a new territory in the West – that began the chain of events that would lead to civil war by 1861.

By 1890 and the Battle of Wounded Knee, the Indian Wars had come to an end. In Chicago, historian Frederick Jackson Turner declared in 1893 that the Frontier had also come to an end. Yet the spirit of expansion survived. From the 1890s, many Americans began to look for expansion outside North America. This desire was an important factor behind the Spanish–American War. As a result of the war, the USA acquired a colonial empire in the Philippines and Puerto Rico. From 1898, the USA was becoming a world power.

The end of westward expansion helped to launch the USA on to the world stage. With vast mineral wealth, extensive agriculture and industry, the USA rivalled Britain and Germany. The nineteenth century had been based on westward expansion; the twentieth century saw US influence expand across the world.

1.3 What impact did immigration have on the development of America?

Apart from Native Americans, the entire population of the USA is descended from immigrants – people who arrive from another country or continent to live and work in a different country. Up to the time of the American War of Independence, the majority of immigrants came from the British Isles and Germany. Many came for economic reasons, to acquire land and to improve their economic and social standing. Others came to avoid religious persecution – such as the Pilgrim Fathers to Massachusetts, the Quakers to Pennsylvania and the German Amish and Mennonite sects. Those who signed the Declaration of Independence came predominantly from White, Anglo-Saxon, Protestant (WASP) backgrounds.

Immigration came to the USA in two huge waves. Between the 1840s and the Civil War, the 'old immigration' came from Scandinavia, Germany

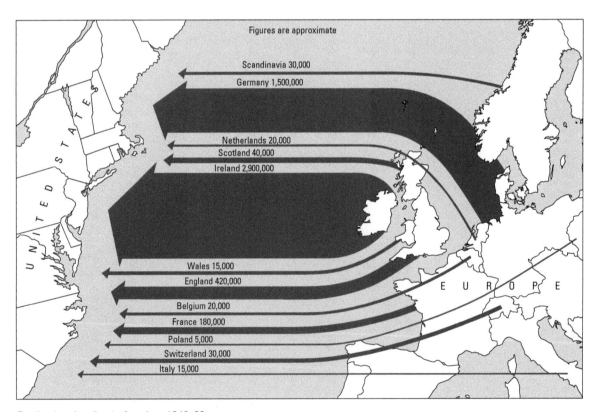

Foreign immigration to America, 1840–60

Growth of US population and area

Census	Population	Land area (square miles)	Population/square mile	% age of population Urban	Rural
1790	3,929,214	867,980	4.5	5.1	94.9
1800	5,308,483	867,980	6.1	6.1	93.9
1810	7,239,881	1,685,865	4.3	7.2	92.8
1820	9,638,453	1,753,588	5.5	7.2	92.8
1830	12,866,020	1,753,588	7.3	8.8	91.2
1840	17,069,453	1,753,588	9.7	10.8	89.2
1850	23,191,876	2,944,337	7.9	15.3	84.7
1860	31,433,321	2,973,965	10.6	19.8	80.2
1870	39,818,449	2,973,965	13.4	24.9	75.1
1880	50,155,783	2,973,965	16.9	28.2	71.8
1890	62,947,714	2,973,965	21.2	35.1	64.9
1900	75,994,575	2,974,159	25.6	39.1	60.3
1910	91,972,266	2,973,890	30.9	45.7	54.3
1920	105,710,620	2,973,776	35.5	51.2	48.8

Source: Census Bureau, *Historical Statistics of the United States*, updated by relevant Statistical Abstract of the United States

Nativist: A supporter of the idea that the USA should be a country of White Anglo-Saxon Protestants (WASPs).

and Ireland. The Irish came mainly as a result of the Great Famine of 1845–49. They were destitute when they arrived in the USA, and the vast majority were Roman Catholic. This sparked off a recurrent theme in 19th- and 20th-century American history: the reaction of WASPs or **Nativist** Americans to the different religions and cultures of the immigrants. In the 1850s, Catholic Irish immigration led to the rise of the 'Know Nothing' party which was anti-Catholic.

After the Civil War, the 'new immigration' began. Not only did it include immigrants from Germany, Ireland and Scandinavia, it also included Jews from Eastern Europe, Italians, Poles and Russians.

Welcome to the Land of the Free. Illustration from 1887.

These immigrant groups had a large impact on US society:

- They provided the cheap labour required to fuel the rapid economic growth of the USA.

- They brought with them skills that were needed for economic development.

- They also brought their own religions and culture.

Cities such as New York and Chicago developed ethnic neighbourhoods inhabited almost exclusively by Italians, Poles, Jews or the Irish.

The WASP resistance to immigration took a variety of forms. The rise of the prohibition movement (see Chapter 3) was in part due to opposition to the drinking excesses of the new immigrants. By the time of the First World War and the 1920s, Nativist opposition seemed to be triumphant. National prohibition was passed in 1918. The Ku Klux Klan was re-formed in 1915. It added Jews and Catholics to the list of groups it opposed and intimidated. Finally, in 1924, immigration was severely restricted. No longer would the words on the Statue of Liberty ring true: 'Bring me your huddled masses yearning to be free.'

These waves of immigration have been met by resistance, but this has not stopped the USA becoming a 'melting pot' of races. However, the 'melting pot' has found it extremely difficult to incorporate one of America's oldest ethnic minorities, African-Americans.

1.4 Why did America develop into a major economic power?

Subsistence agriculture: Growing enough food for personal consumption rather than for surplus and profit.

In 1740 most of what became the United States was wilderness, inhabited by Native American (Indian) tribes who were engaged in hunting and fishing and **subsistence agriculture**. The 13 Colonies which developed on the eastern seaboard were overwhelmingly agricultural, with farming being supplemented by fishing in the coastal states. The Southern colonies developed farming of cash crops, such as cotton and tobacco. On the frontier, the settlers followed economic pursuits not dissimilar to the Native Americans.

But by 1919 the USA was the world's greatest economic power. It dominated world manufacturing and was a major producer of energy and cash crops. How did this transformation occur?

One of the reasons was 'Yankee ingenuity' – the ability of Americans to develop new ways of producing goods. An early exponent was Eli Whitney who, in the 1790s, invented the 'Cotton Gin', a device for separating cotton from the cotton seed, greatly speeding up the process of producing raw cotton. In the nineteenth century, Americans were involved in the development of the telephone, the light bulb, the phonograph and the typewriter. In the early twentieth century, Henry Ford pioneered the production line.

Associated with this ingenuity was the American work ethnic. Waves of immigrants entered America in search of 'the American Dream', which suggested that anyone, whatever their background, could be wealthy in America through hard work and ability. American history is full of examples of how ordinary people rose to be multimillionaires. Andrew Carnegie, for example, and John D. Rockefeller, Henry Ford and J.P. Morgan, all rose from relatively humble origins to the top of US society. America was also blessed with abundant natural resources – huge forests for timber, coal, iron-ore deposits, oil, and great grasslands for the production of grain. All these factors helped the USA to become the world's greatest industrial and agricultural power by 1919.

To exploit its economic potential, the USA needed a constant supply of cheap labour. This was provided by waves of immigration from Europe. In the first half of the nineteenth century the 'old immigration' saw Irish, Germans and Scandinavians join the British as America's White population. After the Civil War, the 'new immigration' saw these groups joined by Italians and Eastern Europeans.

America also had large navigable rivers and lakes to provide the basis of a transportation system. The Mississippi and Ohio rivers allowed produce such as cotton and tobacco to be transported downstream to the port of New Orleans for export. In the early nineteenth century, rivers were supplemented by canals. The Erie Canal, for example, linked the Hudson River in New York State with Lake Erie, easing the move westward. But the great change came with the development of railways in the 1840s. Railways transformed the American economy, because they allowed the easy and relatively speedy transportation of goods from the interior to the east coast ports for export. Railways also helped unite America. In 1869 at Promontory Point, Utah the first transcontinental railway was completed. It was now possible to travel by train from the east to the west coast of the USA in days. Previously, such a journey – by covered wagon – would have taken months.

The economic development was spectacular, but it wasn't achieved without problems. Immigrants lived in very poor housing and suffered poor working conditions. In the South, economic prosperity was dependent upon slave labour until 1865, and even after that date many African-Americans lived in extreme poverty. In an attempt to protect workers' rights, trade unions began to develop. Unlike in Britain, the history of American trade unions was associated with violence and racial division. The Homestead steel strike of 1892, for example, saw units of the US army battle with armed trade unionists. Industrial development also caused tensions between industry and farming. By 1892 farmers formed the backbone of the 'Populist Movement', which aimed to protect farmers through limiting the power of railroads and 'big business'.

The social and economic tensions associated with industrialisation helped create the 'Progressive Movement' of the first decade of the twentieth century. And at the same time, during the presidency of Theodore Roosevelt, important social legislation was passed.

By 1919 the USA was one of the world's greatest producers of oil, coal, grain, cotton, and iron and steel. In addition, it pioneered new industries such as motor car manufacture and the film industry. Not only was America an economic giant, but the quality of life of ordinary Americans was superior to any other nation on Earth.

1. Draw a timeline from 1740 to 1919 and include on it what you regard as the main landmarks in American history.

2. What do you regard as the major problems facing America in the period 1740 to 1919?

3. Why do you think the USA became a major economic power by 1919?

2 The loss of the American colonies, 1740–1789

Key Issues

Framework of Events

1744	King George's War begins
1748	Treaty of Aix La Chapelle
1754	French and Indian War begins
1759	Wolfe captures Quebec
1760	George III becomes king
1763	Treaty of Paris
1764	Sugar Act
1765	Stamp Act
1767	Townshend Duties
1770	Boston Massacre
	Lord North becomes prime minister
1773	Quebec Act
	Boston Tea Party
1775	Outbreak of American War
1776	Declaration of Independence
1777	France declares war on Britain
1779	Spain and the United Provinces (Holland) declare war on Britain
1781	Fall of Yorktown
1783	Treaties of Paris and Versailles
1787	Constitutional Convention in Philadelphia
1789	George Washington becomes first US president.

Overview

IN 1740 Britain had an important colonial empire in North America. In addition to the northern colonies in modern-day Canada – such as Prince Edward Island, Nova Scotia, Newfoundland and Ontario – Britain possessed thirteen colonies further south, along the eastern seaboard. These colonies, which had been established between 1607 and 1733, were, from the north southwards: New

Hampshire, Massachusetts, Connecticut, Rhode Island, New York, Pennsylvania, Delaware, Maryland, Virginia, North Carolina, South Carolina and Georgia. They possessed colonial governors appointed by the King of England and locally elected colonial assemblies. But by 1789 the position of Britain in North America had changed dramatically.

Between 1740 and 1763 Britain defeated its major colonial rival, France, in a series of wars, culminating in North America in the 'French and Indian War' of 1754 to 1763. Britain now seemed to reign supreme over eastern North America. Yet the great British victories over France sowed the seeds for future conflict between Britain and the thirteen colonies. There were growing tensions over westward expansion and colonial trade, but the main source of conflict was over who should pay for the administration and military protection of the thirteen colonies. Between 1763 and 1775, British policies towards the colonies veered between coercion and conciliation. On occasion, British policy was reversed because of colonial opposition – in 1765, for example, over the Stamp Tax, and in 1770 over the Townshend Duties.

By the early 1770s, Britain was trying to reassert its authority over its colonial empire in North America. At the same time, colonial opposition to British policy had brought the colonies closer together in self-defence.

In 1775 armed conflict erupted between the colonies and the British, and in 1776 the thirteen colonies took the dramatic step of declaring their independence from Britain. What ensued was a long-drawn-out war, lasting until 1783, which also involved France, Spain and the United Provinces all joining the American side.

By 1783, Britain had suffered its greatest ever military defeat. That year, in the Treaty of Paris, Britain recognised American independence, handing over to the 'United States' all British territory east of the Mississippi River.

In Britain, the loss of the American colonies ruined the careers of several prime ministers, most notably Lord North. It was also held responsible for George III's insanity which afflicted him from 1788. In North America, the loss led loyalists in the thirteen colonies to move north to British colonies in Canada.

From 1783 the newly independent United States grappled with the problems of creating a new country. By 1787 a **Constitution** was drawn up which was **ratified** in 1788 and became the basis of US government to the present day.

Constitution: A document which contains the procedures on how a country is to be governed.

Ratified: A formal process of agreement. (In the case of the Constitution, over half the thirteen colonies had to agree to it, which was achieved in 1788 when Delaware became the seventh.)

Give reasons why you think the loss of the American colonies was a major landmark in British history in the eighteenth century.

2.1 Britain and North America in 1740

In 1740, Britain was one of four major European powers with colonial territory in North America. In the far north west, Russia had established trading bases in what is now Alaska. In the south and south west, the Spanish had created colonies in Florida and to the west of the Mississippi River. In the east, the process of colonisation involved two great European rivals, Britain and France.

France had begun to explore the St Lawrence River in the 1530s, under Jacques Cartier. The centre of French colonisation was the creation of Quebec in 1608. French traders – 'les voyageurs' – helped develop a vast trading empire which covered the Great Lakes area and extended down the Mississippi River to New Orleans.

Britain had established colonies along the eastern seaboard of North America and in the area of modern Canada known as Ontario and the island of Newfoundland. In 1713, Britain also acquired Arcadia from

France and renamed it 'Nova Scotia'. The British colonial presence on the east coast had begun in 1607, with the establishment of Jamestown in Virginia. And in 1620, extreme Protestants, known as Puritans, established their own colony near Cape Cod which eventually became New England.

The creation of the thirteen colonies

By 1740 Britain had thirteen separate colonies in eastern North America, in what became the United States. These were settled by different groups, and due to their widely different climate and geography, developed different economies.

The 'New England' colonies (New Hampshire, Massachusetts, Rhode Island, and Connecticut) were rich in forests. The farmland was not particularly good and the small farms mainly just provided food for individual families. There were numerous harbours in the region, however, and besides lumbering and fur trading, New England flourished because of its fishing, shipbuilding and trading of goods with Europe. New England played a part in a form of 'trade triangle' (see below) making rum, using molasses from the West Indies. The rum was then shipped to Britain. In New England, small towns were the centres of local government. In 1643, Massachusetts Bay, Plymouth, Connecticut, and New Haven formed the New England Confederation to provide a defence against Indians, Dutch, and the French. This was the first attempt to form a union between colonies.

The thirteen colonies and their dates of permanent settlement

- **Virginia** (1607) – Established by the London Company.
- **New Jersey** (1618) – Originally settled by the Dutch, but seized by the English in 1664.
- **Massachusetts** (1620) – Founded as two colonies: Plymouth Colony (1620) and Massachusetts Bay Colony (1630). They were united in 1691, and annexed Maine, which had been colonised by the New England Council in the 1620s.
- **New Hampshire** (1622) – Originally part of Maine, then a colony from 1629 until annexed by Massachusetts, 1641–43. It became a separate colony again in 1679.
- **Pennsylvania** (1623) – Originally settled by Dutch and Swedes. Came under English control in 1664 and was granted to William Penn by Charles II in 1681.
- **New York** (1624) – Originally founded as the New Netherlands by the Dutch West India Company. Seized by the English in 1664 in the Second Anglo-Dutch War and renamed after the Duke of York, the future James II.
- **Maryland** (1634) – Granted to Lord Baltimore by Charles I, it became colonised by Catholics from England.
- **Connecticut** (1635) – Founded by settlers from Massachusetts. New Haven Colony, founded by settlers from Massachusetts in 1638, was annexed to Connecticut in 1662, when the older colony was granted a royal charter.
- **Rhode Island** (1636) – Settled by two groups from Massachusetts and united in 1644. It was given a charter to establish itself as a separate colony by King Charles II in 1663.
- **Delaware** (1638) – Originally settled by Sweden, then seized by the Dutch in 1655, and by Britain in 1664.
- **North Carolina** (1653) – Settled by pioneers from other colonies. Carolina was separated from Virginia and granted to a private company in 1663. It was divided into two colonies in 1711, North and South Carolina. It became a 'royal' colony in 1729.
- **South Carolina** (1670) – Originally part of Carolina Colony, it was separated from North Carolina in 1711, and became a 'royal' colony in 1729.
- **Georgia** (1733) – Established by Essex soldier James Oglethorpe. He was granted the right to establish a colony by George II, partly to protect the Carolinas from Spanish attack. The first settlement was the seaport of Savannah.

The 'Middle' colonies (New York, New Jersey, Pennsylvania and Delaware) had good farmland, where farmers grew grain and raised live-stock, and they had good harbours. Like New England, they practised trade, but typically they were trading raw materials for manufactured items.

The 'Southern' colonies (Maryland, Virginia, North Carolina, South Carolina, and Georgia) grew their own food, along with growing three major cash crops: tobacco, rice, and indigo. These were grown on planta-tions typically worked by slaves and **indentured servants**. The main commerce of the South was with Britain.

Indentured servant: A white person whose passage to the thirteen colonies was paid for by their future master. They then had to work for him until they had paid for their travel. Once freed from their 'indenture' they usually sought land on the western frontier of the colonies.

Trade with Britain

An important link between Britain and the thirteen colonies was trade. British trade was based on 'mercantilism' which was based on the idea that the world's economic wealth was finite. To gain extra wealth, a country had to establish colonies with which to trade, or take land and trade from a rival. Countries also employed a number of measures to protect their trade. In 1650, for example, Britain passed the Navigation Act, stating that British goods could only be transported in British ships. In addition, British colonies could only trade with Britain. By 1740 Britain had established a large trading empire in North America. An important aspect was the 'trade triangle'. British ships, carrying British-made goods would trade with West Africa. In

Trade and commerce in Manhattan, 1790.

return for these goods the British would purchase African slaves. The slaves would be transported across the Atlantic to the West Indies and the Southern colonies and would be sold for goods, such as rum, sugar, tobacco and cotton. These goods would then be shipped back to Britain, where ports such as Bristol and Liverpool grew wealthy on this trade.

Colonial government

- Each of the thirteen colonies had a slightly different form of internal government.
- A common feature was a 'Colonial Governor' appointed by the King of England. He ran the colonial administration.
- Colonies also had elected assemblies, although the right to vote varied from colony to colony.

The growth of the thirteen colonies

Between 1700 and 1763 the population of the thirteen colonies increased eightfold, reaching two million – about a third of the size of the population of England and Wales at the time. Up to 1700, the vast majority of the immigrants were English, but in the eighteenth century new immigrants appeared. From Germany came religious groups who had suffered persecution in their own land, such as Amish, Dunkers and Mennonites. However, the largest influx of new immigrants was the 'Scotch-Irish', Scottish Protestants who had settled in Ulster but had then decided to move on to North America. By 1776 there were 250,000 Scotch-Irish, mainly in the frontier areas of western North Carolina and Pennsylvania.

1. Describe how British colonies developed in North America by the mid-eighteenth century.

2. In what ways were the thirteen colonies similar, and in what ways were they different?

2.2 What were the main issues affecting Britain and the American colonies, 1740–63?

Early conflict, 1702–48

In the period 1740 to 1763, Britain and the American colonies were affected by a variety of issues, the main one being Anglo-French rivalry, when North America became part of the global conflict between Britain and France.

The centre of this conflict was Europe, which Britain feared might be dominated by the French. The conflict in North America was partly an overspill of this issue, but it had other causes too. The French laid claim to the St Lawrence River, the Great Lakes and the Mississippi river basin – the planned territory of a vast French trading empire. However, these French ambitions stood in the way of the westward movement of British colonists from the eastern seaboard. By 1750, colonists had begun to enter the area which would eventually become Kentucky. Between 1702 and 1713 Britain and France fought each other – in Europe and in North America – in the War of the Spanish Succession. (In North America this was known as 'Queen Anne's War'.) The main result of this war for the British presence in North America was the acquisition of Arcadia. French settlers were removed, many going to Louisiana. In their place, the area was colonised by Scots, becoming the new colony of Nova Scotia.

In 1740 the War of the Austrian Succession broke out in Europe. It involved warfare between Prussia and France, on one side, and Austria on the other. In 1744, Britain became involved in the war when the French occupied the Austrian Netherlands, now known as Belgium. As in Queen

Anne's War, this conflict spilt over into North America. From 1744 to 1748 British and colonial forces fought the French, in what was known as 'King George's War'. Both sides in the conflict employed Indian allies. In 1745 the French and their Indian allies destroyed the New York settlement of Saratoga, killing a hundred settlers, and three years later, France's Indian allies attacked Schenectady, New York. The impact of these raids was to force the settlers to abandon their frontier settlements along the borders with French Canada. The major event in the war was the British capture of the French fortress of Louisbourg on Cape Breton Island. This fortress guarded the entrance to the St Lawrence River and, with it, the whole French colonial empire in North America. The decision to attack Louisbourg was made by the Colonial Governor of Massachusetts, William Shirley. The colonial forces, under the command of William Pepperell of Maine worked closely with the Royal Navy to capture the fortress after a six-week siege on 17 June 1745. Although a great military triumph, the capture of Louisbourg brought limited benefit to Britain's position in North America. In the peace treaty of Aix la Chapelle, in 1748, Louisbourg was returned to France in return for the French evacuation of the Austrian Netherlands, which was regarded as far more important for British security.

The French and Indian War, 1754–63

Although war between Britain and France ended in Europe, colonial rivalry continued in North America. Under the leadership of Roland-Michel Barrin, Marquis de La Galissonière, governor of New France (1747–49) the French attempted to restore their position in North America by advancing up the Ohio River valley. Barrin's policy was adopted by his successors, and in 1749 Pierre-Joseph Céloron de Blainville led an expedition down the Ohio to claim the valley for France. This confined the English colonists and their fur trade to the east of the Appalachian Mountains. The British colonists from New York to Virginia immediately felt the threat to their trade, expansion, and settlement. In 1749 the Ohio Company was formed in London with English and American support, and the fortress of Halifax in Nova Scotia was built to counter the French fort at Louisbourg, now back in French hands. In 1750, British and French representatives met in Paris to try to solve these territorial disputes, but no progress was made. In 1752, the Marquis Duquesne was made governor of New France, with specific instructions to take possession of the Ohio Valley, removing all British presence from the area. The following year, he sent troops to western Pennsylvania where they built forts at Presque Island (Erie) and on the Rivière aux Boeufs (Waterford). At the same time, Robert Dinwiddie, Lieutenant Governor of Virginia, was granting land in the Ohio Valley to citizens of his colony, setting in motion the events which inevitably led to the French and Indian War. In 1754, the future US President, George Washington, then a junior officer in the Virginia militia, established a British fort on the Ohio River called Fort Prince George. But the French captured the fort and renamed it Fort Duquesne, leading to the outbreak of fighting in 1755.

Much of the fighting in the French and Indian War was centred in upper New York, which bordered French Canada, but the war reached its height further north in 1758 and 1759. In 1758 British and colonial troops recaptured Louisbourg, and in September 1759 General Wolfe made a spectacular attack on the capital of New France, Quebec. The capture of the city was the turning-point in the war, and the following year, 1760, the British captured Montreal.

The Treaty of Paris in February 1763 marked the triumph of Britain in North America. All North America, east of the Mississippi River was given to Britain – including Spanish Florida. In addition, France handed over

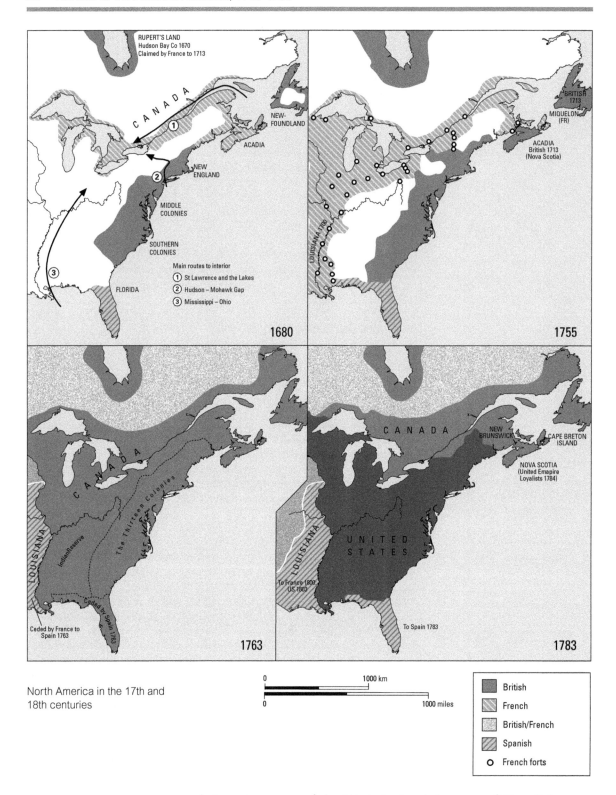

North America in the 17th and
18th centuries

their territory west of the Mississippi and the town of New Orleans to
Spain. Through its victory over France, Britain had removed the French
threat from the thirteen colonies. However, this did not mean an end to
Indian threats. In 1763 a major uprising, Pontiac's Rebellion, threatened
British control south of the Great Lakes, but it was defeated in 1764.

The French and Indian War, therefore, was a combination of the global conflict between Britain and France and a conflict between British and French settlers. Britain fought France in Europe between 1756 and 1763, where the conflict was known as the Seven Years War. Fighting also occurred between the two powers in India and the West Indies. In many ways it was the first 'world war'. Britain won for many reasons:

- Britain had control of the seas. The British capture of Louisbourg in 1758 blocked off the entrance to the St Lawrence River. The Royal Navy also blockaded the main French naval base of Brest, France, in 1758–59. When the French fleet attempted to break out they were soundly defeated in the Battle of Quiberon Bay. In the same year, the French Mediterranean fleet was also defeated in the Battle of Lagos Bay, Portugal. Without supplies from Europe, New France found it difficult to continue the war. British command of the sea also resulted in victory in the West Indies – in 1762 Britain captured Havana, Cuba, from France's ally, Spain.

- The British forces in North America were led by a brilliant commander, General James Wolfe. In September 1759, when the British besieged Quebec, he took the risk of a surprise attack up steep cliffs to the Plains of Abraham, which overlooked the city. In a battle lasting no more than twenty minutes, the British and their Indian allies routed the French army. The French commander in North America, the Maquis de Montcalm was killed, and so was Wolfe. The result of the battle was to destroy French control of the St Lawrence River.

- France had to fight a major war in Europe against Britain and Prussia. This absorbed considerable amounts of men and military material.

- The British war effort was led effectively by William Pitt the Elder, the prime minister. It was Pitt who developed the strategy of preventing French forces reaching North America by blockading French naval bases.

1. How did Anglo-French rivalry affect the thirteen colonies in the period 1702 to 1763?

2. Why was Britain successful in its conflict with France?

2.3 What were the causes of the American Revolution?

In 1763, hardly any American colonists had thoughts of independence. Yet within just twenty years, a new independent state, the United States, had been created after a protracted and bloody war with Britain.

The importance of this break with Britain cannot be overstated. The United States went on to become the greatest military and economic power in world history. Britain, having created by 1763 a large empire in North America – at the expense of France and Spain – managed to lose a significant portion of it by 1783. The loss of the American colonies was felt throughout Britain. (At the time it was even felt that it had contributed to the madness of George III in 1788.) But why did the American Revolution take place?

British policies towards the thirteen colonies, 1763 to 1770

Britain's crushing victory over France in the French and Indian War created many problems. The British colonists in North America were now no longer dependent on British military protection. The French threat had been removed. Britain now had to absorb 80,000 French Canadians, with their different language and their Catholic religion. Also, Britain had acquired large amounts of new territory from France, east of the

Mississippi River and in Canada. In the area west of the Appalachian mountains, Britain now faced the new problem of westward-moving settlers and Indian tribes. In many ways, the aftermath of the French and Indian War laid the foundations of what was to become the American Revolution.

Westward expansion

In a Royal Proclamation, issued in October 1763, the new territories acquired in the 1763 Treaty of Paris were organised into four areas: Quebec, East Florida, West Florida and the island of Grenada. The lands west of the Appalachians were reserved for the Indians. These lands weren't part of any of the colonies, settlement of them was forbidden, and land negotiations with the Indians were prohibited – the right to arrange surrender of Indian lands being reserved for Britain. The Indians, according to their own laws, administered this territory, though non-Indian fugitives could be followed and apprehended.

This 'barrier' caused great resentment among the colonists. A central feature of colonial history had been the westward movement of colonists from the eastern seaboard inland. By 1770, colonists had established the town of Pittsburgh and a small village had appeared at Wheeling. And in 1774 Daniel Boone led colonists through the Cumberland Gap, in the Appalachians, into the area which became Kentucky.

Financing the British presence in the thirteen colonies

The French and Indian War had cost Britain a considerable amount, and the cost of colonial administration rose from £70,000 in 1748 to £350,000 in 1763. Then there was the additional cost of maintaining an army of 10,000 men in North America. The French may have been defeated in 1763 but the Indians still posed a problem. In 1763–64 Britain was faced by Pontiac's Rebellion, and Pontiac did not make peace until 1766. Even after the rebellion, settlers faced periodic attacks by Indians along the frontier. A substantial, and expensive, army was still needed in North America.

The person who attempted to resolve the financial problems was George III's chief minister, George Grenville. In 1764 he introduced the Sugar Act, which was the first law aimed strictly at raising American money to pay the costs. It increased duties on goods imported into the colonies that were not of British origin. This was followed by the Currency Act, 1764, which barred the colonies from printing their own currency. Both these Acts created resentment in the thirteen colonies. The Sugar Act interfered with an increasing aspect of colonial trade. During the eighteenth century the colonies turned their backs on the British policy of mercantilism and started developing their own trading links with French and Spanish colonies in the West Indies. The Currency Act was unpopular because it threatened to limit the amount of money in circulation. This would have an adverse effect on the colonial economy, which was already suffering signs of recession following the end of the French and Indian War. In addition, many colonists were suspicious of the need to maintain a large standing army of 10,000 in North America. The combined effect of all these policies raised issues about the relationship of the thirteen colonies to Britain. In one town meeting in Massachusetts, a suggestion was made that there should be no taxation without representation. This hit at the centre of British–colonial relations.

The Stamp Act, 1765

While the Sugar Act and the Currency Act caused resentment, the Stamp Act of 1765 led to outright opposition and violence in the thirteen colonies. The Sugar Act had upset trade in New England, but the Stamp Act antagonised all the colonies. The Stamp Act required revenue stamps to be affixed to newspapers, legal documents, ships' papers, insurance policies and licences for taverns. This was a tax which hit at the heart of colonial life. In the Virginia House of Burgesses, Patrick Henry claimed that only Virginians could tax Virginians, not Britain. And within a short time the Stamp Act was suspended because of the mob violence.

In October 1765, the first ever joint meeting of the colonies took place, when nine colonies were represented at the Stamp Tax Congress in Albany, New York. The Congress petitioned the king to repeal the Stamp Act, and it gave an impetus to the boycott of British goods.

In 1766, the Stamp Act was repealed. George III had dismissed Grenville on a domestic issue and had replaced him with Rockingham. The repeal, however, was linked to the Declaratory Act which asserted the full power of Britain's parliament to make laws for the thirteen colonies.

Townshend Duties, 1767

In May and June 1767, the chancellor of the exchequer, Charles Townshend, passed a series of acts which aimed to assert British control over the colonies by raising extra revenue from them and ensuring that colonial legislatures did not block British policy.

Instead of bringing stability to the situation, Townshend's measures only helped to increase opposition. In 1767, a Philadelphia lawyer, John Dickenson, in *Letters from a Farmer in Pennsylvania*, claimed that Britain had no right to raise taxes for revenue purposes. In Massachusetts, John Adams, formed the 'Sons of Liberty', claiming that Britain had no right to legislate for the colonies and, in 1769, the Virginia House of Burgesses passed a resolution reasserting its exclusive right to tax Virginians. As a result of its actions, the House was dissolved by the Governor of Virginia.

Boston Massacre, 1770

The height of opposition came on 5 March 1770, when a mob assembled in central Boston, Massachusetts. The mob was met by British troops who opened fire, killing five civilians. The first person shot was a runaway African-American slave, Crispus Attucks. The event caused outrage in the thirteen colonies – and in Britain. Eight soldiers were put on trial, of which six were acquitted. The other two soldiers were found guilty of manslaughter, but were released after being branded on the hand. In Britain, the Townshend Duties were repealed by the new prime minister, Lord North.

Following the French and Indian War, therefore, Britain faced major financial problems in administering the thirteen colonies and the new lands acquired from France. British attempts at solving these problems were met by increasing opposition from within the thirteen colonies. The development of British policy was not aided by the frequent changes in ministry during the 1760s. As a result, in 1766 and again in 1770, an incoming ministry reversed the policy of its predecessor. British policy seemed to be a mixture of attempts to tax the colonists and conciliatory measures. The effect of this inconsistent policy was to embolden the colonists.

From 1770 Britain had a long period of ministerial stability, with Lord North remaining as prime minister until 1782. But the conflict between the thirteen colonies and Britain only intensified.

1. From the information contained above, identify whether you think the British were responsible for the outbreak of the American War of Independence.

2. How far were the colonists to blame for the deteriorating relations with Britain from 1763 to 1770?

3. What do you regard as the most important reason for the deterioration in relations between Britain and the thirteen colonies in the period 1763 to 1770?

1. Place the factors in the mind map in order of importance in causing the outbreak of the American War of Independence.

2. Can you identify any links between the factors in the mind map? If so, give reasons to support your choice.

British prime ministers 1760–1783

Duke of Newcastle	June 1757 – May 1762
Earl of Bute	May 1762 – April 1763
George Grenville	April 1763 – July 1765
Marquis of Rockingham	July 1765 – July 1766
William Pitt the Elder (Earl of Chatham)	July 1766 – October 1768
Duke of Grafton	October 1768 – January 1770
Lord North	January 1770 – March 1782
Marquis of Rockingham	March 1782 – July 1782
Lord Shelburne	July 1782 – March 1783

The drift to war, 1770–75

The repeal of the Townshend Duties brought over two years of calm to British-colonial relations. In 1772, however, the calm was broken when the British customs schooner Gaspee ran aground near Providence, Rhode Island and was attacked by several boatloads of colonists. The Royal Governor of Rhode Island issued a reward for the capture of the offenders, but this only fuelled the colonists' outrage against Britain.

The Boston Tea Party, 1773

A major deterioration in relations occurred with the passage of the Tea Act in 1773, part of the government's plan to rescue the East India Tea Company from possible bankruptcy. The Act decreased the tax on imported British tea and, in effect, gave the British merchants an edge – they could now undersell any other tea obtainable in the colonies, including smuggled tea. This development, however, caused outrage across the colonies. In New York and Philadelphia the imported tea was

Illustration of the Boston Tea
Party.

promptly sent back to Britain. But in Boston, on 16 December 1773, colonists, under the direction of John Adams – and disguised as Indians – boarded the tea ships and threw their cargo into the harbour.

The Coercive (or Intolerable) Acts

The British government retaliated with the Coercive Acts (known as the Intolerable Acts in the thirteen colonies) of 1774. The Boston Port Act closed the port from 1 June 1774. The Act for the Impartial Administration of Justice allowed the Governor to transfer to Britain for trial any official accused of committing an offence in the line of duty – this was to prevent government officials been imprisoned by colonial juries. A Quartering Act directed local authorities in the colonies to ensure that British troops had adequate lodging, which included lodging in private homes. Finally, the Massachusetts Government Act made all that colony's senior administrators appointees of the Governor.

The Quebec Act, 1774

If the Coercive Acts were not enough, in June 1774, the British passed the Quebec Act, which recognised the privileged position of the Roman Catholic Church in Quebec. It also recognised the French legal system in that colony. Finally, and most controversially, the province's boundaries were extended south and west to include the Ohio and Mississippi river valleys. This Act was seen as a major affront to the colonies. It gave special privileges to the Catholic Church, which the vast majority of Protestant colonists viewed with extreme suspicion. It also seemed to act as a major obstacle to westward expansion.

The First Continental Congress, 1774

On 5 September 1774 representatives of the thirteen colonies met in Philadelphia. This Congress had been called before the terms of the Quebec Act were known, but when delegates learned of them during the Congress, their suspicions of British intentions were only confirmed. The Congress resolved to fight the Coercive Acts and petitioned George III and the British parliament to repeal them. More significantly, the Congress issued a 'Declaration of Rights' and organised a campaign against the importation of British goods.

After the dissolution of the Congress, in November 1774, the more militant colonists began organising military units, and the prospect of an open rebellion against British rule began to develop.

North's Resolution, 1775

In February 1775, Lord North's government attempted to calm the developing crisis by claiming that the British parliament would only raise taxes to regulate trade, and would give each colony the right to raise its own taxes, as long as all the colonies contributed to the cost of defence. However, North's conciliatory actions were too little, too late.

The opening shots

In April 1775, the new British military commander in the colonies and newly appointed Governor of Massachusetts, Thomas Gage, sent 700 troops from Boston to seize ammunition and guns held by colonists in Concord, New Hampshire. The colonists were forewarned by Paul Revere and William Dawes, who rode from Boston to Concord to give the alert. On 19 April, at Lexington, the route of the British troops was blocked by armed colonials. Shots were exchanged before the British force moved on to Concord where more serious fighting occurred. Outnumbered by armed colonials, the British force suffered casualties before retiring to Boston. This turned out to be the first engagement of the American War of Independence. The British lost 273 killed and wounded, out of their force of 700, while the colonials lost 93.

The events at Lexington and Concord were used effectively by anti-British colonials to whip up support for opposition and rebellion.

The Second Continental Congress, 1775

The Congress met again at Philadelphia in May 1775. This time the Congress declared to raise a Continental Army of 20,000 men and on 15 June, a Virginian, George Washington, was given overall command. On 6 July the Congress issued the 'Declaration of the Causes and Necessities of Taking Up Arms'. The Congress specifically stated, however, that it had no intention of separating from Britain, and it adopted the 'Olive Branch Petition' to George III which asked the king to end hostilities and engage in reconciliation with the thirteen colonies.

But even before the Olive Branch Petition was delivered, a bloody encounter between the British and the colonists occurred at the battle of Bunker Hill, (actually fought on Breed's Hill) near Boston on 17 June 1775. The British suffered 1,054 casualties compared to approximately 400 on the colonial side, but it was a British victory, and Boston was besieged by British forces. The war had begun.

By the end of 1775, war had broken out in the thirteen colonies. Both sides had somehow drifted into a major conflict. In an attempt to reassert British control, North's policies had simply made matters worse. Events at

Lexington and Concord quickly escalated into more open warfare.

The Declaration by the Second Continental Congress fell on deaf ears. On 22 December 1775 the British parliament passed the Prohibitory Act which declared that the rebellious colonies were outside the protection of the king and put an embargo on all colonial trade.

In January 1776 the British Radical, Thomas Paine, issued a pamphlet entitled 'Common Sense'. He suggested that independence was the only way forward, and the pamphlet sold 120,000 copies within a month. On 6 April 1776 the Continental Congress opened colonial ports to shipping of all nations except Britain. On 2 July the Congress passed the resolution, put forward by Patrick Henry of Virginia, that the thirteen colonies should separate from Britain. Two days later, it accepted a 'Declaration of Independence' which had been written by the Virginian, Thomas Jefferson. The Declaration transformed a colonial war into a revolution.

1. What actions did the British government take which contributed directly to the outbreak of war by 1775?

2. What do you regard as the most important reason for the outbreak of war between Britain and the thirteen colonies by 1775? Give reasons for your answer.

Timeline: The road to revolution 1760–1776

1763	Royal Proclamation on Western Lands
1764	Sugar Act and Currency Act
1765	Stamp Act, repealed in 1766; Stamp Act Congress
1767	Townshend Duties, repealed in 1770
1770	Boston Massacre
1773	Boston Tea Party
1774	First Continental Congress
	Quebec Act
1775	Fighting begins at Lexington and Concord
	Second Continental Congress
1776	Declaration of Independence

The Declaration of Independence [4 July 1776]

The Unanimous Declaration of the Thirteen United States of America

We hold these truths to be self-evident, that all men are created equal, that they are endowed by their Creator with certain unalienable rights, that among these are life, liberty and the pursuit of happiness. That to secure these rights, governments are instituted among men, deriving their just powers from the consent of the governed. That whenever any form of government becomes destructive to these ends, it is the right of the people to alter or to abolish it, and to institute new government, laying its foundation on such principles and organizing its powers in such form, as to them shall seem most likely to effect their safety and happiness.

Prudence will dictate that governments long established should not be changed for light and transient causes. But when a long train of abuses reduces them under absolute despotism, it is their right, it is their duty, to throw off such government, and to provide new guards for their future security. The history of the present King of Great Britain is a history of repeated injuries, all having the object of the establishment of an absolute tyranny over these states.

1. What reasons are given for the decision of the thirteen colonies to separate from Britain in the Declaration of Independence?

No Taxation without Representation

A major criticism of Britain by the American colonists before 1775 was that they were taxed by an authority (the British Parliament) in which they had no representation.

'No taxation without representation' was a protest with a long tradition within England. One reason for the Civil Wars of 1642–49 was the attempt by the king to tax without the support and permission of Parliament.

In 1688 the Glorious Revolution occurred in Britain when James II was replaced by William and Mary. The Bill of Rights of 1689 laid down that these joint monarchs had to rule with Parliament. It was the beginning of Britain's Constitutional Monarchy.

In 1689–90 the English political philosopher, John Locke, published his *Two Treatises on Civil Government* which attacked the idea that kings were appointed by God, and clearly put forward the idea that the government could only govern with the consent of the governed.

By the middle of the eighteenth century this concept had support across the thirteen colonies. The colonists did not deny the right of George III to raise taxes, but he had to gain the consent of the taxpayers.

2.4 Why did Britain lose the American War of 1775–83?

The American War of Independence was a war between two very unequal sides. On one side, was Britain and her Empire. Britain had vast economic and military resources, compared to the thirteen colonies. Britain had the largest navy on earth. In 1776, Britain had 32,000 troops in North America (including 9000 German mercenaries) to put down the rebellion. On the other side were the colonists, who had approximately 19,000 troops, including militia (part-time troops). Usually Washington had an army of 5000 men.

Many of the officers who joined Washington's 'Continental Army' had military experience in the French and Indian War, but the Congress had very little money and the soldiers lacked formal training. In addition, not all colonists supported separation from Britain. Loyalists, known as Tories, were found in every one of the thirteen colonies but especially in the South. Also, British colonial possessions in Canada – such as Newfoundland, Nova Scotia, Quebec and Upper Canada (Ontario) – did not separate.

In many ways, the War of Independence was a dual conflict. It was a war between Britain and the thirteen colonies, and it was also a 'civil war' within the colonies, between those who wanted separation and those who did not. To many contemporaries, it seemed only a matter of time before Britain reasserted its control. Yet in 1783, in the Treaty of Paris, the thirteen colonies won their independence to become the United States. The war was Britain's greatest military defeat of the eighteenth century. But why did Britain lose?

The terrain

Today it takes about six hours to fly from Britain to the USA. In 1776 it took five or six to weeks to sail across the Atlantic. In addition, it is over a thousand miles from the northernmost colony, New Hampshire, to Georgia in the south.

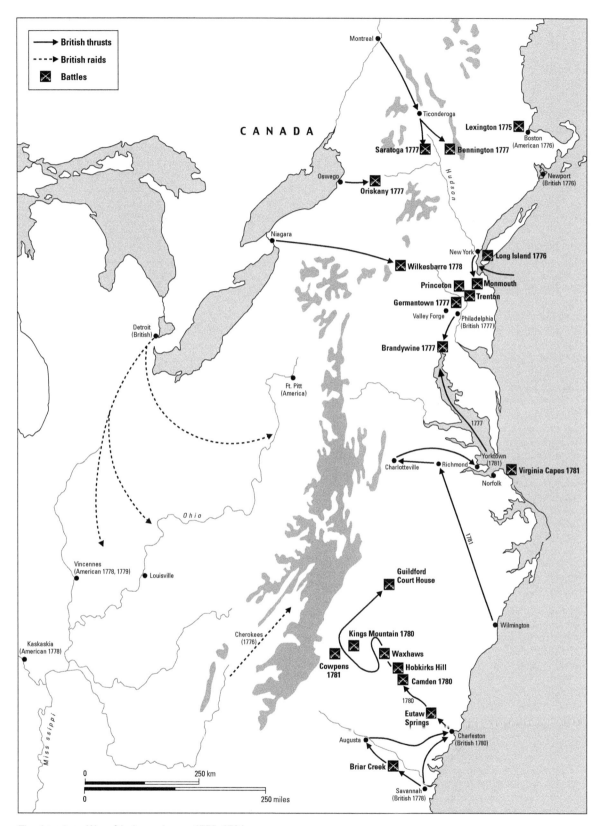

The American War of Independence, 1775–1781

'The American War of Independence: main events 1775–1783'

April 1775
Fighting begins between colonists and British troops – the Lexington massacre in Massachusetts is followed by more outbreaks at Concord.

17 June 1775
British control hills overlooking Charlestown and Boston, although 1,000 British soldiers are killed in Battle of Bunker Hill (three times the American casualties).

July 1776
The British leave Boston to the rebels. Instead, they use New York as their centre of operations, amply supplied by 35,000 troops and 500 ships. They easily outnumber the 18,000 men assembled by Washington.

December 1776
Defeat of the colonials at the Battle of Long Island, out of New York, only narrowly avoided becoming a rout when Washington is able to escape to Manhattan, and from there to New Jersey. The British commander, General Howe, complacently chooses not to pursue the Americans, allowing Washington's troops to cross the Delaware river on Christmas Day and attack an encampment of British soldiers on 26 December.

3 January 1777
Another American victory at Princeton. In a few weeks, General George Washington has turned around the situation and shown the British that a quick victory was far from assured.

The British focus now turns to upstate New York with an attempt to capture Albany and the river valley of the Hudson. Capturing the Hudson would divide troublesome New England from the other colonies and provide a useful link between New York and Canada. Two British forces advance from the north at the start of 1777: General Burgoyne leads the major force of 7,000 from Lake Champlain, whilst a smaller force under Colonel Barry St Leger begins an advance from the west via Lake Ontario. It is expected that Howe will advance up the Hudson from New York if needed.

August–October 1777
The action goes wrong from the start. Instead of moving up the Hudson, Howe moves south-west to Philadelphia, defeating Washington at the battles of Brandywine Creek and Germantown in October and easily capturing the rebel capital. Howe's successes in Pennsylvania mean that Washington's army is forced to endure a miserable winter at Valley Forge. It also means Burgoyne is left alone when he begins to run into difficulties by the autumn. St Leger is checked at Oriskany in August and by October Burgoyne is trapped at Saratoga. (Desperate but effective action by Benedict Arnold in October of 1776 on Lake Champlain prevents the British from retaking the fortress of Ticonderoga until 1777, so delaying Burgoyne's march south. The difficult march through inhospitable terrain is time-consuming and morale-draining with rebel militia men harassing the British as they advance.) On 17 October, Burgoyne is forced to surrender, with 5,000 men at Saratoga, to the American Horatio Gates. Any advantage gained by Howe in Pennsylvania is quickly lost. The British suddenly look vulnerable.

Saratoga is significant, for it is the American military success that prompts the French to intervene directly in the war. The French have been watching events in North America carefully, encouraged by the American ambassador in Paris, Benjamin Franklin. They have been secretly supplying the colonials since 1776, keen to see Britain weakened in its empire. France is also attracted to the ideals of liberty that the American struggle seems to represent, especially after the Declaration of Independence. However they are anxious to avoid direct help for fear that the British will declare war on France itself – a war that France cannot afford to fight.

6 February 1778
The Declaration of Independence and the Battle of Saratoga convince the French that the rebel leaders are serious in their fighting and stand a chance of victory. In such circumstances, the French Government offer to recognise the independence of the colonies as well as a military and commercial alliance (signed on 6 February 1778).

1778–1780
The British withdraw from Philadelphia to New York in 1778 and choose to concentrate on the southern states. Between 1778 and 1780, the British enjoy some success there, taking Georgia and the major ports of the Carolinas. They receive another boost, in October 1780, when rebel hero Benedict Arnold turns traitor and almost succeeds in handing over the key fortress of West Point to the British. But the tide has turned in the South and the British commander, Lord Cornwallis, despite winning most engagements, fails to gain control of the interior.

October 1781
By 1781, Cornwallis withdraws to the North, leaving the loyalists in Georgia and South Carolina to look after themselves. In the west, most Indian tribes side with the British and launch a series of attacks against American settlers of the 1770s.

Although the small American navy makes little impact against the British navy, Britain's merchant fleet suffers, especially from privateers (pirates).

The French fleet is more concerned with protecting the French West Indies from the British fleet than with helping the colonials. This changes in 1781 when the French fleet is made available to assist Washington (who also has the support of a French land force of 6,000 troops). Cornwallis' troops are withdrawn from Virginia to Chesapeake Bay, awaiting reinforcements. Surrounded by Washington and the French army on land and at sea, Cornwallis has no alternative but to surrender, which he does at Yorktown on 19 October 1781.

Fighting continues for over a year. The British remain in control of New York, Savannah and Charleston with 32,000 men stationed in the colonies, but the major fighting on the continent has come to an end.

The American War of Independence was a distant colonial war which involved huge logistical problems in supplying the British forces. In contrast, the American colonists were fighting on their own land.

British troops, experienced at fighting in Europe, were faced with a completely different theatre of war. Forests, swamps, and long and wide rivers provided natural obstacles which prevented British forces fighting a conventional European-style war. In addition, the Americans sometimes adopted guerrilla tactics, which were very difficult to counter.

The leadership of George Washington

Throughout the war, the Americans found it extremely difficult to raise sufficient funds to pay for the army. Congress printed $250,000 of paper money and the individual colonial governments raised a further $200,000. But because this paper money was not backed by gold or silver, it led to inflation. To get colonists to enlist, therefore Congress also offered a bounty of 100 acres of land, as well as $20.

One of Washington's great accomplishments as General was keeping his army intact. He acted swiftly when he realised that the British were attempting to encircle his troops in the area around the city of New York in 1776, withdrawing his troops through New Jersey to Pennsylvania.

A testing time for Washington came in the winter of 1776–77 when he barely kept his army together in its winter quarters at Valley Forge, near Philadelphia. Without Washington, the Americans may have not been able to continue the fight into 1777. During the rest of the war, Washington had to battle for support from the Congress and the individual colonial governments. In a complex situation, Washington proved to be one of the few uniting forces on the American side.

British mistakes

1777 proved to be the turning-point in the war. From Canada, the British launched an invasion of the colony of New York, under General Burgoyne, with 7000 troops. But Burgoyne was ill-equipped to fight in the forested and mountain terrain he encountered, and on 6 August 1777 he was attacked by American militia and their Indian allies near Oriskany. Burgoyne then made the fatal mistake of withdrawing to Saratoga, where he was surrounded by the American forces led by General Horatio Gates, and forced to surrender on 16 October 1777. This was the first major military victory for the colonists. The British prime minister, Lord North, believed the war could not be won and offered to resign, but George III refused. News of the Saratoga surrender also persuaded the French to intervene.

Foreign intervention, 1778–83

On 6 February 1778, France signed two treaties with the American colonists. One was a commercial agreement, but the other, more importantly, was a defensive alliance. France then declared war on Britain in 1778, transforming the situation. The war had developed into a major conflict. From 1778, right through to 1783 (two years after the defeat of Cornwallis at Yorktown) French forces fought the British – in the West Indies, Africa and India. In 1779, Spain and the United Provinces (Holland) also declared war on Britain. From 1779 Britain lost the naval control of the North Atlantic – the only time in the eighteenth and nineteenth centuries. At the same time, Britain faced a major invasion scare, which diverted large amounts of military equipment and personnel to defend Britain against possible French invasion.

French military aid was also a decisive factor in the American victory. French land and sea forces fought on the side of the American colonists against the British. At the same time, British and French (and to a lesser extent, Dutch and Spanish) forces fought for colonial wealth and empire around the world. The high point of French support was the landing of five battalions of French infantry and artillery in Rhode Island in 1780. In 1781, these French troops, under the command of Count Rochambeau, marched south to Virginia where they joined Continental forces under Washington and Lafayette. The British leader, Cornwallis, encamped on the Yorktown peninsula, hoped to be rescued by the British navy. A French fleet under the command of Admiral DeGrasse intercepted and, after a fierce battle lasting several days, defeated the British fleet and forced it to withdraw. This left the French navy to land heavy siege cannon and other supplies and to trap Cornwallis on the Yorktown peninsula. At that point, the defeat of Cornwallis was essentially a matter of time. On 14 September 1781, the French and Continental armies completed their 700—mile march and laid siege to the British positions. After a number of weeks – and several brief but intense engagements – Cornwallis, besieged on the peninsula by the large and well-equipped French–American army, and stricken by dysentery, decided to surrender his army. On 19 October 1781, the British forces marched out between the silent ranks of the Americans and French, arrayed in parallel lines a mile long, and cast down their arms.

The fall of Yorktown was the last major engagement of the war. But it took two years of negotiation to bring the conflict to its official end. The

The United States in 1783

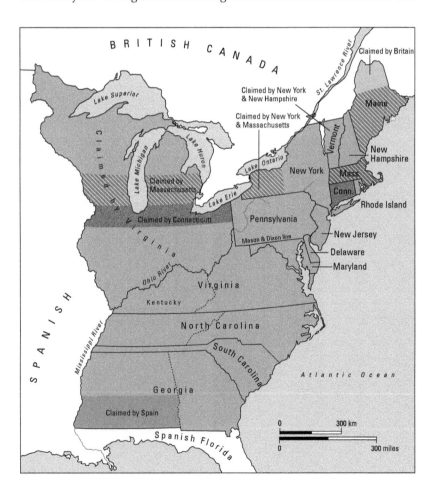

Peace of Paris was signed on 3 September 1783. Britain recognised the independence of the thirteen colonies as the 'United States'. It also agreed to hand over to the United States all British territory south of the Great Lakes and west of the Mississippi River. Florida was handed back to Spain (having been been taken by Britain in 1763).

Historians debate whether the independence movement which resulted in the creation of the United States was a revolution, that is, a movement which changed the fundamental political, economic, and social arrangements of the society, or whether it was primarily a political rearrangement. Although a small radical minority had been pushing for independence since the 1760s, they did not have much support in 1775. The incidents at Lexington and Concord, especially the shedding of blood and deaths, got more colonials off the fence, for they tended to force people to choose sides. Most people in Massachusetts did not want to risk life, limb, or property by fighting the British army, so they waited. Others were radicalised by British actions in the war. The war transformed George Washington into a national hero amongst Americans. It also cost Lord North his position as prime minister – he resigned in 1782.

1. What difficulties did Britain face in fighting the American War of Independence?

2. 'Without France the Americans would have lost the War of Independence.' Assess this view.

1. What do you regard as the most important reason why Britain lost the war?

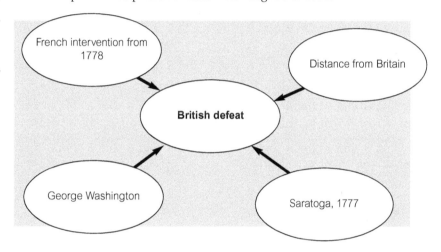

2.5 How did the United States develop in the years 1783 to 1789?

Although independent from Britain in 1783, the United States faced an uncertain future. What had brought the thirteen colonies together had been their opposition to Britain. But now Britain had been removed. The thirteen colonies all had their own governments and they had widely different economic structures. The new country had also acquired new lands in the West that did not belong to any colony. What was to happen to this land?

In what ways did the Articles of Confederation fail to provide strong government?

In the summer of 1776, Congress appointed a committee to provide a framework for national government. Some of the colonial leaders, such as John Dickinson, wanted a strong central government. Instead, they produced Articles that went to the opposite extreme of preserving the rights of states and creating a weak national government.

The Articles of Confederation were finally adopted in 1781, when Maryland agreed to sign. They provided a one-chambered (unicameral) Congress in which each state, irrespective of size, would have one vote. A committee of 13 would provide the government – one delegate from each state. In order to amend (change) the Articles, all 13 states had to agree.

The government had the power to make war and to make treaties. It also had the power to admit new states. However, it did not have the power to raise taxes, raise troops or regulate commerce.

From the start, many colonists were unhappy with the form of government under the Articles. In 1783, in the Newburgh Conspiracy, some colonial leaders approached the army second-in-command, Horatio Gates, to force the states to surrender more power to the central government.

By 1785, a meeting at George Washington's house, of representatives from Maryland, Virginia, Pennsylvania and Delaware, called for a discussion on the problems of government. In September 1786, only five states sent representatives to the Annapolis Convention, but they called all states to attend a Constitutional Convention in Philadelphia in 1787 to revise the Articles of Confederation.

1. How was power divided between the state and national government under the Articles of Confederation?

2. Why do you think many Americans were dissatisfied with the Articles of Confederation?

Strengthening the Central Government

Under Articles of Confederation	Under Federal Constitution
A loose confederation of states	A firm union of people
One vote in Congress for each state	Two votes in Senate for each state; representation by population in House of Representatives
Two-thirds vote (9 states) in Congress for all important measures	Simple majority vote in Congress, subject to presidential veto
Laws executed by committees of Congress	Laws executed by powerful President
No Congressional power over trade	Congress to regulate both foreign and inter-state trade
No Congressional power to levy taxes	Extensive power in Congress to levy taxes
No federal courts	Federal courts, capped by Supreme Court
Unanimity of states for amendment	Amendment less difficult
No authority to act directly upon individuals, and no power to coerce states	Ample power to enforce laws by coercion of individuals and to some extent of states

In what ways did the Constitution of 1787 change the US political system?

The Constitution that was produced at Philadelphia was a compromise between the views of the delegates.

James Madison proposed the 'Virginia Plan'. This suggested that Congress should have two houses, each based on size of population. The smaller states feared they would lose influence under the plan. So William Patterson produced the 'New Jersey Plan'. This would involve keeping the one-chambered Congress of the Articles of Confederation, with equal representation for all states. He also suggested a large increase in the powers of the national government. In the end, a 'great compromise' was reached. The Congress would comprise two houses:

● In one house – the Senate – all states, irrespective of size, would have two seats.

- The House of Representatives would be based on size of population.

Another issue of debate was slavery. A compromise was reached, where the Constitution neither supported nor condemned slavery. For the purposes of calculating representation in the House of Representatives, slaves would count as three-fifths of a freeman. They did not have the right to vote.

The third compromise came over the presidency. George Washington was certain to be first President. He was trusted not to abuse his power, so the President was given control over foreign policy and the right to veto Congress's legislation. In the unlikely event of the President or senior government officially acting unlawfully, a system of removal was included. This was the impeachment process. The House of Representatives has the right to begin impeachment proceedings. Then the Senate tries the individual. If convicted, the person is removed from office. No President has been successfully impeached. Only two – Andrew Johnson in 1868 and Bill Clinton in 1999 – have been tried for impeachment.

As a result of the decisions in Philadelphia, the United States was

---

Outline of the United States Constitution

Preamble
'We the people of the United States in order to form a more perfect union, establish justice, ensure domestic tranquillity, provide for the common defence, promote the general welfare, and secure the blessings of liberty to ourselves and our posterity, do ordain and confirm the Constitution for the United States of America.'

Article I: The Legislature (Congress)
Congress is divided into two parts:
1. The House of Representatives: 435 members determined by population.
2. The Senate: 100 members since 1959 – two from each state.

The House of Representatives:
- may start impeachment against a President or other high government officials.
- All bills that deal with money must begin in the House.
- Speaker of the House presides over proceedings.
- Members, known as Congressmen, are elected every two years (minimum age: 25).

The Senate:
- was originally elected by state legislatures, but since Seventeenth Amendment in 1913 they are directly elected.
- approves or rejects nominations from President for senior government officials and Supreme Court justices (Advice and Consent Power).
- approves or rejects treaties with other countries (Advice and Consent Power).
- Debate is unlimited.

- The Vice-President presides over proceedings and can only vote in the event of a tie.
- Senators are elected for six years (citizens over 30 years). A third are elected every two years.

Article II: The Executive (President and Government)
President is elected every four years. Originally elected without limit. Since the Twenty-Second Amendment, can only serve two terms. Must be native born and at least 35 years of age.

President is:
- Commander-in-Chief of the armed forces
- Chief Executive (Head of Government)
- Head of State
- Chief lawmaker.

Article III: The Judiciary
US Supreme Court created as highest court of appeal for federal and state cases. Precise composition of Courts defined by Judiciary Act of 1789.

Article IV: Inter-state relations
- All states are guaranteed a republican form of government.
- Any new state is equal to the original 13 states.
- Each state shall respect the laws of the other states.

Article V: Amending the Constitution
Amendments must receive two-thirds support from both Houses of Congress and three-quarters of the states before they become law.

Article VI: Ratification of the Constitution
Nine of the original 13 states had to accept the Constitution before it could become law.

confirmed as a federal state. This meant political power was divided between a national (federal) government and state government (see below). In 1787, such a decision was inevitable. The United States had been created out of a voluntary union of 13 separate states. As the country grew and more states were admitted, the size and geography of the USA meant that the federal system of government was the only logical form of government. No national government based in Washington DC could make laws for over 250 million people living in a country over 3,000 miles wide which embraced deserts, mountains and farmland.

To emphasise the federal nature of the political system, the President and Vice-President were chosen by an **electoral college**. In a presidential election, each state would vote separately. Whichever candidate won the state's popular vote, won all the electoral college votes. The electoral college votes were based on the number of Senators and Congressman a state had in Congress. In 1992, for example, Wyoming had three electoral college votes because it had two senators and one Congressman; California had 53 electoral college votes because it had two senators and 51 Congressmen.

As a result, in a presidential election it was possible for a candidate to get the most popular votes but lose in the electoral college. This happened in 1876 when Samuel Tilden polled most votes, but Rutherland B. Hayes won the electoral college by one vote. It also occurred in 2000 when George W. Bush became President.

To avoid the abuse of power, a central principle of the Constitution was the separation of powers. Political power was divided between federal and state government (see panel below). It was also divided within the federal government. For instance, in passing laws, both the Senate and the House of Representatives had to agree. Then the President had to agree. He could veto the Bill. However, Congress could override the veto if two-thirds of both Houses agreed. Even then, the US Supreme Court might declare the law unconstitutional if it believed it contravened the Constitution. Also, no member of the Executive (government) could be a member of Congress.

The Senate was given advice and consent power over the appointment of senior government officials and Supreme Court justices. The President had the right to nominate them, but the Senate had to agree. Similarly, the President negotiated treaties with foreign states but the Senate could reject them. In 1919, the Senate rejected the Treaty of Versailles with Germany.

Electoral college: Method of choosing a President and Vice-President. Each state votes separately. The winner in a state gets all the state's electoral college votes. These votes are calculated by adding the number of senators allotted to each state to the number of Congressmen.

---

1. Explain the meaning of 'federal state' as it applied to the USA.

2. What was the 'separation of powers'? Explain how it divided power between the states and federal government and between the three branches of the federal government: President, Congress and Supreme Court.

3. Explain how the electoral college is involved in electing the President and Vice-President. What are its drawbacks?

The separation of powers between the federal and state governments

Powers reserved for the federal government alone
- Regulation of foreign trade
- Regulation of inter-state commerce
- Minting money
- Running the post office
- Regulating immigration
- Granting copyrights and patents
- Declaring war and peace
- Admitting new states
- Fixing weights and measures
- Organising the armed forces
- Governing the federal capital, Washington DC
- Conducting foreign relations.

Powers reserved for state governments only
- Conducting elections
- Establishing voter qualifications
- Providing local government
- Regulating contracts
- Regulating trade within the state
- Providing education
- Maintaining a police force and internal law and order.

Powers shared by federal and state governments
- Taxation
- Controlling the state militia, later known as the National Guard.

Further Reading

Texts designed for AS and A2 students

1776, The American Challenge by R.C. Birth (Longman Seminar Study series, 1976).

The War of American Independence by Esmond Wright (Historical Association, 1976).

George Washington by Paul Johnson (Eminent Lives, 2004).

The Enduring Vision, Part 1 to 1865 by P. Boyer *et al.* (Houghton Mifflin, 2001).

The Longman History of the United States by Hugh Brogan (Longman,1999).

America by G. Tindall and D. Shi (Norton, 2007).

The Limits of Liberty by Maldwyn Jones (Oxford University Press,1995).

More advanced reading

The Causes of the American War of Independence by Claude van Tyne (Macmillan, 2001).

The War of Independence from 1760 to the Surrender of Yorktown, 1781 by Samuel Griffith (University of Illinois Press, 2002).

The Glorious Cause: The American Revolution, 1763 to 1789 by Robert Middlekauf (Oxford University Press,1982).

3 Westward expansion in the 19th century

Key Issues

- Why did so many Americans move west in the 19th century?

- What were the consequences of the westward expansion?

- Why was Plains Indian society destroyed?

3.1 Why did it become possible to move west?

3.2 Who went west, and why?

3.3 What are the reasons for the destruction of Native-American society?

3.4 What was the extent of federal government involvement in westward expansion?

3.5 How did westward expansion affect American attitudes?

Framework of Events

1803	Louisiana Purchase
1804–1806	Lewis and Clark Expedition to Pacific North-West
1811	Tecumseh's Confederacy defeated at Battle of Tippecanoe
1819	Adams–Onis Treaty cedes Florida to USA from Spain
1820	Missouri Compromise
1825	Completion of Erie Canal
1830	Indian Removal Act: removal of south-east Indians to Indian Territory
1832	Oregon Trail becomes main route West
1836	War between Mexico and Texan settlers; leads to independence of Texas following Battle of San Jacinto
1846	Mexican Wars begin
	Brigham Young leads Mormons on trek to Utah
1848	Treaty of Guadeloupe-Hidalgo ends Mexican War: USA acquires California, Nevada, New Mexico, Arizona, Utah and parts of Colorado
	Gold is discovered in California
1849	California Gold Rush
1853	Gadsden Purchase
1854	Kansas–Nebraska Act
1858	Comstock Silver Lode is discovered in Nevada
1860	Pony Express
1862	Homestead Act provides cheap land in West
1867	Indian Peace Commission establishes Indian reservation policy
1868	Laramie Treaty between USA and Sioux
1869	First transcontinental railroad is completed at Promontory Point Utah where Union Pacific meets Central Pacific railroads
1876	Battle of Little Big Horn between US army and Sioux/Cheyenne
1890	Battle of Wounded Knee; end of Indian Wars
	Turner Thesis on West.

Overview

THE development of the West is a major theme in the history of the United States of America. It helped to transform the country from a small state clinging the eastern seaboard to a vast continental power stretching from the Atlantic Ocean to the Pacific.

The process of expansion was partly achieved through the clever purchase of land. In 1803, Jefferson purchased the vast Louisiana territory for $15 million from Emperor Napoleon I of France. In 1853, the USA acquired the Gadsden Purchase of land in the Gila Desert, from Mexico, as a possible route for a transcontinental railroad.

However, land was also acquired through war. In 1819, the USA acquired Florida from Spain and, in 1848, large areas in the South-West and West from Mexico.

Even though the USA had acquired large areas of land, there had to be reasons for Americans wanting to move westward. Part of the reason lay in the vast mineral wealth of the West. Gold and silver led to thousands heading west to become rich. Others went west to farm. The Mormons were forced west because of religious persecution.

To aid movement west, Americans used a variety of transportation. River travel took them part of the way, usually to St Joseph or Independence, Missouri. To get further west, they organised themselves into wagon trains. From the end of the Civil War, the main way west was by train. The nation was joined from Pacific Ocean to Atlantic Ocean by a transcontinental railroad in 1869. This allowed tens of thousands to move west.

In the process of moving west, Americans came into conflict with Native-American society. The story of westward expansion is the history of armed conflict between whites and Indians. To provide the basis for the destruction of Native-American society, many believed it was the 'Manifest Destiny' of the USA to conquer and colonise the whole continent.

Many Indian tribes were initially moved west of the Mississippi river, in the 1830s, to occupy Indian Territory (later the state of Oklahoma). However, after the Civil War, open conflict occurred between the USA and the Plains Indians. It took until 1890 for the Plains Indians to be defeated. That date stands out as the end of westward expansion – the end of the 'Frontier'. In 1890, in Chicago, the historian Frederick Jackson Turner provided an interpretation of American history in which the desire to move westward was a central theme. Once the Frontier had come to an end, many Americans looked outside the continent for further expansion of American influence.

What do you regard as the most important reason in the mind map why westward movement occurred?

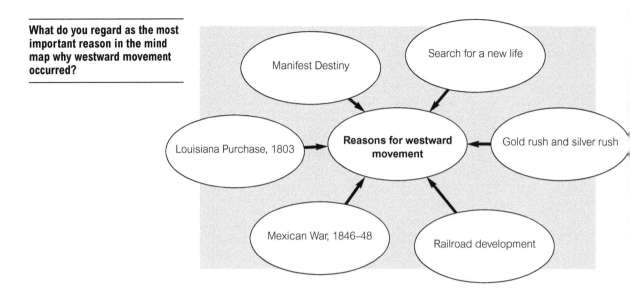

3.1 Why did it become possible to move west?

In the half-century from 1803 to 1853, the USA was transformed. Within a period of 50 years, the United States changed from a republic of 16 states to the east of the Mississippi into the major regional power that stretched from the Atlantic to the Pacific – three times the size and almost five times as populous. The number of American citizens living west of the Appalachian mountain range went from 2.5 million in 1820 to over 5 million in 1830; from 25 to 40 per cent of the total population. This significant territorial increase was, of course, important for population expansion westward. So, before one investigates why so many Americans moved west, one must first understand why it became possible to do so. The answer lies in a combination of the territorial expansion of the growing republic and changes in transport and communications that made moving out west increasingly viable.

Territorial expansion

The Louisiana Purchase, 1803
In 1803, President Thomas Jefferson supported the purchase of the Louisiana territory for the bargain sum of $15 million. In doing so, the size of the United States doubled overnight, adding 828,000 square miles to the **republic**. The whole process came about rather unexpectedly. In 1800, Spain ceded (gave) the territory to France whose leader, Napoleon Bonaparte, had dreams of restoring a colonial empire in North America. Jefferson, though generally a supporter of Republican France, was well

Republic: A country whose system of government is based on the idea that every citizen has equal status, so that there is no king or queen and no aristocracy.

Thomas Jefferson (1743–1826)			
3rd President of the USA (1801–09), founder of the Democratic-Republican Party. As a member of the Continental Congress (1775–76), Jefferson was largely responsible for	drafting the Declaration of Independence. He was the first President to be inaugurated in Washington DC. Jefferson supported the French Revolution and spent 4 years in France (1785–89). Upon his return to the United States, he	was Secretary of State (1789–93) and Vice-President (1797–1801). His political philosophy of 'agrarian democracy' placed responsibility for upholding a virtuous American republic mainly upon the yeoman farmers.	Ironically, his two terms as President saw the adoption of some of the ideals of his opponents, the Federalists. This period also witnessed the Louisiana Purchase (1803) and the abolition of the slave trade (1808).

aware of the importance of New Orleans to American trade, situated as it was at the mouth of the Mississippi river (down which frontier farmers transported their produce) and already a major port.

Suggestions, in 1802, that the rights of Americans to trade through New Orleans might be limited, prompted Jefferson to send James Monroe to France to negotiate the purchase of the port and any lands to the east. By the time of his arrival in France, Napoleon had already abandoned his colonial plans and informed the American Minister in Paris, Robert Livingston, that he was willing to sell the whole of Louisiana for $15 million. Livingston and Monroe, having been authorised to spend up to $10 million on New Orleans and lands to the East, were now being offered almost half of the remaining continent in the West, of which New Orleans was a tiny but significant part. Without time to consult and fearing Napoleon might change his mind, they quickly signed the Treaty. The **Senate** ratified this in October. It led to the formal transfer of this vast tract of land by the end of the year.

The **Louisiana Purchase** was a significant moment in American history. Overnight the idea of a nation stretching from the Atlantic to the Pacific coasts of America suddenly seemed possible and the foundations of a major power were laid. Furthermore, the United States now controlled both banks of one of the most fertile river valleys in the world. Jefferson's ideal of a republic of self-sufficient farmers could now spread down this 'Valley of Democracy'.

During the following decades, the rush for further territorial expansion died down, although there were always some voices keeping the issue

Senate: The smaller and more important of the two councils that form the law-making part of the government in some countries, e.g. the USA and Australia.

Louisiana Purchase: This was the biggest land sale in history. In April 1803, the size of the USA doubled when the federal government bought the whole of the Mississippi Valley up to the Rocky Mountains from France – an area of 828,000 square miles (2,144,522 square kilometres or 2,145 hectares). The US government paid $15 million for this land. The American Minister in Paris, Robert Livingston, and the future President, James Monroe, negotiated the treaty.

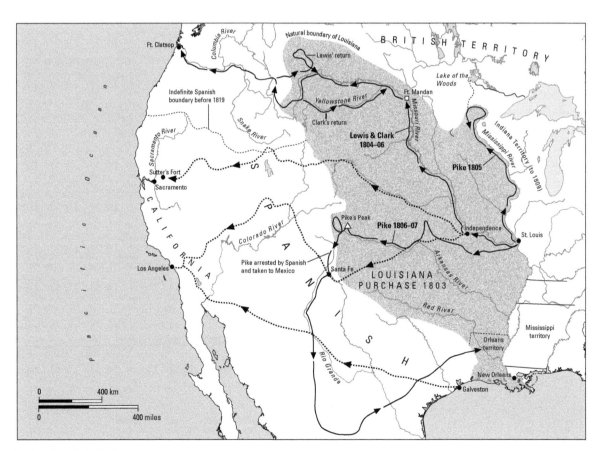

Explorations in the West

'Manifest Destiny': The belief of many white Americans in the early 1800s that all land could be owned. Expansion westwards was seen as a natural right. The ideology of 'Manifest Destiny' was used to justify forcing Indians off their ancient lands, and thus allowing the white occupation of the American West.

Expansionism: Seeking to enlarge the area of the world under your control, not always by internationally acceptable means.

Dictator: A ruler who has complete power in a country, especially power which was obtained by force. As well as Santa Anna in Mexico, other examples include Adolf Hitler in German (in the 1930s) and Fidel Castro in Cuba.

Annexation: Taking possession of territory and adding it on to an existing state. The annexed areas are then integrated into the state and ruled as part of it.

James Knox Polk (1795–1849)
11th President of the USA (1845–49), a Democrat. He allowed Texas into the Union, and forced the war with Mexico that resulted in the annexation of California and New Mexico.

---

alive. The 1840s, especially after the election of James Polk as President in 1844, saw renewed interest in westward expansion. Indeed, by the end of the decade, US territory extended to the Pacific coast, justified and encouraged by the popular idea of '**Manifest Destiny**'. This expansion was due to diverse policies regarding Texas, Oregon and Mexico that had the common theme of seeking to extend American influence and power westwards (see map on page 47).

Florida, 1819

Under the colonial control of the Spanish, Florida was always going to be vulnerable to US **expansionism**. Already, during the war of 1812 when Spain had been allied with Britain, Americans had seized the opportunity to take control of the most westerly parts of Florida around Mobile and Baton Rouge. As Spain was forced to deal with a series of revolts in its South American colonies, troops were removed from Florida and the area became a centre for outlaws and runaway slaves, as well as the Seminole Indians. In 1817, General Andrew Jackson was asked by the federal government to pursue these groups, after a series of raids over the border in Georgia and the Mississippi territory. Although the government had not ordered Jackson to attack Spanish posts, this is what the triumphant general did when he seized Pensacola and St Mark's in 1818. Spain could do little to resist and, struggling to maintain its empire elsewhere, it gave up Florida in 1819, as well as abandoning any claims to the Oregon territory in the North-West.

Texas, 1836–1845

The future of Texas was the source of many political debates following its securing of a tenuous independence from Mexico in 1836. Mexico's **dictator**, Santa Anna, had accepted Texan independence when captured by Sam Houston in 1836, at the Battle of San Jacinto. However, since that time, he had refused to accept Texan independence. Texans feared it was only a matter of time before Mexico sought to retake the province. President Andrew Jackson recognised Texan independence in 1837. Ever since then, there had been support for Texas to be annexed to the United States, not least from the Texans themselves (who hoped for greater security from Mexico). There was also support from most southerners and expansionists who feared that an independent Texas might be susceptible to British influence and act as a block to westward expansion of the United States. Many in the North feared Texan annexation, however. Many of those who had moved to Texas when it was part of Mexico had gone from the South with their slaves. The admission into the Union of a territory the size of Texas would significantly extend slavery in the Union, especially if it broke up into several states. This might well lead to war with Mexico.

In 1844, a treaty for **annexation** was supported by the Texans but defeated in the Senate. With the election of James Polk as a committed 'annexer' the same year, it seemed only a matter of time before Texas joined the Union. A joint resolution (a constitutional device, since a joint resolution does not need a two-thirds majority, as a treaty does) was put to Congress. Reassuring some northerners by insisting that Texas would not be divided up, so only adding two slave-state votes to the Senate, the resolution passed Congress in just three days. By the end of the year, Texas had entered the Union as the 28th state.

Oregon, 1846

When James Polk was elected President in 1844, he made clear his desire to secure Oregon – an area in the North-West that had ill-defined boundaries. It had been occupied jointly by Britain and the USA since 1818, when attempts to divide the region had failed. At the time the territory had been largely empty of settlers from either nation, but since 1830 there had been considerable settlement by American **pioneers** who followed the 'Oregon Trail' as **missionaries** and farmers. By 1845, around 5,000 Americans were living in Oregon, compared with less than 1,000 British. In the 1844 election, Polk had called for the occupation of all of Oregon up to the 54° 40′ line of latitude North and there was talk of war if the British did not cooperate. In the end, a compromise was worked out that saw the territory divided at the 49th Parallel, which then formed the northern border of the USA with Canada. There was some discontent with Polk for compromising on his tough campaign line over Oregon, especially from some northerners who felt that the President was favouring expansion to the South over the North. However, the advantages of securing a route to the Pacific without a single shot having been fired, and without upsetting the world's strongest power, suggests the Oregon Treaty of 1846 suited the United States well. The fact that by the time the Senate approved the treaty the USA was already at war with Mexico may well have encouraged a spirit of compromise in the North-West.

War with Mexico, 1846–1848

President Polk, with his firm belief in 'Manifest Destiny', could not help but be tempted by the vast territories still held by Mexico. Calculating that the United States could easily win a conflict with Mexico and secure significant territorial prizes, he put pressure on the Mexicans from the start in the hope of provoking a conflict or securing concessions.

California was the most attractive prize Mexico had to offer. Many Americans were aware of its possibilities as a gateway to the Pacific, as well as its being a lush agricultural prospect. There were some Americans living in California, as there had been in Texas before the revolt there, but it seemed unlikely that they would rise up against Mexico as the Texans had done. Besides, Spanish Mexicans and Native Americans easily outnumbered them. Polk's hopes that he might settle the issue peacefully came to nothing, despite sending a minister to Mexico City, in 1845, with the offer of up to $25 million for California and the territory that would link it to Texas. The Mexicans were still upset over Texas and were not about to negotiate away more territory.

Polk now became deliberately provocative. In 1846, he sent 4,000 troops under General Zachary Taylor to a disputed area around the Rio Grande, which both Mexico and Texas claimed was theirs. He had already positioned a US naval squadron off the Californian coast and had sent an expeditionary force under Captain John Fremont into California to make '**topographical and scientific observations**'. Polk was anxious to maximise support for war by having the Mexicans make the first attack. He moved quickly when, in May 1846, news reached Washington that General Taylor's troops had been attacked by Mexican troops who had crossed the Rio Grande on 25 April.

Polk issued a war message to Congress which, with minimal opposition, authorised the President to raise 50,000 men to fight Mexico and voted him $10 million for the campaign. He had deliberately provoked a war with Mexico in a determined effort to secure California by force, once it became clear the Mexicans would not sell. It was, in the words of the historian Hugh Brogan, a 'disgraceful affair'. The action faced severe criticism from many **New Englanders** who saw it as a southern adventure.

Polk now intended to fight a war as quickly as possible. Quick victories by Taylor in 1846 saw the United States capture the port of Matamoros. The area south of the Rio Grande was all in US hands by February 1847

Pioneers: Some of the first people to live, farm etc. in the unknown areas of America.

Missionaries: People who are sent to a foreign country or area to teach about Christianity (religion based on the teachings of Jesus Christ and the belief that he was the son of God).

Topographical and scientific observations: A study of the area for producing maps.

New Englanders: Those Americans who lived in the six north-eastern states of Vermont, New Hampshire, Massachusetts, Maine, Rhode Island and Connecticut.

with the capture of Buena Vista, despite being outnumbered 4 to 1. Meanwhile, Santa Fe had been captured in the north and Fremont had done his work in California, working with local Americans to overthrow Mexican rule there by the end of 1846. Polk was determined to force the Mexicans to retreat. He sent a second army under General Winfield Scott to attack Mexico City in November 1846.

A brilliant campaign saw the Mexican capital fall by September 1847 and a treaty was quickly drawn up – the Treaty of Guadalupe-Hidalgo – in February 1848. Polk secured the approval of the Senate in March by a majority of 38 to 14, with opposition from both southern expansionists who clamoured for all of Mexico and anti-slavery Whigs who feared the spread of slavery and had been uncomfortable with the war from its start.

Indemnity: Amount of money or goods received by someone or some nation as compensation for some damage or loss they have received.

The 1848 Treaty of Guadalupe-Hidalgo was an extraordinary triumph for Polk. For an **indemnity** of $15 million, America was confirmed in Texas and secured the entire area to the West, including California. Mexico had lost almost half its land mass overnight, whilst the USA increased by a further third, incorporating territory even larger than the Louisiana Purchase. That it had been achieved in rather dubious circumstances, and the way in which it now opened up the slavery issue and paved the way for the sectional strife of the 1850s, were of little immediate consequence to the expansionists around Polk. They could rejoice in the final achievement of 'Manifest Destiny', as the still young republic now stretched from coast to coast and was the undoubted power in the region.

The Gadsden Purchase, 1853

Railroad magnate: An owner of a large number of railroads (railways).

The final piece of the jigsaw was inserted in 1853 when James Gadsden, a **railroad magnate** from South Carolina, was sent by the government to negotiate the purchase of some land to the south of New Mexico that would allow the construction of a southern transcontinental railroad to California. Although arousing some opposition in the North, where attempts to get the first transcontinental railroad built would soon lead to the troubles of Kansas–Nebraska (see page 81), Gadsden found the Mexicans eager for the $10 million on offer. The purchase was made in a treaty of 1853 that was approved by the Senate in the same year.

Taming the wilderness

Although a number of hardy individuals were always likely to move out west, it is hard to imagine any major western settlement without the improvements in technology and communication that made life on the frontier a manageable family experience. As well as acquiring the western territories, governments, settlers and **entrepreneurs** set their minds to making westward movement a viable option for the growing American population.

Entrepreneurs: People who set up business deals in order to make a profit for themselves.

Exploring and opening up the West

As soon as Jefferson had secured the Louisiana Purchase, he was keen to explore the new territory and consider its viability as land for settlement. In 1804, he secretly secured $2,500 from Congress to fund an expedition into the new territory led by his private secretary, Meriwether Lewis, and a young army officer, William Clark. The men, accompanied by the Shoshone princess Sacajawea and a party of 50, explored the territory for the next two and a half years. They learnt much about the terrain and inhabitants of the land and found the route to the Pacific via Oregon that would open up the 'Oregon Trail' in the ensuing decades. They were the best known of several explorers who opened up the interior and came back with vital intelligence and a love for the rich lands to the West that aroused the passion of potential pioneers. In 1805, Lieutenant Zebulon Pike

Pony Express, in 1861

explored the upper Mississippi and, in 1806, trekked to the eastern Rockies of modern-day Colorado.

Communications

If the West was to attract anything more than explorers and trappers, an effective and secure route to the area had to be opened up. Trails such as that to Oregon saw forts spring up along their course as protection from Indian tribes. Supply centres also developed and the routes out west became increasingly well worn. In 1811, the federal government began the construction of the Cumberland road – a highway that, by its completion in 1852, stretched almost 600 miles from Maryland to Illinois and which opened up the Mid-West to relatively easy settlement.

By the time of the American Civil War (see Chapter 4), there were numerous trails across the West (see map on page 47), carrying horse-drawn stagecoaches as pioneers headed west. By the end of the Civil War, the stagecoach entrepreneur Ben Holladay had built up 5,000 miles of stage routes across America. The stagecoaches also formed the basis of the earliest communication and postage systems. In 1857, the federal transcontinental mail contract was awarded to a **syndicate** headed by John Butterfield who, for an annual subsidy of $600,000, provided a twice-weekly mail service in each direction linking St Louis in the East with San Francisco in the West – a distance of 2,800 miles. The first service ran in 1858. Despite considerable costs, overland communication with California had superseded sea transport in popularity by 1860.

More dramatic was the Pony Express service, established in April 1860, that ran from St Joseph, Missouri, to Sacramento – a distance of 2,000 miles which was covered in a staggering ten days as intrepid horsemen galloped between stations about ten miles apart. The service only lasted 18 months, suffering from a lack of funding and from the arrival of the telegraph. In October 1861, the first transcontinental telegraph line was established. Thereafter, communications between East and West would be less dramatic but far more immediate, reliable and affordable. With the widespread development of the telegraph, pioneers could now set forth west without a sense that they would never be heard of again. The plains would still be wild, but less lonely from now on.

Syndicate: A group of people or organisations that is formed for business purposes or in order to carry out a project.

The development of the steamboat also did much to open up the West, especially around the Mississippi and its tributaries. The first steamboat was launched by Robert Fulton in 1807, and by 1860 there were over a thousand chugging up and down the Mississippi. The steamboats were not subject to the tides and currents of the major rivers. With a speed of around ten miles per hour, they became reliable for transporting goods, especially timber and minerals, from the West to the markets of the East.

The impact of the railroads

For all the importance of stagecoach routes, trails, telegraph lines and steamboats, nothing could compare with the importance of the railroads in opening up the western lands of the USA. Westerners had to wait some time for their coming for, despite the acknowledgement that a transcontinental route was desirable as early as the 1840s, the vast expense in construction meant that only one line could be contemplated initially. There was also hot competition over where the terminal should be. The development of California and the Gadsden Purchase were pursued by Southerners anxious to compete with the expanding North, whilst Douglas' ill-fated Kansas–Nebraska Act (see page 81) had its origins in the desire to settle territory that would allow the construction of a line to terminate in Chicago. In the end, the matter could only be settled once the southern states had seceded and Congress could easily pass a bill that would see the construction of a northern transcontinental line. On 1 July 1862, the First Pacific Railroad Act chartered two companies to start building: the Union Pacific Railroad, westward from Omaha; and the Central Pacific Railroad, eastwards from Sacramento. The incentives were in the form of very large land grants, giving the companies a 400-feet

Construction of the Union Pacific Railroad on the Nebraska plains in 1867.

(122-metre) right of way and alternate sections of land for each completed mile of track. Thus an incentive was created for the two companies to build as much track as they could.

Even then, investment was slow and construction only began in 1864 when the land grant was doubled and government money was provided as a loan to attract further investors. Construction was difficult with all the raw materials, plus food and supplies for thousands of workers, having to be transported out west. As well as significant natural obstacles such as the 7,000-feet (2,134-metre) Sierra Nevada mountains to contend with, the railroad builders also faced Indian attacks and a hostile environment. Many of those constructing the railroad arrived as **immigrants**: Chinese contract workers in the West, Irish immigrants to the East. In the end, the track was completed in the spring of 1869 at Promontary, Utah, with the Union Pacific laying 1,086 miles of railroad to the Central Pacific's 689 miles. The speed with which the line was constructed meant that in places it was not especially secure, but the rapid use made of the line encouraged the quick construction of other lines.

Immigrants: People who arrive to live and work in a country from another country or continent.

By the end of the century, there were four more transcontinental lines: the Northern Pacific; Southern Pacific; Atchison, Topeka and Santa Fe; and the Great Northern. These major lines spawned a major network across the West. Western railroad mileage had increased from 3,000 miles of track west of the Mississippi in 1865 to 87,000 miles by 1900 (see page 145). Following a series of scandals involving financing the railroads, the government stopped making loans to companies. However, the land grants remained significant, with the federal government giving 131 million acres away in all and a further 48 million acres being offered by the states' governments.

1. Explain why the USA was able to acquire so much land in the West between 1803 and 1854.

2. Explain the changes in transport that allowed Americans to move West after 1803.

3.2 Who went west, and why?

The lure of the West

At the start of the 19th century, the area to the West of the Mississippi was unknown and in the possession of European powers. Apart from the Native-American tribes who roamed the plains, the only humans who ventured there were traders, trappers and explorers. Even by mid-century the vast majority of western lands were unexplored and uninhabited, with the exception by then of California, which had suddenly filled with gold prospectors in 1849, and the Mormon base at Salt Lake City in modern-day Utah. The farming frontier was slowly advancing, however. The development of communications and of improved farming methods (as mentioned above) saw settlers move into the 1,500-mile wilderness in the subsequent decades.

Independent yeomanry: Farmers who owned, rather than rented, a small plot of land.

Many pioneers were motivated by the prospect of financial gain, though others were escaping the growing urban centres of the East and of Europe. The move west was encouraged by politicians and writers in the East who saw the West as the place where real American values continued to survive, where the Jeffersonian ideal of an **independent yeomanry** was most likely to flourish. Expansionist presidents such as James Polk and Franklin Pierce were keen to see their newly-acquired lands inhabited. Indeed, Polk deliberately encouraged the rush to California in 1849 with his announcement of the discovery of gold there. Writers like Mark Twain told of the liberation of life on the frontier with his popular accounts of Huckleberry Finn and Tom Sawyer. The influential New York journalist, Horace Greeley, used his 'New York Tribune' to publicise stories of frontier life following his journey from New York to San Francisco. 'Go West, young man, and grow up in the country', he urged in 1859 and published an account, 'The Plains as I Crossed Them', in 1869. Settlers were not only attracted by romantic notions of the wilderness and of self-advancement, there were also numerous incentives offered by both federal and state governments and by railroad companies eager to get people to settle on the land they had acquired from the government during construction. Indeed, a number of railroad companies had agents actively recruiting immigrants in Europe by the end of the 19th century. For the most part, people went west as farmers or miners, establishing mining, cattle and homestead frontiers, with the exception of the Mormons who had fled West to escape persecution in the East.

The Mormons go west

The Mormons, or Church of Jesus Christ of Latter-Day Saints, was a new, American-born religion founded in 1830 by Joseph Smith after he reported receiving golden plates from an angel that translated into the Book of Mormon. Many religious groups and **sects** have established themselves before and since in the USA, but the Mormons suffered serious prejudice in mid-19th-century America. It was more to do with their social practices than their religious beliefs. The Mormons operated as cooperatives, voting as a unit, establishing their own **militia** and practising **polygamy**. Other Americans could not accept such a group. Congress passed an anti-polygamy law in 1862.

The Mormons increasingly settled together and, although this was a way of surviving, it only served to emphasise their distinctiveness still more. In 1844, Joseph Smith and his brother were killed by a mob in Carthage, Illinois, near to their settlement of Nauvoo. Smith's successor, Brigham Young, proved to be a more vigorous and charismatic leader. In 1846, he persuaded the Mormons to leave their settlements and head West to set up a new republic free from their hostile neighbours. The great Mormon trek of 1846–47 saw pioneer Mormons march 1,300 miles westwards and settle in the desert valley of the Great Salt Lake, then part of Mexico. They quickly established themselves in the Utah territory. By the end of 1848, 5,000 Mormons had established themselves in their colony of Deseret (see map on next page). With strong leadership and a cooperative approach to farming, the Mormons prospered. Many thousands of Mormons, from Europe and the Mid-West, trekked westward to join Deseret and the settlements that spread out from the Salt Lake down to southern California.

America's acquisition of the territory in 1848 saw Young being made territorial governor of Utah in 1850, though the community still did not fit in with American society. In 1857, a federal army was sent against the Mormons before an accommodation was reached. The Mormons, nonetheless, maintained their cooperative and polygamous practices (Young had almost 30 wives) and so Utah did not achieve statehood until 1896. The Mormon settlements in the Utah desert developed largely independently of any other movements out West, as the hostile territory made the area unsuitable for cultivation or hunting.

The mining frontier

Perhaps the best known of all western pioneers are the 'Forty-niners' who flocked to California in search of gold, following its discovery and the announcement by Polk in 1848. Many prospectors for precious metals went west in the earliest days of the frontiers. The 'Forty-niners' were the first discernible group to head west and settle. There were a series of gold and silver strikes in the 1860s and 1870s: the largest deposit of precious

---

Joseph Smith (1805–1844)
Founder of the Mormon religious sect. He received his first religious call in 1820, and in 1827 claimed to have been granted the revelation of the 'Book of Mormon' (an ancient American prophet), inscribed on gold plates and concealed a thousand years before in a hill near Palmyra, New Jersey. Smith founded the Church of Jesus Christ of Latter-day Saints in 1830 in Fayette, New York. The Mormons were persecuted for their beliefs. Smith and his brother were killed by an angry mob in Illinois in 1844.

Sects: Groups of people that have a particular set of religious beliefs. Many sects have separated themselves from a larger group in order to follow their strongly held, or some would say, extreme beliefs.

Militia: Organisation that operates like an army but whose members are not professional soldiers.

Polygamy: The custom in some societies of marriage to more than one person at the same time.

Brigham Young (1801–1877)
Mormon religious leader who succeeded Joseph Smith. He joined the Mormon Church in 1832 and was appointed an apostle three years later. After a successful recruiting mission to Liverpool, England, he returned to the USA. He led the Mormon migration to the Great Salt Lake in Utah (1846), where he headed the colony until his death.

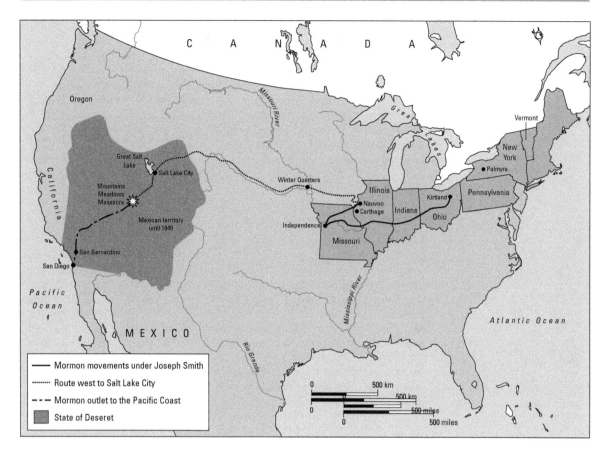

The westward route of the Mormons

metals was found at Comstock Lode, Nevada, in 1859 and the last major strike provoked a gold rush to Dakota in 1874.

The development of mining towns followed a similar pattern across the West. An initial, disorderly rush of prospectors, usually men, would establish camps around gold deposits. Early mining would consist of the basic 'placer mining', which involved washing the surface-deposit gold out of the rocks. These camps would soon attract a collection of hangers-on who sought to exploit the predominantly male and lawless pioneers. Saloons, brothels and gambling dens quickly sprung up to give the hard-living miners an outlet for their money and energy. A good example is Virginia City which emerged from the discovery of the Comstock Lode in 1859. From nowhere, the town had a population of 38,000 by 1878, complete with four banks, six churches and 150 liquor stores (off-licences).

Mining towns often lived up to their reputation for being the 'Wild West'. Gunfights, vigilante action and stagecoach robberies were frequent, though the more established towns had to develop their own rudimentary justice systems quickly in order to rule in mining disputes and to administer basic law. Many of the towns were home to European and Mexican immigrants. Almost a third of Cornwall's tin miners left Britain in search of western gold in the 1860s. Of the 1,966 miners at Comstock Lode in 1880, 1,234 were of British origin. As the deposits dried up, miners would simply pack up and move on, leaving a trail of 'ghost towns' in their wake.

Gradually, the surface deposits dried up and more ambitious deep-level mining developed. Such mining required machinery, skill and capital outlay. This was not likely to develop on an individual basis. By the end of the 19th century, the traditional miner became obsolete, as large-scale businesses developed out West – the most significant of which was the Anaconda Mining Corporation of Montana.

The early pioneers either moved on to new areas, such as those of the gold rushes in Canada at the end of the century, returned to the East or found themselves working as more skilled labour with the new, large-scale companies. The mining frontier opened up stretches of the United States that were not likely to develop agriculturally and, in that sense, was crucial in the settlement of the mountainous West. Most significant of all was the major movement and development of California. Within two years of the discovery of gold, 90,000 settlers had moved to California. It became a state in 1850, without going through the process of organising itself as a territory.

The cattle frontier

The decades immediately after the Civil War marked the 'golden age' of the cowboy, who ranged across the plains of the South-West driving his cattle to the developing railroad towns of the Mid-West. In the 1860s, there were around five million longhorn cattle roaming wild in Texas (they had been introduced by the Spanish in the 18th century). Worth only $3 or $4 per head in Texas, they could fetch ten times as much in the northern meat markets, centred on Chicago. The issue was how to get them there. In 1866, a group of Texans herded some cattle 1,000 miles to the terminus of the Missouri–Pacific railroad at Sedalia, Missouri. Heavy losses en route made them change routes the following year and herd to Abilene, Kansas, where the cattle were loaded on to the Kansas–Pacific railroad at its western terminus and transported to Chicago. It was the beginning of a major trade for Abilene, which saw 35,000 cattle pass through in 1867, rising to 700,000 by 1871. Abilene was a popular choice, due to the decision of lifestock dealer Joseph McCoy (the real 'Real McCoy') to run a line from Chicago to Abilene and to the liberal **quarantine** laws in Kansas that allowed transport of live cattle. This practice of ranging cattle over two or three months from Texas to the Mid-West railheads spread quickly. Soon 'cow towns' such as Abilene, Dodge City in Kansas and Miles City in Montana emerged as the transportation centres for cattle. Between 1866 and 1888, almost ten million cattle were driven by cowboys to these stations, and America became a beef-eating nation.

Not all cowboys herded cows. There was considerable sheep-herding too in the north around Oregon and Montana, and about a quarter of the herders were former black slaves finding a free life out West. In many ways, cowboy life is the most potent image of life on the frontier, but cowboys lived a dangerous yet predictable life with wages rarely going beyond $30 per month. Two-month journeys entirely outdoors with little comfort and facing natural hazards as well as rustlers and Indian attacks were the standard lifestyle. Then at the end the cow towns were rarely as wild as their mining cousins. Indeed, Kansas adopted **prohibition** as early as 1880.

The ranging lifestyle did not last long, however. The spread of railroads made it easier for cattle farmers to transport cattle from nearer home. The invention of barbed wire, in 1873, allowed the formation of large ranches where cattle could roam free without drifting off. Moreover, a series of outbreaks of splenic fever in cattle yards and severe winters in the mid-1880s – that saw cattle exposed to other herds and to the elements respectively – encouraged farmers to protect their cattle with winter shelter. As ranches developed and water supplies were fenced off, so it became harder to maintain a ranging lifestyle at all. By the 1880s, almost all cowboys found themselves working on ranches as little more than

Quarantine: Period of time during which animals that may have a disease are kept separate from other animals. This prevents the disease spreading to other animals.

Prohibition: A rule or law, which states that a particular thing is not allowed. It usually refers to the sale and consumption of alcohol.

farmhands. Just as mining opened up California, so the range and ranch systems brought settlement and identity to Texas and the South-West. The 'Lone Star' state of Texas was soon integrated into the US system.

The farming frontier

By far the least glamorous, but most significant, settlement out West was that of the farmers who gradually cultivated the western lands around and then beyond the Mississippi. They created a wheat belt which, by the end of the American Civil War, was set to supply not only the United States but a hungry global market too. Land could be acquired by several methods: straightforward private purchase; grants from federal or state governments; or land from the railroads, keen to establish settlement alongside their own lines. Initially, the federal government had sold land in large plots allowing **land speculation**. There was growing pressure by mid-century for a homestead act that would allow families to purchase affordable plots of land that would sustain one farm. This was finally achieved by the Homestead Act of 1862 which was passed whilst Congress was free of southerners, who rightly feared that small-scale farming would prevent the development of plantations and so slavery. The Act allowed farmers to acquire 160 acres in one of two ways:

Land speculation: Where people who buy land sell it again for a profit.

1. either a settler could stake a claim and live on the land for five years, after which it was his;

2. or the settler could live there for six months and then pay $1.25 per acre.

Between 1862 and 1900, 600,000 settlers claimed their homesteads and, although it was subject to widespread abuse with speculators and companies putting in numerous dummy applications, the Homestead Act did allow small-scale settlement to develop. Problems linked to the inappropriate size of the homesteads in areas where the terrain was poor were resolved by the Desert Land Act of 1877, and the Timber and Stone Act a year later. The former Act allowed the purchase of 640 acres at $1.25 per acre provided the homesteader established an **irrigation** scheme. The Timber and Stone Act of 1878 allowed the purchase of land unfit for cultivation for mining and lumbering. Although these federal land acts did stimulate settlement, most homesteaders still purchased their land from the states or railroad companies.

Irrigation: The supply of water through ditches or pipes that are specially put there in order to help crops to grow.

Perhaps of greater significance was the Morrill Act, also passed in 1862, which granted public land to states to provide for agricultural colleges that might help farmers learn new and improved techniques. Life on the farms was hard, made more difficult by the start-up costs which, at around $1,000 for an average homestead, meant many farmers faced chronic debts. Life was wild and frequently homesteaders lived many miles from their nearest neighbours. The treeless and dry region saw homesteaders living in houses scraped from the earth and resorting to animal dung for fuel. Railroads and the telegraph made life more bearable as the century wore on, but farmers were highly vulnerable to drought, fire, tornadoes and grasshopper plagues, as well as Indian attacks in the early years. There were even occasional battles to be fought against rangers who resented the fencing off of the plains and water supplies they had traditionally used.

Most of the early farmers in the West began as subsistence farmers and struggled to break the virgin soils of the plains. A series of new inventions and techniques allowed this to change dramatically as farming became more mechanised. Farmers could cultivate wider areas and achieve higher yields than they needed for themselves or even, by mid-century, the needs of the entire United States.

Sickle and scythe: Simple farm implements for cutting corn.

The breakthrough came in the 1830s, most notably with the development of the first steel plough by John Deere of Illinois in 1837 and the patenting of the McCormick Reaper in 1834 by Cyrus McCormick. McCormick's reaper provided a mechanical means of harvesting that replaced the **sickle and scythe**. It allowed two men with horses to harvest 20 acres of wheat per day, covering five times as much ground as was the case previously. Deere's plough opened up new soils to planting as it became possible to cut through soil formerly resistant to the wooden plough. This was further strengthened by the chilled-iron plough invented by James Oliver in 1868 and known as the 'sod buster' for its ability to cut through the toughest soil.

One of the most significant inventions was barbed wire, invented by Joseph Glidden in 1873 and popularised by John Gates. Barbed wire provided a cheap and efficient means of fencing off vast tracts of less productive grazing land in the South-West and Texas. It encouraged settled livestock farming, as opposed to the ranging that had featured previously. Other new techniques included 'dry-farming' – the practice of deep ploughing and frequent harrowing that checked evaporation and so helped cultivation in drier climates – and the development of spring and winter wheat harvests. Irrigation schemes did not emerge effectively until the 20th century, though awareness of the need to preserve moisture and the potential for irrigation was growing from the 1870s onwards.

Such inventions and developments in technique lightened the load for farmers, but they added further to the need for capital outlay that was often beyond the resources of the small-scale farmer. Increasingly large farms developed, known as 'bonanza farms', out in the prairies of Minnesota and the Dakotas. Farming there became a large-scale industry and small-scale farmers found themselves bought out. They either moved away or became employed as farmhands.

There was a pattern to western settlement that can be seen in all three accounts above. Initial small-scale enterprises of individual pioneers developed by the end of the century into large-scale productions. The independent-minded yeoman farmer or miner, although he existed, did not dominate the Valley of Democracy as Jefferson and others had hoped.

Who were the settlers?

Traditionally, there had been an assumption that many of those who went west had come from the towns in the East and so eased the tensions of the cities, meaning America avoided much of the urban unrest that characterised urban Europe in the 19th century. This theory does not stand up to critical examination. Determining exactly who was moving west in the 19th century is not as easy as working out what they were doing there. Certainly, the West was a more diversely populated region than popular films and television suggest. Up to a quarter of cowboys may well have been former slaves, whilst the construction of the railroads brought thousands of Irish and Chinese workers into the western states. Many of the farmers were already farming in the Mississippi Valley and were simply trying their luck elsewhere; the environment was not suited to city-dwellers with no farming experience. Many, of course, moved directly west having arrived as immigrants; some specifically recruited by the railroad companies. These foreign-born farmers tended to settle in national groups, so that a traveller through the mid-West in the 1840s might well hear as much Swedish or German spoken as English, especially in states such as Wisconsin and Michigan.

Nor did the population grow uniformly. Although the number of white settlers living in the wheat-belt states of Kansas, Nebraska, the Dakotas,

Iowa and Minnesota increased from one million to seven million between 1860 and 1900, the population of Nebraska actually fell between 1890 and 1900. Many westerners – farmers, ranchers or miners – moved around constantly. Of the settlers who entered Kansas in the 1850s, only 35 per cent of them were still there in 1865.

Finally, the western states were overwhelmingly male. In 1880, Colorado had twice as many men as women and Wyoming three times. This was especially the case in the mining towns of the Rockies where the climate was not suited to women in their traditional roles. As a result, those women who did live out West tended to be treated more as equals than their eastern sisters. The daily fight for survival and the rudimentary conditions were not conducive to the maintenance of separate spheres. It is not surprising that the first states to introduce female suffrage were in the West.

> **1. Explain the religious and economic reasons why some Americans went west in the 1840s.**
>
> **2. What do you regard as the main reasons why many Americans wanted to settle in the West? Explain your answer.**

3.3 What are the reasons for the destruction of Native-American society?

Early federal responses to the Native Americans

Early encounters between Native Americans and settlers had been varied. Tribes had responded in various ways to the arrival of the Europeans – from cooperation and integration to outright hostility and warfare. Whatever the course of action, the Europeans had nonetheless had the best of it in the long term for, at the start of the 19th century, the Native Americans found themselves pushed westward into the territories of the **North-West Ordinance**, safely out of the way of the original 13 colonies. There were a few exceptions to this, where Indian tribes were more settled in their farming habits, such as the Cherokee of Georgia. These Indians lived in protected areas, agreed by treaty and beyond the jurisdiction of state or federal authority. The North-West Ordinance had made it clear that the Native Americans were to be left to their own devices in the territories.

> **North-West Ordinance:** A law passed by Congress on 13 July 1787. It allowed north-west territories – including Ohio, Indiana and Illinois – acquired from Britain in 1783 to be colonised and later admitted as states.

> 'The utmost good faith shall always be observed toward the Indians; their land and property shall never be taken away from them without their consent, and in their property, rights and liberty, they shall never be invaded or disturbed, unless in just and lawful wars authorised by Congress.'

There was a clear warning in the final phrase that the United States might not be forever persuaded to ignore the Indians, but it was clear that the federal government had no intention of allowing individual settlers to take matters into their own hands.

Early government policy, under the Federalists and later Thomas Jefferson, had hoped that the Indians might gradually be integrated into settler society via a programme of education and persuasion. Organisations such as the Society for Propagating the Gospel Among Indians, founded in 1787, sent missionaries into Indian villages, and Congress voted money to promote literacy and European farming practices. Jefferson's liberalism encouraged him to be interested in and to study the various tribes. However, it did not extend so far as to see them as the white man's equals. His Secretary for War, Henry Deerborn, was happy to write, in 1803, that 'the government consider it a very important object to introduce among the several Indian nations within the United States the arts of civilisation'.

Tecumseh's Confederacy

Hopes of a gradual and peaceful 'civilisation' of the tribes were dashed in the early 19th century. The Louisiana Purchase meant that millions of

Assimilation: Learning ideas from other people and making use of them.

Tecumseh's Confederacy: A union of Eastern Indian tribes, formed in 1811 to stop the westward advance of Americans. It included Shawnees, Kaskaskias and Cherokees. They were defeated by Governor of Indiana, William Henry Harrison, at the Battle of Tippecanoe on 6 November 1811.

Shaman: A medicine-man of some of the north-west American Indians.

Andrew Jackson (1767–1845)
7th President of the USA (1829–37), a Democrat. Major General in the war of 1812, he defeated a British force at New Orleans (1815) and was involved in the war that led to the purchase of Florida (1819). Elected President, at the second attempt, in 1829 – the first election in which electors were chosen directly by voters rather than state legislators. He demanded loyalty from his Cabinet members. The political organisation he built was the basis of the modern Democratic Party. Known as an expansionist and the scourge of the Creeks and Seminoles.

acres of land had been acquired by the United States. Substantial settlement was likely to begin in the area between the Appalachians and the Mississippi river, especially in the lush farming areas around modern-day Kentucky and Ohio. Jefferson might continue to talk of **assimilation** and civilisation but, as President, he was as clear as anyone else that Indian claims to hunting grounds in the North-West Territory were illegal. If the tribes were to reject 'civilisation', then their only alternative was to move to the West.

As tribal leaders saw white settlers move further and further into their traditional hunting grounds, a resistance movement began to take shape which would culminate in the most united resistance the Native Americans ever managed against the settlers – **Tecumseh's Confederacy**. The Shawnee chief Tecumseh, together with his **shaman** brother Tenskwatawa (the 'Prophet') concluded that this was the last opportunity for the Indians to resist settler encroachment for good. They managed to unite the many tribes to the east of the Mississippi in a pan-Indian alliance against the white man. Tecumseh used his organisational skills and eloquence to put together the largest concerted resistance the Americans were ever to face. He told the governor of Indiana territory, William Henry Harrison, how the 'paleface' intruders had 'driven us from the sea to the lakes – we can go no further'. As well as being a respected warrior, Tecumseh was aware of the difficulties and importance of maintaining Indian unity. He argued passionately that the tribes should renounce those elements of European life which some had adopted. Textile clothing and alcohol were to be discarded and negotiation over land rejected. Land was a general commodity, not subject to specific ownership in the American sense.

The uprising soon found itself entangled with the war of 1812 against the British. Indeed, British arming of the Indians was partially a cause of the Anglo–American conflict. Before war against the British had broken out, Henry Harrison had managed to destroy the Shawnee base at Tippecanoe, in November 1811, forcing Tecumseh to abandon the village. Tecumseh himself, having been appointed Brigadier General in the British army, was killed fighting alongside the British at the Battle of the Thames in 1813.

With Tecumseh dead, the Confederacy died with him, though several tribes fought on for several more months. Andrew Jackson was active on the southern frontiers, defeating a Creek army at the Battle of Horseshoe Bend in 1814 before turning his attention to the Spanish and the British. Tecumseh's revolt and the support the Indians gave to the British ensured that, thereafter, American attitudes to the Native Americans would be more hostile. Several treaties were drawn up, forcing the Indians in the North to move west of the Mississippi, whilst in the South the First Seminole War (1817–18) saw action against the Seminoles in the marshes of Florida. As Jefferson wrote ruefully in 1813:

'They would have mixed their blood with ours and been amalgamated and identified with us within no distant period of time [but] the cruel massacres they have committed on the women and children of our frontiers taken by surprise will oblige us now to pursue them to extermination or drive them to new seats beyond our reach.'

Andrew Jackson and Indian Removal

Those Indians who remained east of the Mississippi now found themselves as small islands surrounded by covetous settlers. By 1830, most territory east of the Mississippi had been settled as states – for example, Illinois

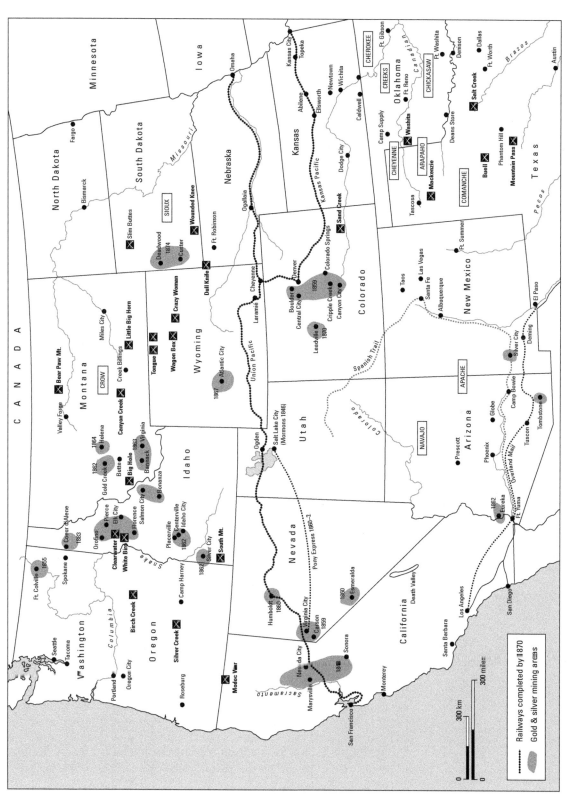

Native American tribes (names of tribes in boxes)

joined in 1818 and Alabama in 1819. It was unlikely that the 125,000 Native Americans still living in the East could survive much longer, especially following the election of Andrew Jackson as President in 1829. Jackson is traditionally seen as one of the Presidents most hostile to the Indians, but his attitude is more complex than seems at first, since he adopted an Indian boy. He respected Indian values, even if he did not see how the tribes could continue to exist within the civilised borders of the United States. On his election, he championed the idea of removal, which came to fruition with the Indian Removal Act of 1830. The Act allowed for the removal out west of all Indians living to the east of the Mississippi. In 1834, modern-day Oklahoma was designated Indian territory (see map on page 61). There they were to be left 'permanently free' in an area no one expected the white man to penetrate.

In a sense, Jackson's policies were more progressive than Jefferson's. Although he was no more prepared than his predecessors to see Indians denying land to white settlers, he did acknowledge and respect the Indian way of life and genuinely assumed that it could be continued after their removal. The subsequent removals were not always accepted peacefully by the Indian tribes. In Illinois, the Sauk and Fox Indians under Chief Black Hawk fought unsuccessfully against the militia in the Black Hawk War of 1832. The federal government was forced into a long and not totally successful war against the Seminoles in Florida between 1835–42, which saw 1,500 US casualties and which cost the Treasury $30 million. Most significantly, the removal policy saw the forced march of the 'five civilised tribes' of the Cherokees, Chickasaws, Choctaws, Creeks and Seminoles out of their southern lands to the Indian reservation in Oklahoma. The Cherokees, in particular, had reason to be unimpressed. Having adopted a settled agricultural life in Georgia, that even saw them owning several hundred black slaves in the 1820s, the state of Georgia tried to move them out in 1828.

Despite the Supreme Court, under the Chief Justice John Marshall, ruling in their favour on three occasions, the Cherokees were eventually forced out by federal troops, who marched 15,000 of them over the winter of 1838–39 to the Indian territories. The conditions on the march – known to history as the Trail of Tears – were so terrible that a quarter died on route. Jackson had made his own views on the Cherokees perfectly clear. On hearing that the Supreme Court had supported the Cherokees, he is reported to have replied, 'John Marshall has made his decision; now let him enforce it.'

By 1840, almost all Indians had been moved to the 'Great Desert' beyond the Mississippi. There, supplies and rations were administered by the Bureau of Indian Affairs, established in 1836 and supported by the US army.

The Indian Wars of the 1860s and 1870s

By mid-century, around 300,000 Indians lived on the Great Plains. Some of the tribes had always lived there, whilst others had been moved there during the removals of the previous decades. These Indians maintained their tribes and, for the most part, their traditions. Thus, with the exception of the 'civilised tribes' of the South, most operated in bands. There were tribal subdivisions of between 300 and 500 who lived a nomadic lifestyle, living off the buffalo herds and hunting on horseback. They would be as likely to fight one another as the settlers. Until 1850, they could for the most part ignore the settlers who passed through on trails to Oregon, California and Utah.

This began to change as mineral discoveries, improvements in farming techniques and the development of the Texas cattle industry opened up the

Major conflicts of the Indian Wars

- In 1862 an uprising of the eastern Sioux, led by Little Crow, saw 500 settlers massacred in Minnesota before the militia re-established control and hanged the ringleaders.

- In 1864 the Cheyennes, who had been launching occasional raids in Colorado, were persuaded to gather at Fort Lyon on Sand Creek to discuss peace terms. There, 450 men, women and children were massacred by Colonel John Chivington, a Methodist minister who took delight in exhibiting the scalps he collected from the massacre. The massacre, one of the most notorious events of the Indian Wars, did lead to the survivors giving up their lands the following year.

- Between 1865 and 1867, the western Sioux harassed soldiers building a road through their hunting territory in Montana. This led, in December 1866, to the Fetterman Massacre when 82 soldiers under Captain Fetterman were ambushed and murdered.

- The Red River War of 1874–75 marked southern tribal hostility to the reservation policy being implemented at the time. A winter campaign under General Sheridan saw the Indians eventually forced to accept the terms.

- Perhaps the most famous incident of the Indian Wars was part of a campaign against the Sioux in the Black Hills of Dakota in 1876. The Sioux were resisting settler encroachment into their territories because of the discovery of gold there. During the campaign, General Custer found the main Sioux encampment on the Little Big Horn river in Montana. In June, he and his small band of 265 men were surrounded and totally destroyed by 2,500 Sioux Indians led by Sitting Bull and Crazy Horse. Even then, the Sioux did not capitalise on their victory. The following year, the Sioux were forced to give up their hunting grounds, despite having been promised them less than a decade earlier.

Sioux chief Sitting Bull.

central plains of America, previously written off as the Great American Desert, to settlers. The 'permanent freedom' of the Indians began to look less secure. Treaties continued to be made – such as the agreements at Fort Laramie in 1851, when the major Indian chiefs agreed to accept certain fixed tribal boundaries in return for goods and supplies. However, Indian chiefs treated such agreements with growing distrust. Many would agree with the words of Chief Spotted Tail of the Sioux when he observed, in the 1870s, that '... since the Great Father promised that we should never be removed we have been removed five times ... I think that you had better put the Indians on wheels and you can run them about wherever you wish.'

Although Spotted Tail tended to support peaceful coexistence with the white men, there now erupted a series of wars in the West as Indian tribes became frustrated. These were not coordinated uprisings, like Tecumseh's, but occurred across the frontier from the 1860s to the 1880s. Although the Indians managed to secure some short-term victories, they were no match in the long term for the superior technology of the settlers, state militias and the US army. A number of conflicts broke out during and immediately after the Civil War when, because of the absence of the US army in most places, Indians felt emboldened and local militia less observed. Several conflicts followed (see above).

There were a few sporadic outbursts across the Plains and Rockies in the final years of the 19th century, but it was clear to the Native Americans that the battle had been lost. The Blackfoots and Crows were pushed out of Montana, the Utes lost their lands in Colorado after a brief war in 1879. Geronimo, chief of the Apaches, was caught in 1886 after 15 years of fighting. The Nez Perces were finally pushed out of Idaho when, despite a brilliant campaign by their chief Joseph, he was captured in 1877. His surrender speech eloquently reflects the resignation of the proud warriors:

> 'I am tired. My heart is sick and sad. From where the sun now stands I will fight no more forever.'

Reservations and Americanisation

Whilst the wars were taking place in the West, the federal government was trying to work out a new policy to deal with the fact that, with western settlement across the continent, removal was no longer an option. In 1867, an Indian Peace Commission was established that was to set up and police a reservation policy. This led to Indians being moved to protected federal lands in modern-day Dakota and Oklahoma, the latter already established as a place of Indian settlement. Indians, not surprisingly, were unhappy about the reservation policy and a number of the wars documented above were the result of resistance to removal to the reservations.

Humanitarians: People concerned about the welfare of other people. The aim of humanitarianism is to improve life for people and to lessen their pain and suffering.

The later decades of the century saw a return to Jefferson's assimilationist ideas. Eastern **humanitarians**, horrified at the accounts of the physical destruction, turned their well-meaning but culturally arrogant minds to policies collectively known as 'Americanisation'. Boarding schools, such as the Carlisle Institute in Pennsylvania, were established to teach Indians civilised ways, before sending them back to the reservations to educate their elders. Indian practices and dress were outlawed and instruction in the virtues of independent farming and private ownership encouraged. In 1887, the Dawes Act broke the reservation lands up into family holdings and granted citizenship to all property holders after 25 years. In 1901, the five civilised tribes of Oklahoma received citizenship automatically.

Most of these policies were motivated by genuine liberal sentiment, but they resulted in the loss of millions of acres by Indians who were tricked into surrendering their land by fraudsters before they understood the concept of ownership. Between 1887 and 1934, Native Americans lost almost two-thirds of the land they had been granted. More to the point, their way of life and customs were being gradually destroyed. They may not have been physically destroyed but in terms of the Indian way of life it was as much a cultural **genocide** as the massacres of settlers on the plains.

Genocide: The deliberate and systematic killing of an ethnic or national group.

Why was Native-American society destroyed?

The destruction of the Native Americans has tended to be seen as inevitable once the settlers began to move West, but it is important to consider the factors at work in order to decide if the destruction of the native culture, and triumph of the European/American culture, was really unavoidable. Several factors can be identified.

● **The incompatibility of nomadic and settler cultures**
It is important to establish first of all that, once settlers moved west, a clash of some kind between settlers and Native Americans was inevitable. That is not to say that the settlers were bound to win that struggle, but the

nomadic lifestyle of the Indian tribes could not really exist side by side with settlers who were fencing off land and so depriving tribes of traditional water and hunting resources. Some tribes did adapt, such as the Cherokees, and there are examples of white traders accepting elements of Indian culture too. However, it is difficult to see how this could have operated on a wide-scale basis without the Indians effectively ceasing to operate as an independent nation.

● **The development of transport and farming methods that opened up the frontier**

It is clear that some easterners assumed that the removal method was a long-term solution. This was based on an assumption that the Indians were being moved to territory that no settler would want to inhabit. New agricultural techniques, developments in transport and communications, and the expansion of the USA to the Pacific changed this. It made the idea of two fundamentally opposed social systems co-existing on one continent impossible to sustain.

● **The lure of Indian lands to settlers**

Not only were settlers moving into the Great Desert, but also the lands set aside for Indian reservations were not secure for the Indians. This was most graphically illustrated in the 1870s when the discovery of gold in the Dakota hills, though part of the northern reservation, drew numerous white settlers into the territory and the US army did nothing to protect Indian rights there.

● **The destruction of the buffalo**

The destruction of the buffalo dealt a serious blow to the Indians who depended on them not just for food but for clothing, fuel, hunting and cooking utensils. A craze for buffalo robes and leather in the East, together with railroads opening up the hunting of the buffalo (William Cody, or Buffalo Bill, was reputed to have killed over 4,000 buffalo in 18 months), saw their numbers decline rapidly. From an estimated 13 million buffalo on the plains in 1865, they were almost extinct by the end of the century. It is unclear if the extinction policy was deliberate, but federal officials were well aware of the implication of their destruction for the Indians. For example, General Sheridan commented, 'let them kill, skin and sell until the buffalo is exterminated as it is the only way to bring lasting peace and allow civilisation to advance'.

● **Indian divisions**

After the death of Tecumseh in 1813, there was no further coherent Indian resistance to settler advance and at times tribes were fighting one another rather than the Americans.

● **Broken promises and assurances**

Inevitably, some Indian chiefs only realised too late that the treaties they drew up were worthless. Even when there was an attempt to get them enforced – as seen with the Cherokees in Georgia – it required executive or army support to see justice done. That was unlikely given the general attitude of the federal government to Indian policy. As the western states secured representation in Congress and enjoyed political influence, this became even less likely. At times, the federal army intervened explicitly on the side of the settlers, even sometimes in the face of instructions from back east. The Civil War helped further, as eastern minds were turned elsewhere.

1. How did President Andrew Jackson deal with Native Americans in the 1830s?

2. Why did it take so long to defeat the Plains Indians?

3. Draw a mind map showing the reasons why Native-American society was destroyed.

4. Did the Americans engage in genocide against Native Americans?

● **Technological advantages of the settlers**

For all their bravery, speed and skills, the Indian tribes could not match the impact of the telegraph and railroad that the settlers could use for transport and communication, nor the repeating Winchester rifle and Colt revolver that they could use in the field.

● **The cultural destruction of assimilation and Americanisation**

Even those Americans who sympathised with the plight of the Native Americans saw the solution in terms of assimilation or Americanisation. Thus the best the Indians could hope for was to survive physically: once the western lands were coveted by the settlers, their only alternative was to fight or adapt.

3.4 What was the extent of federal government involvement in westward expansion?

For the most part, the federal government encouraged westward expansion and did much to facilitate the movement west.

In some obvious ways, the government helped settlement. The North-West Ordinance, for example, established a clear and encouraging system to allow states to join the Union easily. The actions of Presidents generally favoured settlement, from the Indian removal policies of Andrew Jackson to the deliberately expansionist actions of James Polk over Mexico and Texas. The federal government also passed a number of Acts to encourage people to move West, most notably the Homestead Act and the Morrill Land Act of 1862. Financial assistance and substantial land grants were made to transcontinental railroad companies and Butterfield's stagecoach route was also subsidised by the federal government. In some ways, government inaction was as telling as any legislation passed, not least the blind eye that was turned to some settler actions against Native Americans in the middle decades, and even the specific collaboration of federal army units and posts out West from time to time. There was a general mood of encouragement and support for 'Manifest Destiny' that became even easier after the sore of slavery had been removed by the Civil War and the free/slave state tensions of westward expansion had long since gone.

However, there were moments and issues that saw the federal government at least putting a brake on expansion. Certainly, some settlers came to resent the unhelpful interference, as they saw it, of the federal government in their affairs. There were three areas in particular where, from time to time, the federal government got in the way of settler desires:

● slavery disputes and sectional opposition to expansion

● Native American policy

● conservation.

We will now look at these three areas in some detail.

Slavery disputes and sectional opposition to expansion

The most obvious check on expansionism came in the period before the Civil War, when growing **sectionalism** and fears of either slave or free states dominating Congress meant that some of the more expansionist instincts of Presidents and settlers had to be put on hold. The best example of this is the northern restraint on Polk and Pierce in their plans

Sectionalism: The idea that different parts of the USA have a strong regional identity (such as North and South).

for expansion southwards in the 1840s and 1850s. This manifested itself most clearly in 1854 when Pierce was involved in secret negotiations with his **ambassadors** to offer $120 million for Cuba. If Spain refused, they were to go to war over the sugar- and slave-rich colony. Details of the secret plotting – the Ostend Manifesto – leaked out and Pierce was forced to abandon his plans before even making them public, when he was faced with northern anger and opposition. Awareness of such opposition also explains Polk's decision not to press for more territory off Mexico and to secure California and New Mexico quickly, before northern opposition grew.

Earlier in the century, the Federalists had similarly acted as a restraining force on westerners clamouring to take Canada in the war of 1812, fearing most the further growth of Mid-West farming states, which tended to be attracted to the radical politics of Jeffersonian Republicanism. As long as sectionalism pervaded the federal institutions, then expansionism would always be viewed with a wary eye by one section or the other. This was also seen with policies towards the western settlement. The Homestead and the Transcontinental Railroad Acts, both essential to the substantial population movement westward in the later half of the century, had to wait until the southern secession ensured their passage through Congress.

Native American policy

Although the federal government tended to turn a blind eye to settler violence against Native Americans, and on occasion federal troops played an overt role in moves against them, there were certain policies that at times thwarted, or tried to thwart, anti-Indian moves. Some politicians sought to accommodate Indian concerns or to humanise policy towards them. For instance, President Grant attempted to staff the Indian Affairs Office with pacifist **Quakers**. Also, President Hayes' admitted in 1877, in seeking to strengthen treaties drawn up with the tribes, that 'many, if not most, of our Indian wars have had their origin in broken promises and acts of injustice on our part'. The Supreme Court did, on occasion, intervene in support of treaties when states or individuals seemed to break them, most famously in the 1830s cases when Chief Justice Marshall repeatedly ruled in favour of the Cherokees in their battles against Georgia. For the most part, these interventions were insignificant in the overall scheme of things. However, the federal government did act at certain times as a restraint on the wilder excesses of settlers in their dealings with Native Americans, even if there was fundamental collaboration in the slow extinction of their way of life.

Conservation

As the last stretches of wilderness began to disappear at the end of the century, so the issue of conservation became significant as some Americans began to wake up to the possibility that the West was not inexhaustible. The destruction of wildlife, woodland and mineral wealth, as well as the exhaustion of the soil, became an issue and there were several federal attempts to preserve lands and resources out West. Pressure grew after the Civil War for some action to protect American timber reserves. In 1873, the Timber Culture Act acknowledged the issue when it offered 160-acre plots to settlers prepared to plant a quarter of their land with trees. Attempts to introduce a forest management system, as existed in Canada, were resisted until 1897 when the Forest Management Act established the Bureau of Forestry, initially under the Swiss expert Gifford Pinchot. By 1910, the Bureau managed 149 protected national forests, after a process of setting aside public lands initiated by President Benjamin Harrison in the Forest Reserve Act of 1891.

The setting aside of land for preservation and public enjoyment had received a boost several decades earlier when, in 1872, two million acres of Wyoming were set aside to create Yellowstone National Park for 'the benefit and enjoyment of the people'. Yellowstone was the first of several national parks, with three being established in California alone in 1890: Yosemite, Sequoia and General Grant. Initially, it was difficult to ensure that the national parks and national forests were policed and protected from indignant settlers who saw the land as theirs. Hence the creation of the Bureau of Forestry and later the National Park Scheme, complete with rangers, in 1916.

Irrigation was a policy more likely than the national parks to secure the support of westerners. Though even here there was a reluctance to take the issue seriously until a series of droughts, in the 1880s, gave greater credence and urgency to the warnings of soil erosion issued by geologists such as Major John Wesley Powell. He urged the federal government to develop water reserves out West before the soils were eroded and exhausted for good. It was not until 1902 that the appropriately named Senator Newlands secured the passage of the National Reclamation Act. This established the principle of federal management of the waterways and authorised the federal government to build and maintain irrigation projects out West. The resulting Bureau of Reclamation acted quickly. By 1914, over a million acres had been reclaimed for farmland from schemes such as the Buffalo Bill Dam in Wyoming and the Theodore Roosevelt and Boulder (later Hoover) dams in Arizona. Conservation was one of the major achievements of the Progressive era, but it was done for the most part against the instincts of western settlers, who generally resented federal interference and ownership of lands which they viewed as their own.

1. Why are there differing views on why the federal government became involved in westward expansion?

2. What do you regard as the most important reasons why the federal government became involved in westward expansion? Explain your answer.

Without federal action – through territorial expansion, military protection and financial support – the rapid westward expansion of the USA could not have taken place. Nevertheless, the federal government did not always act in unison and there were times when settlers had to force the issues themselves. It is also important to recognise that, for all the support and encouragement the federal government might have given, it still required brave pioneers and risk-taking entrepreneurs to act upon the opportunities the federal government presented.

3.5 How did westward expansion affect American attitudes?
A CASE STUDY IN HISTORICAL INTERPRETATION

The Turner Thesis

The impact of the major population movement westwards in the 19th century was not limited to the western lands themselves. Historians have been concerned ever since with the extent to which westward expansion and 'Manifest Destiny' have shaped the modern American mind. Certainly, writers concerned with American 'exceptionalism' have been attracted to the idea of a frontier mentality affecting American social and political attitudes which make them distinct from European attitudes. It is also the case that the West has produced more than its fair share of American myths, most often promoted by Hollywood and the 'spaghetti western'. The individualistic, anti-government streak in the American character has been well fed by tales of Custer's Last Stand, Wyatt Earp, Buffalo Bill and Davy Crockett.

The first historian to consider these issues directly was Frederick Jackson Turner in his lecture 'The Significance of the Frontier in American

American Progress by John Gast, 1873. The woman in a white robe is the symbol of 'Manifest Destiny'. She floats over the prairie holding a school book and a coil of telegraph wire, which she is stringing out behind her. On the ground below, Native Americans and bison run in front of her. Behind her are signs of westward expansion: trains, ships, covered wagons, and pioneer settlers.

History' delivered to the American Historical Association in 1893. Turner, a historian at Wisconsin University, presented his thesis ('The Turner Thesis') following the announcement by the Census Bureau, in 1890, that the frontier had effectively ended and that all western regions were sufficiently inhabited not to be seen as wilderness. It is worth quoting Turner:

> 'It is to the frontier that the American intellect owes its striking characteristics. That coarseness and strength combined with acuteness and inquisitiveness; that practical, inventive turn of mind, quick to find expedients; that masterful grasp of material things, lacking in the artistic but powerful to effect great ends; that restless, nervous energy; that dominant individualism, working for good and for evil, and with all that buoyancy and exuberance which comes with freedom – these are the traits of the frontier, or traits called out elsewhere because of the existence of the frontier.'

Turner was thus suggesting that the frontier had been the source of a number of what might be seen as American values, including democratic ideals, an open society, rugged individualism and unrestricted economic activity. He was also proposing that American characteristics commented upon by Europeans, such as individualism, inventiveness and expansionism, had their roots in the frontier. Turner suggested that the frontier had acted as a safety valve for America, in times of potential economic strife, by providing an escape from urban centres for otherwise discontented citizens. He concluded by seeing the ending of the frontier as a significant turning point in American history:

'The frontier has gone and with its going has closed the first period of American history.'

Turner's Thesis has its merits. One can see, for instance, the ideals of Jeffersonian democracy functioning far better in the West, and it is true that certain movements in US history – such as temperance reform, populism and women's rights – all had their origins in the West. However, historians have since raised objections to the thesis.

Whilst the earliest settlement did tend to involve pioneering individuals acting alone, most westward expansion gradually involved whole communities working together; for example, the development of ranches and mining enterprises. Farmers increasingly formed alliances, such as the Granger and Populist movements, to work together. The most distinct group to move west, the Mormons, actually went because their community-style society did not fit with American values in the East.

Individual democratic ideals can be seen as having their origins in the Whiggism of 17th-century England. The values of the Declaration of Independence and the Constitution – developed when the USA essentially looked East – were certainly dominated by the elites of New England and Virginia.

The idea of westward expansion as a safety valve for urban dwellers does not stand up to scrutiny when one notes that most of those moving West were already farmers, either in Europe or in the Mississippi Valley. The attraction of moving west was that of better lands on which to continue farming, not to start up a farming life from scratch.

The ideal that Turner's Thesis suggests ignores the vast diversity of cultures and backgrounds that were to be found out West. Not only did Native Americans play their role out West, but the West saw Mormons, Hispanics, free blacks, Irish labourers, Scandinavian farmers and Chinese immigrants all bringing their unique cultures and identities into the western melting-pot. The idea of the hard-living, white male pioneer is a legitimate stereotype, but cannot be seen as typifying all western settlers.

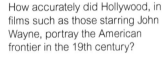

How accurately did Hollywood, in films such as those starring John Wayne, portray the American frontier in the 19th century?

If Turner was correct, then one ought to detect a change after 1890 in the direction of US history, but that does not seem to have occurred and there remain today distinct differences in the attitudes of Americans living in different sections of the Union. There may then have been a western frame of mind, but the idea that it shaped the views of others is exaggerated.

However, just as it is perhaps best not to accept all that Turner had to say as an all-embracing philosophy, so it is fair to see some elements of truth in his observations. It is certainly possible to argue that it is no coincidence that shortly after the closing of the frontier, Americans began to look further west still. They began the process, hesitant at first but confident later, of acquiring an overseas empire. 'Manifest Destiny' had seen the Americans overwhelm colonial powers and native settlers in the space of less than a century. Westward expansion had given America status as a world power. The USA, and the world, would spend much of the next century trying to come to terms with that reality.

1. Explain Frederick Jackson Turner's Thesis on the role of the West in American history.

2. Using information from this chapter, how far do you think Turner's views on the role of the West are correct?

Source-based questions: The causes of the Mexican War of 1846–1848

SOURCE A

Care has been taken – that all our military and naval movements shall be strictly defensive. We will not be the aggressor upon Mexico – but if her army shall cross the [Rio Grande] del Norte and invade Texas, we will if we can drive her army – to her territory. We invite Texas to unite her destinies with our own.

Letter from President James K. Polk to William H. Haywood,
August 1845

SOURCE B

Sir, I am directed by the President to instruct you to advance and occupy with the troops under your command, positions on or near the east bank of the Rio [Grande] del Norte as soon as it can be conveniently done with reference to the season and the routes by which your movements must be made.

It is not designed, in our present relations with Mexico, that you should treat her as an enemy; but, should she assume that character by a declaration of war, or an open act of hostility towards us, you will not act merely on the defensive.

Order from Secretary of War, William L. Marcy, to General
Zachary Taylor of the US Army, 13 January 1846

SOURCE C

The strong desire to establish peace with Mexico on liberal and honourable terms, and the readiness of this Government to regulate and adjust our boundary induced me last September to seek a reopening of diplomatic relations between the two countries. An envoy of the USA [went] to Mexico with full powers to adjust every existing difference. His mission was unavailing. The Mexican government not only refused to receive him or listen to his propositions, but have at last invaded our territory and shed the blood of our fellow-citizens on our own soil.

President Polk's War Message to Congress, 11 May 1846

---

1. Study Sources A and B.

How far do these two sources agree on the role of the US army in possibly starting a war with Mexico?

2. Study Source C.

How reliable is this source as evidence of the reason why the Mexican War took place in 1846?

3. Study Sources A, B and C, and use information from this chapter.

'The USA went to war with Mexico out of self-defence.'

Assess the validity of this statement.

Further Reading

Texts designed for AS Level students

The Enduring Vision by P. Boyer and others (D.C. Heath and Co., 1992)

Texts for A2 and advanced study

The Limits of Liberty by Maldwyn Jones (Oxford University Press, 1995)
America by G.D. Tindall and D. Shi (W.W. Norton & Co., 1993)
Bury My Heart at Wounded Knee by Dee Brown (Pan Books, 1971)
The Indian Frontier of the American West by Roger Utley (University of New
    Mexico Press, 1984)

Television and DVD

'The Way West' – a documentary written and produced by Ric Burns (1995);
    shown on BBC as 'The Wild West' divided into six one-hour episodes. Covers
    Westward expansion from the 1840s to 1890, but concentrates on
    1860s–1890.
'The West' – produced by Stephen Ives and written by G. Ward and D. Duncan
    (1996); divided into eight one-hour episodes. Covers Westward expansion
    during whole of 19th century. Available from DD Video, 5 Churchill Court,
    Station Road, North Harrow, Middlesex HA2 7SA.
'Into the West' – A miniseries produced by Steven Spielberg (2005). Intertwining
    real and fictional characters, the plot follows the story of two families, one
    Native American, the other white American, as their lives become mingled
    through the momentous events of the American expansion. Available on DVD.

4 The origins and course of the American Civil War, 1820–1865

Key Issues

- Why were there growing sectional tensions in the 1840s and 1850s?

- Why did civil war break out in 1861?

- Why did the North win the Civil War?

4.1 How did slavery cause problems during western expansion?

4.2 Why did sectionalism grow in the 1850s?

4.3 Why did Lincoln win the presidential election of 1860?

4.4 How did the election of Lincoln lead to the outbreak of war?

4.5 What were the strengths of the two sides on the eve of war?

4.6 How did the two sides perform in the military campaigns?

4.7 What opposition did the political leadership face during the Civil War?

4.8 How did foreign powers respond to the war?

4.9 What was the importance of the Emancipation Proclamation?

4.10 Historical interpretation: Why did the North win the Civil War?

4.11 To what extent was the Civil War the 'first modern war'?

Framework of Events

1820	Missouri Compromise
1844	Polk is elected President
1846	Start of Mexican War
	Wilmot Proviso
1847	Calhoun Doctrine
1849	California ratifies a free state constitution
1850	Compromise measures pass Congress
1851	*Uncle Tom's Cabin* is published
1852	Pierce is elected President
1854	Kansas–Nebraska Act
	Emergence of Republican and 'Know Nothing' parties
1854–1856	'Bleeding Kansas'
1856	Beating of Sumner; Buchanan is elected President
1857	Dred Scott decision in Supreme Court
	'Panic of 1857'
	Kansas elects a free state legislature and Lecompton slave constitution
1858	Lincoln–Douglas debates in Illinois
1859	John Brown's Raid
1860	Lincoln is elected President
	Secession of South Carolina
1861	February: Deep South secedes; establishment of Confederacy
	April: Shots fired at Fort Sumter
	Secession of the Upper South
	Battle of First Manassas (Bull Run)
1862	April: Battle of Shiloh
	2 June: Robert E. Lee takes command of Army of North Virginia
	McClellan's Penisula Campaign

	Battle of Second Manassas (Bull Run)
	September: Battle of Antietam
	Lincoln issues Emancipation Proclamation
	13 December: Battle of Fredericksburg
1863	May: Battle of Chancellorsville
	July: Battle of Gettysburg
	4 July: Union captures Vicksburg
	July: Riots in New York City against compulsory military service (the draft)
	September: Battle of Chickamauga
	October: Battle of Chattanooga
1864	September: Union army under Sherman captures Atlanta
	November: Lincoln is re-elected President
	November: Confederate army under Hood routed at Battle of Nashville
	November–December: Sherman's 'March through Georgia'
1865	9 April: Lee surrenders at Appomattox
	15 April: Assassination of Abraham Lincoln.

Overview

Cotton gin: A machine invented by Eli Whitney in Georgia, in 1793. It consists of two rollers: one, covered in spikes, tears the cotton-wool away from the seed; the other, covered with bristles, brushes the cotton off the first roller.

Constitution: A legal statement of limitations upon the power of the government, and upon the rights and freedoms of the governed.

Secession: The formal separation of a region or state from a larger group or country. In this instance, the southern states of America wanted to break away from the Union (i.e. the USA) and form their own group of states (to be known as the Confederacy).

Confederacy: The name given to the breakaway southern states of America, under the presidency of Jefferson Davis, during the period of the Civil War.

States' rights: Belief that the state government rather than the federal government had the final say in policy and decision making.

THE war between North and South came as a surprise to many. It had its origins in several decades of growing tensions between the two sections of the young republic. For economic and geographical reasons, slavery remained the dominant economic system in the plantation South long after it had died out in the northern states. It was given a further boost by the invention of the **cotton gin** in 1793. Whilst both sections could accept different systems in the old states, tensions grew over the spread of slavery as the United States expanded westwards. The extent to which slavery could continue to grow in the newly acquired territories was an issue that kept raising its ugly head. Initially, the issue was resolved by compromise; in the **Constitution**, in the 1820 Missouri Compromise and the Compromise of 1850. However, by the 1850s the two sections were growing increasingly uneasy about one another's intentions. The Wilmot Proviso and the Calhoun doctrines – both issued in the late 1840s – raised the stakes on both sides and the work of northern abolitionists became more prominent, most notably with the publication of *Uncle Tom's Cabin*.

A series of events in the 1850s saw both sections move to more extreme positions, made more likely by the decline of the national two-party system. The emergence of the sectional Republican Party, which only sought support in the North, as well as the increasing domination of the Democratic Party by southerners (followed by its formal split in 1860), meant that the forum and will for compromise was diminished. Clashes over the future of Kansas–Nebraska territory gave rise to civil war in the area between 1854 and 1856. There was also violence on the Senate floor when an angry southern Congressman, Charles Sumner, was beaten up by a northern senator. Matters came to a head in 1860 when Republican Abraham Lincoln was elected President without a single southern state supporting him. South Carolina led the way for a southern **secession** from the Union and for the formation of the **Confederacy**, which Lincoln refused to recognise. The failure of compromise in 1861 led to Lincoln resorting to violence in order to force the southern states back into the Union, which in turn caused four more slave states to secede in the cause of 'states' rights'.

Neither side expected the ensuing war to last the four years it did (1861–65). In fighting it, the United States introduced to the world the horrors and destruction of modern warfare. Initial southern successes were not enough to overcome northern morale or resources, strengthened by Lincoln's determination to win. A series of northern victories on the battlefield in 1863, and the appointment of Ulysses Grant to overall military control in 1864 (the same year as Lincoln's re-election), saw the tide turn in the North's favour. The exhausted South was forced to surrender to the North in April 1865. The Civil War had transformed the **Union** forever, causing some historians to refer to it as the Second American Revolution. Slavery disappeared following Lincoln's Emancipation Proclamation and the northern success marked a victory for the proponents of strong central power over the supporters of states' rights. It also marked the beginnings of further westward expansion and the development of a more industrialised economy and society.

Union: The name given to the northern states of America, under President Lincoln, during the Civil War.

What do you regard are (a) the long-term causes of the Civil War, and (b) the short-term causes? Give reasons to support you view.

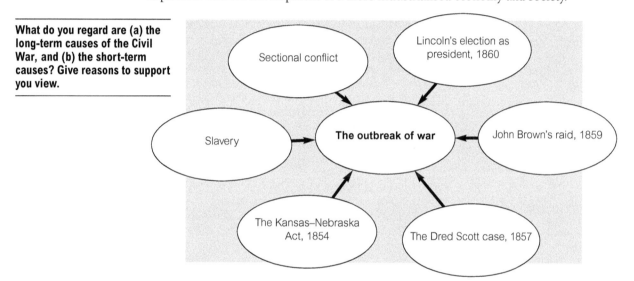

4.1 How did slavery cause problems during western expansion?

In a sense, the American Civil War was caused neither by slavery nor by western expansion, but rather by the way in which these two key issues of the 19th century intertwined. Slavery had existed initially throughout the United States, but had gradually been abolished in the northern states so that by the beginning of the 19th century it was concentrated in the southern part of the USA. Although there were active campaigners against slavery, known as **abolitionists**, the majority of Americans were happy to accept that there were different economic and social systems existing within their country. A number expected slavery gradually to die out as, state by state, planters would come to prefer different systems. However, this hope was destroyed by the invention of the cotton gin by Eli Whitney in 1793. The cotton gin made possible a massive expansion inland of cotton production and the figures for cotton production rose dramatically:

Abolitionists: People who are in favour of abolishing a particular system or practice. In this instance, the abolitionists wanted to abolish slavery.

1790	3,000 bales (one bale is 500 lb / 227 kg)
1801	100,000 bales
1820	400,000 bales
1860	c. 4,000,000 bales

The close relationship between cotton production and slavery was encouraged further by the development of effective labour systems which made slavery a highly productive way of working the southern economy. With the purchase of the vast Louisiana territory from France in 1803, the pattern of slave distribution also changed. In the 18th century, half of the slaves in the USA were in Virginia. By the 1850s, the largest concentrations were to be found in eastern Virginia and the Deep South, in a belt stretching from South Carolina across to the Mississippi and the state of Louisiana (see map on page 95).

The abolition of the slave trade in 1808 did not lead to a decline in slavery. Instead, the value of slaves increased as the supply from Africa ceased. The value of the average slave hand increased from $300 in the 1790s to almost $2,000 by the 1850s. The majority of southerners were not slave-holders. In 1860, there were almost 400,000 slave-holders out of a white population of around eight million in the South, but only about 50,000 of them could be called planters (i.e. owning more than 20 slaves on a plantation). Despite this, most people living in the South accepted slavery as part of their way of life. They might well have aspired to own slaves even if they did not do so themselves.

The existence of slaves also acted as a reminder to poorer whites that there was a social class below them in society. Slavery was thus seen very much as part of the Southern way of life – its 'peculiar institution' as it was later referred to. Attacks on slavery were seen as attacks on the South as a whole.

Not that slavery came under much attack in the early decades of the 19th century. The American Colonisation Society had been founded in 1817 with the aim of returning freed slaves to Africa. The first group arrived in Liberia in 1822, but by 1860 only 15,000 black Americans had actually made the journey. In 1831, the northern radical William Lloyd Garrison first published a weekly abolitionist newspaper, 'The Liberator'. A year later, he founded the New England Anti-Slavery Society. The

Slave family in a cotton field near Savannah in the 1860s.

American Anti-Slavery Society was established by Arthur and Lewis Tappan in 1833. However, neither organisation attracted mainstream support in the North or the South until the 1850s, and the movement was initially troubled by divisions. Northerners were no less racist than their southern brothers and there are plenty of examples of **discrimination** against freed and escaped slaves in the northern states. Workers, especially immigrants, feared the economic competition of freed blacks, and abolitionists were the subject of attacks in their own states throughout the 1830s. That is not to say that there were not important voices speaking out against slavery, on both moral and economic grounds, during the period. It is simply that their influence can be exaggerated.

The Missouri Compromise

Whilst few northerners felt the need to abolish slavery, this tolerance did not extend to agreeing to the expansion of slavery into the western territories. The first tensions were seen in 1819, as **Congress** considered the entry of the southern territory of Missouri into the Union. Missouri easily qualified for statehood but, when it applied to join the Union, the House of Representatives passed the **Tallmadge Amendment**. This called for a ban on any more slaves entering Missouri and anticipated gradual **emancipation** by stating that any children born to slaves should be free. This was not acceptable to the slave-holding Missourians, nor to southerners generally, so the Amendment was defeated in the Senate. The issue went beyond Missouri, however.

As the USA developed, the North was emerging as the more populous, more economically diverse and more wealthy section, whilst the South identified itself more and more with slavery and plantation agriculture. As a consequence, the North began to dominate in the House of Representatives, which was constituted according to population. In 1819, there were 11 free states and 11 slave states, so the balance in the Senate – where each state had two senators regardless of size – was even. Southerners became concerned that, with the Tallmadge Amendment, the North might at some point begin to use its population advantage to limit or even abolish slavery in the South and certainly in the expanding territories. For this reason, they were determined to maintain the slave/free state balance in the Senate as a counterweight to northern dominance of the House. In the end, a compromise was found – the Missouri Compromise of 1820. This stated:

> 'Missouri would be admitted as a slave state. Maine, a free-soil area that had been part of Massachusetts, would be admitted as a separate state, so preserving the balance in the Senate.
>
> Slavery would not be permitted in the future in any territories that were created out of the Louisiana Purchase above the line of 36 degree-30 – which constituted the whole of the territories of the USA as existed in 1820.'

Although neither side was entirely happy with the solution, both houses of Congress accepted it (although a majority of southern Congressmen opposed it). Wiser heads were not convinced that the issue had been resolved. Former President John Quincy Adams saw the issue as 'a title-page to a great tragic volume', whilst Thomas Jefferson feared the Compromise as 'the most [portentous] question which ever yet threatened our Union'.

The impact of the expansion of the 1840s

The slavery issue went quiet in the 1820s and 1830s, but by the end of the

Discrimination: The practice of treating one person or group of people less fairly than others.

Congress: The elected group of politicians that is responsible for making the law in the USA. It is the American parliament and has two houses: the House of Representatives and the Senate (see page 41).

Tallmadge Amendment: In 1819 it was proposed that the territory of Missouri be admitted to the Union as a slave state. Congressman James Tallmadge of New York proposed an amendment that Missouri should be accepted as a slave state only if it undertook to forbid further slave immigration and to free its slaves gradually, as the northern states had done earlier. Tallmadge and his associates had two objectives: to reserve as much as possible of the Louisiana Purchase (see page 46) for free, white labour; and to weaken the political ascendancy in the Union which the South had enjoyed since independence.

Emancipation: The freeing of people from the social, political or legal restrictions that are considered to be degrading or unnecessary. In this instance, it refers to the freeing of slaves.

1840s it was threatening to destroy the Union altogether. Between 1836 and 1848, three slave states and three free states had been admitted to the Union, so preserving the sectional balance in the Senate achieved in the Missouri Compromise. However, the acquisition of Oregon in 1846 and of California and New Mexico in 1848, the discovery of gold in California in 1848 and migration of the Mormons to Utah ensured that there would soon be large populations out West. This forced the issue of whether the new states should be free or slave. A number of northern Congressmen were already concerned that the Democratic President, James Polk, appeared to be favouring the South (he had compromised with Britain over Oregon in the North-West, but was fighting a provoked war against Mexico). This would mean more territory susceptible to slavery was likely to be added to the Union. The northern Congressmen were anxious to prevent slavery from spreading into the new territories. In August 1846, David Wilmot, a Democrat from Pennsylvania, proposed an amendment to a war bill that became known as the 'Wilmot Proviso'.

The Proviso proposed to exclude slavery from any territory acquired from Mexico, whether from war or purchase. The House of Representatives passed it but it was defeated in the Senate, with voting more on sectional than party lines – the majority of northern Congressmen voted for the proposal; all but two southerners voted against.

Senator John Calhoun of South Carolina most eloquently expressed the southern response to the Wilmot Proviso and growing sectional tensions. He issued a series of resolutions, in February 1847, that later came to be known as the 'Calhoun Doctrine' or 'The **Platform** of the South'. The main points were:

Platform: Collection of policies put forward by a political party during an election; otherwise known as a manifesto.

● Territories were the common property of all the states.

● Any US citizen should be able to settle in any territory with their property (including slaves) as guaranteed by the Constitution.

● Each state was sovereign and had the right to leave the Union (secede) if it chose to do so.

● If northerners continued to ignore southern interests and threaten slavery, then the South would be justified in leaving the Union.

Between the two extremes of the Wilmot Proviso and the Calhoun Doctrine lay a large group of talented and moderate politicians who were committed to the Union and who were determined to find a solution to the controversy. They were helped by the fact that the two main political parties, the Whigs and the Democrats, contained members from both sections of the Union. The two most likely solutions were:

● either to extend the 36 degree-30 line agreed in the Missouri Compromise to the Pacific coast and so include any new territory secured;

● or to adopt the doctrine of **popular sovereignty**, proposed by the northern Democrat Lewis Cass.

Popular sovereignty: This would allow the people living in a territory to decide whether they wished to become a slave or free state at the point of applying for statehood.

Democracy: A political system in which there are many parties and the people get to choose their government through voting. There is free speech and a free press. The United States and the United Kingdom are democracies.

Popular sovereignty was a solution that fitted in with the commitment to federalism and **democracy**. It provided enough ambiguity so that southerners could feel that slavery was permitted to expand, whilst northerners could be reassured that, given the terrain out west and nature of the settlers, a vote for slavery in the new territories was unlikely. Cass, as Democratic Presidential candidate in 1848, campaigned on the idea. His Whig opponent, Zachary Taylor, expressed no views on the subject – a conscious decision by the Whigs, who wanted to avoid the divisive issue arising during the campaign.

Ominously, a third party – the Free Soil Party – also contested the election and secured 10 per cent of the popular vote, on a platform supporting the Wilmot Proviso and calling for resistance to southern influence and slavery expansion. Taylor won the election and carried states equally in the North and the South, but the issue of slavery expansion remained there for Congress to resolve. Within weeks, the House of Representatives had reaffirmed the Wilmot Proviso and condemned the slave trade in Washington DC, whilst Calhoun had issued another statement supporting slavery that was signed by a third of slave-state representatives.

Tensions were given a specific focus in 1849 when both Californian gold prospectors and Mormons around Salt Lake City applied for statehood. Taylor encouraged them to establish constitutions and apply immediately for statehood. Despite being a southerner and slave-owner himself, Taylor alienated most of his Whig supporters in the South by his refusal to seek compensation for the South if the two states were to be admitted as free states. By the autumn of 1849, the situation was looking very tense. In October of that year, Mississippi urged all slave states to send representatives to a convention to discuss some way of resisting 'Northern aggression'.

When Congress met in December 1849 many southerners were talking openly of secession and invoking the Calhoun Doctrine. Northerners began to raise the stakes over slavery in Washington DC and southerners complained of the non-enforcement of the Slave Fugitive Law (see box).

The 1850 Compromise

The situation in 1850 needed all the reserves of skill and diplomacy that could be mustered if secession or war was to be avoided. Over the next few months, politics was dominated by the 'Great Debate' which finally led to the 'Compromise of 1850'. This was an acceptance by the two main parties and the majority of the country of its 'finality'. In the debate, three of the key political figures of the previous decades were to make their final contributions to American politics:

- 72 year-old Henry Clay, who proposed the Compromise

- 68 year-old Daniel Webster, who provided important northern support

- 68 year-old John Calhoun, who made his last great speech against compromise.

Within two years they were all dead.

Compromise of 1850

Concessions to the North

- California should be admitted as a free state.

- Territory disputed by Texas and New Mexico to be surrendered to New Mexico.

- Abolition of the slave trade (but not slavery) in the District of Columbia.

Concessions to the South

- The remainder of the Mexican Cession area to be formed into the territories of New Mexico and Utah, without restriction on slavery – hence open to popular sovereignty.

- Texas to receive $10 million from the federal government as compensation.

- A more stringent Fugitive Slave Law, going beyond that of 1793.

The Omnibus Bill tried to provide something for all sections of the Union. Clay and Webster made eloquent appeals to both sides to compromise for the sake of the greater cause, the Union. Nevertheless, the Bill was defeated as a single package in the Senate, in July 1850. Clay returned to his home state of Kentucky, ill and dejected. This was not the end of the Bill though. The convention called by Mississippi the previous year went ahead, but it soon became clear that the South did not yet have the appetite to fight. Also, President Taylor died suddenly in July 1850 and his successor, Vice-President Millard Fillmore, appointed Webster Secretary of State and threw himself behind the proposals that had just been defeated. The Democratic senator, Stephen Douglas of Illinois, now took up Clay's cause. Douglas recognised that an omnibus bill would attract the opposition of both southern and northern extremists. Instead, he divided the Bill into its five parts and was able to pass each section by combining the support of one section with the moderates who had supported the Omnibus Bill. Thus by September 1850 all of Clay's original proposals had been passed into law. The Compromise of 1850 resolved all the immediate issues that the late 1840s had thrown up. Douglas rejoiced in its passing: 'Each section has maintained its honour and its rights and both have met on the common ground of justice and compromise.'

In the election of 1852, both national parties agreed to accept the 'finality' of the 1850 Compromise and avoided discussing the slavery question. The Free Soil Party polled over 100,000 fewer votes than in 1848, as a spirit of unionism spread across the country.

The confidence of the unionists can, however, be seen as misplaced. After all, the Compromise was only achieved through political skill, rather than through a genuine acceptance of the legitimacy of each section's view by the other. There were no guiding principles established for the future and the South had certainly not abandoned the central beliefs of the Calhoun Doctrine, even if popular support had taken the wind out of secession for the moment. With the admission of California as a free state the North now had a balance in their favour in the Senate. The main sop to the South, the Slave Fugitive Law, was untested and would need the support of northerners to work.

1. How did expansion westward create problems between North and South?

2. Explain why the North and South were able to avoid conflict in the period to 1850?

Thus the 1850 Compromise may have been effective in preventing violence in 1850, but it could only be a permanent solution if subsequent events could be controlled and if the Union had time to establish a spirit of cooperation. It is for these reasons that the historian David Potter has described the Compromise of 1850 as 'an armistice rather than a compromise'. It is also why studying the events that followed is now so critical.

4.2 Why did sectionalism grow in the 1850s?

The Compromise of 1850, however faulty it may have been, did manage to keep a kind of peace for the next ten years. However, some fighting did break out during the Kansas–Nebraska issue and violence increasingly became a tool the two sections were prepared to employ. John Brown's Raid on Harper's Ferry and the beating of Charles Sumner on the Senate floor (see page 82) demonstrated this. The 1850s were an unhappy decade for the USA. What was needed after the patched-up peace of 1850 was a period of stability and calm. What America got instead was a series of events that polarised opinion between North and South. This led to a growing sense of sectionalism, in which the two sections identified more with the North or South than they did with the Union and came to view almost all the actions and pronouncements of the other section as hostile. As this notion grew on both sides, so perceptions became blurred with reality, while perceived slights became actual ones.

The Kansas–Nebraska Bill

Kansas–Nebraska was a large and unsettled region in the early 1850s, although interest in the area was growing in the period as agricultural and irrigation improvements meant that it had agricultural possibilities. The territory covered the likely route that a northern transcontinental railroad might follow.

Senator Stephen Douglas, the chairman of the Senate Committee on Territories and a prominent Northern Democrat from Illinois, proposed the settlement of the territory in his Kansas–Nebraska Bill to Senate in 1854. Ever since the 1840s, Douglas had been a prominent supporter of western expansion and believed such expansion should not be held up because of sectional disputes. He had been a key figure in getting the 1850 Compromise through Congress and now believed that the last major unsettled territory in the West could be settled with minimal sectional conflict. Douglas also stood to gain personally from the Bill, hoping to strengthen his presidential chances by appearing as the champion of western expansion and improving his position in his home state of Illinois by bringing the transcontinental railroad terminus to Chicago.

In proposing the Bill, Douglas was aware that southerners in Congress were unlikely to be enthusiastic. The area was north of the 36° 30′ line (see map on page 95) and so forbidden to slavery under the Missouri Compromise (the land was unlikely to suit slavery anyway, at least in the northern part). A number of southerners were pushing for a southern transcontinental link. They recognised that the Bill would open up the northern route more effectively. Douglas thus proposed that the whole territory should be admitted as just one state (so avoiding a major free state/slave state imbalance in the Senate) and that the issue of slavery should be settled according to the principle of popular sovereignty (i.e. the Bill ignored the Missouri Compromise). In seeking southern support for what Douglas saw as an essentially northern bill, he accepted two southern amendments that included a rejection of the Missouri Compromise. It was agreed that the territory should be divided into two states – Kansas and Nebraska – since southerners felt that there was at least a possibility of voters choosing to introduce slavery in Kansas, the southern part of the territory. Unfortunately for Douglas, his concessions to the South provoked a hostile reaction among the North who saw southern demands as evidence that they did not accept the terms of the 1850 Compromise. Douglas was branded a traitor to the section and various groups united against the Bill.

The South now took up the Kansas–Nebraska Bill as a cause to fight for, assuming that northern hostility confirmed that it was in the southern interest. They campaigned equally energetically against the North and for its passage.

The Bill dominated congressional debates in 1854. As President, Franklin Pierce faced significant pressure to come down on one side. In the end, recognising the importance of the southern votes to the Democratic Party, he tried to make it a party issue and put pressure on some northern Democrats to support Douglas' Bill. The Bill was passed in May 1854, but the section from which a Congressman came was more significant than the party he belonged to in determining his vote. Ninety per cent of all southern Congressmen voted in favour of the Bill and 64 per cent of all northerners, with the northern Democrats in the House split 44 in favour and 43 against.

The Kansas–Nebraska Bill thus served to re-ignite the sectional tensions of 1849–50 and confirmed northern fears of a 'slave power' at work. Perhaps most importantly, the Bill weakened the national reputation of the

---

Stephen Arnold Douglas (1813–1861)
Democrat who served in the House of Representatives (1843–47) and as a senator for Illinois (1837–61). He urged a compromise on slavery. After losing the presidential race to Abraham Lincoln (1860), Douglas pledged his support to Lincoln's Administration (see definition on page 127). He earned the nickname 'Little Giant' for his support for western expansion.

Franklin Pierce (1804–1869)
14th President of the USA (1852–56), a Democrat. Served in the New Hampshire legislature (1829–33), before holding office in the House of Representatives (1833–37) and the Senate (1837–42). Pierce saw action in the Mexican War of 1846–48. Despite his expansionist foreign policy, North–South tensions grew more intense during his Presidency.

Democrats and encouraged politicians in voting according to section rather than party. Coming as it did just as the national Whig Party went into decline, it meant that one of the reasons why sectional tensions tended to be overcome – the non-sectional appeal of the two-party system – had been undermined. As if to confirm this, the 1854 elections were a disaster for the Democrats in the North where they controlled only two northern **legislatures** after the elections, having controlled all but two before. Furthermore, the number of Democrats from free states fell from 91 to 23, compared to a fall from 67 to 63 in slave states. The Democratic Party was becoming a party that increasingly depended on, and appealed to, the South.

Legislatures: The group of people in a particular state who have the power to make and pass laws.

Growing northern concerns

Before the Kansas–Nebraska Bill, many in the North and the South were prepared to accept the terms of the 1850 Compromise even though they disliked certain elements of it. The abandonment of the Missouri Compromise in 1854 changed all that, and mass meetings appeared in the North to protest against elements of federal policy that seemed to favour the South. Already, northerners had felt uneasy about the expansionist policies that Pierce and the Democrats seemed to be supporting:

- in Cuba (which would almost certainly have joined the union as a slave state);
- the Gadsden Purchase in 1853, where the federal government purchased some land off Mexico for $10 million that would allow a transcontinental railroad to run through the southern states.

135,000 SETS, 270,000 VOLUMES SOLD.

UNCLE TOM'S CABIN

FOR SALE HERE.

AN EDITION FOR THE MILLION, COMPLETE IN 1 Vol., PRICE 37 1-2 CENTS.
" " IN GERMAN, IN 1 Vol., PRICE 50 CENTS.
" " IN 2 Vols., CLOTH, 6 PLATES, PRICE $1.50.
SUPERB ILLUSTRATED EDITION, IN 1 Vol., WITH 153 ENGRAVINGS.
PRICES FROM $2.50 TO $5.00.

The Greatest Book of the Age.

A poster advertising *Uncle Tom's Cabin*.

Southerners had opposed attempts to annex Canada and to bring Hawaii into the Union for fear it would have strengthened the free states in Congress, which had also frustrated northerners. As a consequence, arguments that there was a 'slave-power conspiracy' – initially only argued and put about by abolitionists – gained credibility among more moderate northerners, who were prepared to tolerate slavery but did not want to see it spread to the North and threaten the free-labour system there.

The popularity of Harriet Beecher Stowe's anti-slavery novel, *Uncle Tom's Cabin* (which sold 300,000 copies in its first year of publication in 1852), showed a growing concern in the North. It helped to develop the view of slavery as an unacceptable and immoral system that diminished the USA. Northerners were increasingly reluctant to accept the Fugitive Slave Law, especially the requirement that all citizens had to help in the capture and return of runaway slaves. A number of states passed personal liberty laws that prevented local gaols from being used for runaway slaves. There were several outbreaks of violence where mobs tried to prevent federal law officers from returning slaves, especially in the more radical cities such as Boston.

Perhaps the most dramatic illustration of the growing tension between the two sections occurred on the Senate floor itself in May 1856. A southern representative, Preston Brooks, beat unconscious the abolitionist senator Charles Sumner in revenge for a savage verbal attack that Sumner had launched on Senator Andrew Butler, a relative of Brooks. Although fined, Brooks was not expelled and became something of a popular hero in the South. He was re-elected and sent numerous canes with the invitation to hit harder next time. There could have been no clearer image for the North of a brutal southern 'slave power' silencing free speech and challenging the essence of democracy.

'Bleeding Kansas'

It was not long before the simmering tensions boiled over. It was perhaps unsurprising that it should be events in Kansas that were responsible. The settlement of Kansas proceeded far from smoothly and popular sovereignty was found to have delayed, rather than solved, a problem. When it came to voting on a constitution for Kansas, pro-slavery and anti-slavery forces mobilised support both inside and outside the territory to try and influence the outcome. The result was that two different governments and constitutions were established: a pro-slavery one at Shawnee Mission and a free-soil government in Topeka.

Within Kansas, a minor civil war erupted with extreme forces from outside the territory getting involved. Most notorious was the attack on Lawrence, when an attempt to arrest anti-slavery leaders led to several deaths. This was followed by a retaliatory attack on a pro-slavery camp at Pottawatomie Creek by John Brown, who led a small band that murdered five pro-slavery men. The pro-slavery faction now arranged a rigged election for the convention that drew up the constitution of the state, which was boycotted in protest by the anti-slavery faction. As a consequence, the constitution that was drawn up – the **Lecompton Constitution** – protected slave property. By now it was clear to almost everyone that the slavery faction was a minority in the state – a fact supported by both federally appointed governors and by Senator Douglas, the author of the original distress.

Nevertheless, the new Democratic President, James Buchanan, insisted on supporting the Lecompton Constitution and recommended that Kansas enter the Union as a slave state. He was supported in the Senate but the bill failed to pass the House of Representatives and, in a direct referendum in Kansas in 1858, the Constitution was defeated. The troubles within Kansas now died down (Kansas was eventually admitted to the Union in 1861 as a free state, after many southern states had seceded), but a great deal of damage had been done. The issue aroused passions on both sides and created a great deal of anger that now sought outlets. Also, the Democratic Administrations of Pierce and Buchanan had so favoured the slavery view that the Democrats were seriously weakened in the North and looked even more like a party of the South.

The emergence of the Republican Party

By the time of the presidential election of 1856, many northern Democrats were no longer prepared to support their party, especially in the North-West. The Democrat James Buchanan managed to get elected, helped no doubt by his absence while a diplomat in Britain during the Kansas dispute. He did not receive a majority of the popular vote and was helped by the existence of two new parties that had emerged to replace the Whigs: the 'Know Nothing' (American) Party and the Republicans. Both parties began life as single-issue groups that attracted significant support in the North.

The 'Know Nothings' were a nativist party, concerned at the threat they perceived the new immigrants posed to the traditional American way of life. At first, they seemed the most likely to emerge to challenge the Democrats. By 1854, they had over one million members. The Republicans, formally

Lecompton Constitution: A constitution drawn up in 1857 by settlers in Kansas which would have allowed slavery if Kansas became a state. Anti-slavery settlers refused to take part in a referendum on the Lecompton Constitution, but it was theoretically accepted. In 1858, Congress refused to admit Kansas as a state and the Lecompton Constitution was rejected.

James Buchanan (1761–1868)
15th President of the USA (1857–61), a Democrat. Member of the House of Representatives (1821–31) and US minister to Russia (1832–34) when he was elected to the Senate. He left his Senate seat to serve as US Secretary of State during the Mexican War (1846–48). When elected President, he could do little to avert the secession of the South over the issue of slavery. This led to the outbreak of Civil War in 1861.

Free-soilers: People who opposed the extension of slavery westward.

created in 1854, were a disparate group of abolitionists, **free-soilers** and former Whigs and northern Democrats who shared a common concern at the spread of slavery and who feared its expansion out west where it might threaten the capitalist system of 'free labour'. They were increasingly convinced that there was a 'slave power' at work and that southerners had gained control of the Democratic Party and were now using it for their own ends in expanding slavery.

In the 1854 elections, both parties fielded candidates but it is unclear precisely which party best commanded the anti-Democratic vote as a number of candidates simply stood as anti-Democrat or actually supported the agenda of both parties. By 1856 though, the Republicans emerged as the stronger group, helped by sectional divisions that now plagued the 'Know Nothings' too. Republicans also expressed concern over the expansion of slavery at the moment that immigration was declining as an issue. Events in Kansas, and Pierce's responses, seemed to confirm the views of the party to the wider and more moderate electorate. Despite the party only having existed for two years, the Republican candidate for President, John Fremont, polled 33 per cent of the vote, 45 per cent in free states, and gained 114 electoral college votes.

The Republicans now emerged as the only serious challengers to the Democrats and began to prepare for a victory in 1860. The 1856 result was important not only because it marked the emergence of the Republicans but also because it showed that they could win an election without winning any votes in the South at all. Fremont had only won 1,196 votes in all the slave states combined. However, because the free states had far greater populations (and therefore more votes in the electoral college), Fremont only needed to win two or three of the five free states Buchanan had won in 1856 (Pennsylvania, New Jersey, Indiana, Illinois and California) to be elected President. None of this was lost on the Republicans, who now set out to broaden their appeal across the North, or the South.

At this point, it is important to avoid seeing the conflict that followed as inevitable. The Democrats had clearly maintained strong pockets of support in the North, and the Kansas dispute was likely to be the last major issue of western expansion. Although tensions were running high in 1856, and each section was seeing the extremists increase their influence as their claims became more believable, the Republicans depended for their support on northerners continuing to believe in the threat of slavery expansion from the South. If Buchanan could defuse the tensions, then the Republicans would be without an issue. Alas for the Union, Buchanan was not only lacking in ability, but events were to occur that would test him still further.

The Dred Scott Case

Within days of Buchanan's inauguration, the Dred Scott decision raised the controversy over slavery to new heights. Dred Scott was a slave from Missouri who had moved with his owner to the northern part of the western territories, where slavery was forbidden under the terms of the Missouri Compromise. Scott sued for his freedom and the Supreme Court, under Chief Justice Taney, ruled on 6 March 1857 that:

> 'No black slave or descendant could be a US citizen and therefore Scott could not bring a case to a federal court. Since a slave was the property of his master, Congress had no constitutional right to deprive that master of his property in the territories.'

The clear implication was that the Missouri Compromise was unconstitutional. Slavery was protected in all federal territories, allowing slave owners to take their slaves anywhere across the territories and to settle with them. This was a clear victory for the South, though it allowed the Republicans to claim that not only the Presidency but also the Supreme Court was controlled by 'slave power'. With five of the nine justices from slave states, and coming at the same time as the controversy over the Lecompton Constitution, such claims were all the more credible. Moderate opinion became increasingly tuned in to Republican claims.

Economic divisions and arguments

In order to secure victory across the North in the next presidential election, the Republicans recognised that they needed to broaden their appeal to include workers in the major industrial cities who did not see slavery expansion as the main issue to determine their vote. Republicans therefore sought to become a fully sectional party of the North, rather than only concerned with the expansion of slavery. They developed a clear economic programme that included higher tariffs to protect northern manufacturing industry from foreign competition, a transcontinental railroad to link Chicago with California and support for internal improvements in communications and transport. They were helped by responses in the South to abolitionist attacks on slavery – the most worrying of which had been Hinton Rowan Helper's contemporary book *The Impending Crisis in the South, How to Meet It.* Helper was a North Carolinian who argued that small-scale farmers and workers suffered from slavery. His arguments threatened the internal stability of the South. Southerners responded by attacking the northern 'factory system' for making 'industrial slaves' of the workers who were disposable once they had been drained of their energy. They contrasted it with a southern slavery system that provided welfare in return for work. Thus the controversy was being elevated to a clash between two economic systems.

The dispute became more dramatic in 1857 when a financial crisis (the 'Panic of 1857') was followed by an economic depression for northern industry. Republicans were quick to blame the low tariffs of the Democrats for the problem. The South, on the other hand, did not suffer in the depression and felt that their system was even more vindicated. 'King Cotton' became the rallying cry. Southerners became dangerously confident that their economic system was better than the North's and that they could easily survive alone if they had to. Just as the northern Republicans were beginning to convince mainstream opinion of the dangers of the 'slave power', so were southern extremists ('Fire-eaters') making the case for secession if it should come to that.

The Lincoln–Douglas debates of 1858

Until 1858, Abraham Lincoln had been a relatively unknown lawyer and politician from the frontier, serving in the Illinois Legislature but only once (1846–48) in the House of Representatives in Washington. He came to

Abraham Lincoln (1809–1865)

16th president of the USA, a Republican. He was President at a very difficult time. During the Civil War (1861–65), he coordinated the Union campaign against the South, leading the North to victory. He fought hard to end slavery, which was finally abolished in 1865. Lincoln also played a vital role in the 1862 Homestead Act, which was to have a huge impact on settlement in the West (see page 57). He displayed considerable skills in working with people in his government with different beliefs and opinions. Following an announcement that he favoured some blacks having the vote in one state, Lincoln was assassinated by an actor and Confederate sympathiser, John Wilkes Booth.

national prominence in 1858 as the Republican candidate standing against Senator Douglas in the senate race for Illinois. With Douglas' national reputation, the contest received national coverage. This was made more dramatic by a series of debates – seven in all – that took place during the contest. Douglas won the election, but the contest and the debates had an important impact on national politics.

Lincoln came to national prominence as a result. In attacking a skilled and prominent figure, he attracted supporters who saw him as a potential Republican candidate for the Presidency. Supporters began to put forward his name as a challenger and he was sure of good 'name-recognition' when it came to the Republican Convention in 1860.

Douglas' attempts to portray Lincoln as an abolitionist and supporter of racial equality (both clearly untrue when one looks at the speeches) made southerners fear the election of Lincoln as President in 1860 more than they need to have done. Although Lincoln never denied his personal disapproval of slavery, he did not support abolition in the South. Yet the very name of Lincoln became associated, because of press reporting in the South, with the more violent extremes of northern abolitionism.

In order to win moderate votes in Illinois, Douglas was forced to claim that the Dred Scott decision did not mean that slavery could exist in the territories. This view – known as the Freeport Doctrine because the debate took place there – played well in Illinois. It would have been soon forgotten but, because the contest was being watched nationally, it undermined Douglas' standing with southern Democrats, who were now unlikely to endorse him for President.

John Brown and Harper's Ferry

Federal arsenal: A place for storing ammunition and weapons to be used by the US Army.

The attack on a **federal arsenal** at Harper's Ferry, Virginia, in October 1859 by abolitionist John Brown became a defining event of the last year of peace and union. Brown's attack ended in failure and he was hanged, along with other members of his group, in December 1859, having been found guilty of treason. He had hoped to gain enough weapons from Harper's Ferry to launch a slave rebellion in the Upper South. However, he was caught too early and, anyway, there were few signs of slave revolt. Although the Republican leaders, including Lincoln, made clear their opposition to Brown, it became evident that he had received financial support from various prominent abolitionists. Brown was transformed into a martyr by northern abolitionists and writers. For southerners, despite the position of the Republicans, it became further evidence of northern hostility to slavery. The 'fire-eaters' were able to present the incident as proof that the North was committed to the abolition of slavery across the South and not just to the limiting of its expansion.

---

1. What impact did the Kansas–Nebraska Act of 1854 have on the conflict between North and South?

2. To what extent was civil war inevitable by the end of the 1850s?

John Brown (1800–1859)		
US slavery abolitionist. On the night of 16 October 1859, with 18 men, he seized the government arsenal at Harper's Ferry in West Virginia. His apparent intent was to	distribute weapons to runaway slaves who would then defend a stronghold that Brown hoped would become a republic of former slaves. On 18 October, US marines under Colonel	Robert E. Lee stormed the arsenal. Brown was tried and hanged on 2 December, becoming a martyr. He is the hero of the song 'John Brown's Body' (written in about 1860).

4.3 Why did Lincoln win the presidential election of 1860?

The election of Abraham Lincoln as the first Republican President, in November 1860, was very much the trigger for the secession of the Deep South. It set in motion events that would lead directly to the Civil War itself. Within two months of the results being known, South Carolina had passed a resolution for secession. Thus, of all single events that can be seen as a cause of the Civil War, this is in many ways the most critical.

Lincoln had not been favourite to get the Republican nomination, but a determination to prevent the front-runner, William Seward, from being nominated, saw Lincoln emerge as the stop-Seward candidate. He was certainly helped by the Republican Convention being held in Lincoln's home state of Illinois. By the third ballot, Lincoln had overtaken Seward and secured the nomination.

He now faced three rivals for the top job:

● Stephen Douglas, the candidate of the Northern Democrats and his old rival from 1858;

● John Breckinridge, the Southern Democrat and current Vice-President from Kentucky;

● John Bell, fighting for the Constitutional Union, an organisation dedicated to saving the Union by means of compromise.

The Democrats divided

The Democrats needed to be united to have a hope of winning. However, it was clear from the beginning of the year that this last, great, cross-sectional institution was likely to go the way of the Whigs under the strain of an election campaign. Southern Democrats could not stomach the favoured and obvious candidate of most Northerners, Stephen Douglas. Despite his high-profile victory over Lincoln in the 1858 Senate race in Illinois, southerners associated Douglas with the hated Freeport Doctrine voiced in the Kansas–Nebraska dispute. Many in the Deep South were determined to have a specific commitment on slavery in the party programme. These divisions led ultimately to a walkout by many Southern delegates at the Democratic Convention at Charleston in April 1860. Following this, no candidate secured victory to become the presidential candidate despite 57 ballots.

The remaining delegates agreed to meet again, which they did in Baltimore, Maryland, in June. Tempers had not cooled. The Southern delegates, increasingly assertive and determined to defend their 'peculiar institution', were in no mood to accept a Northern candidate, particularly Douglas. They were equally determined to see defence of slavery on the platform. There was another Southern walkout, which at least made it easy for the remaining Democrats to agree on Douglas as their candidate. They quickly adopted popular sovereignty and a defence of the Slave Fugitive Law as their platform. The southern Democrats now held their own convention, also in Baltimore, at which they nominated John Breckinridge of Kentucky. They adopted a platform protecting property (slavery) in the territories and calling for the annexation of Cuba, a slave-holding Spanish colony.

By the summer of 1860, the Democrats had clearly weakened themselves and their chances of victory seemed slim. However, a Republican victory was by no means certain. Breckinridge was not as limited sectionally as one might have thought. Indeed, former Democrat Presidents Pierce and Buchanan and the majority of Northern Democrat Congressmen supported him. Douglas, too, could still win the race. The split of the more extreme southerners actually made him a more effective candidate in the North, whilst it was by no means certain that he could not win some of the border slave states, such as Missouri and Delaware. The Republicans could not be sure of victory just because the Democrats were divided, and it was certainly a possibility that no candidate would get a majority in the electoral college. If that happened, then the decision would go to the House of Representatives – where anything might happen.

The appeal of the Republicans

The Republicans had learnt two important lessons from the 1856 presidential election: that they could win without taking a single slave state and that they would have to broaden their appeal beyond being an anti-slavery expansion party if they were to carry free states that traditionally voted Democrat. In 1856, the only free states that the Republicans did not win were Pennsylvania, Illinois, Indiana, New Jersey and California.

The party platform of the Republicans was deliberately moderate. There was a specific promise not to interfere with slavery where it already existed, and Republican speakers throughout the campaign repeated this. The Republicans even took care to criticise John Brown's raid and one of their leading politicians confirmed his party's opposition to 'hostile aggression upon the constitutional rights of any state'. Lincoln himself was a model moderate for the Republicans, taking mainstream opinions on slavery expansion, prohibition and immigration.

Given our knowledge of what followed, there is a danger of overplaying the importance of slavery and constitutional issues in the election. The Republican Party developed an economic position that deliberately appealed to targeted voters in the critical states. A pledge to introduce free 160-acre homesteads was included with the slogan 'Vote yourself a farm'. A commitment to building, with federal subsidy, a transcontinental railroad was designed to appeal to the two states likely to be at either end – Illinois and California. A programme of higher tariffs was promised and was a vote-winner in the industrial cities of New Jersey and Pennsylvania. Furthermore, a deliberate attempt was made to associate Douglas and Breckinridge with the sleaze and corruption of the previous Buchanan Administration. 'Honest Abe' was an important symbol of a cleaner and fresher start in politics, even if in reality the Republicans had a good number of corruption scandals to keep covered themselves.

Certainly, by the time it came to vote, it could be said that the Republicans had fought a clear and united campaign that appealed to all opinion in the North – not just to radical opponents of slavery and its extension.

The campaign

The actual campaign of 1860 was a strange affair. There were four candidates nationally but it was in fact a contest between Lincoln and Douglas in the North, Bell and Breckinridge in the South. Douglas hoped that he could hold on to the states won by the Democrats in the North in 1856, whilst reassuring the Southern states that he posed no threat to slavery and so securing their vote as the only candidate to stop Lincoln. He even chose as his vice-presidential candidate Herschel V. Johnson, the former Governor of Georgia. Unfortunately, he succeeded in neither aim. As Brian Holden Reid writes, in *The Origins of the American Civil War* (1996), 'the polarisation of voters around sectional issues resulted in Douglas falling through the middle'. Douglas was in danger of coming second everywhere, and therefore not getting the crucial electoral college votes.

Lincoln played the election traditionally, by not entering the fray and by allowing his supporters to present him as the westerner who had risen from the log cabin and was on his way to the White House. Both sides presented the other as extreme and a danger to the other section. Republicans talked again of the dangers of a 'slave power', whilst Democrats spoke of the 'black Republican, free love, free Nigger Party'.

When it seemed, from state elections in October, that the Republicans might win, Douglas all but acknowledged the result and 'went South to save the Union'. He urged Southerners to support Lincoln's inauguration and made a passionate case for maintaining the Union. His campaigns for election and against secession were both in vain.

How big was Lincoln's victory in 1860?

In the electoral college, Lincoln won a convincing victory; there would be no need to resort to the House of Representatives. With 180 votes, he was well ahead of Breckinridge with 72 votes. Douglas had indeed fallen 'through the middle', achieving 30 per cent of the popular vote but securing the electoral college votes of only Missouri and three votes of New Jersey's seven.

1. What message is this cartoon making about Lincoln's possible success as president?

2. How reliable is this cartoon as evidence of Lincoln's victory in the presidential election of 1860?

'The Coming Man's Presidential Career'. Cartoon from 1860, showing Abraham Lincoln carrying an African-American slave on his shoulders as he crosses Niagara Falls on a tightrope.

However, Lincoln was a minority President. He won only 40 per cent of the popular vote. His victory was also confined to the North. In 10 states he secured no popular votes at all and he achieved miserly numbers in Kentucky, Virginia and Maryland. Even in the free states his vote was not conclusive. He got 54 per cent of the vote in the Northern states to Douglas' 36 per cent. Even Breckinridge gained 5 per cent of the votes in the free states. The combined votes of Breckinridge and Douglas, the two Democratic candidates, was 47 per cent, compared with Lincoln's 40 per cent.

Whilst this may give the impression that Lincoln only won because of the split Democratic vote, some historians have been quick to point out that Lincoln would have won in the electoral college even if the Democratic votes had been added together. Lincoln only won three states – New Jersey, Oregon and California – because of split votes and the other states would have been enough to give him victory, albeit by a smaller margin. This is a fair point, but not totally convincing since we must assume that a united Democratic Party would have gone into the election with greater confidence and may well have won more popular votes in such circumstances. The truth is that we will never know. What we do know is that Lincoln now found himself a minority and sectional President. For those in the South who favoured secession, the chance now presented itself.

That the election made secession automatic is not a fair conclusion. The election was not a particularly sectional affair. Breckinridge did not secure a majority of the votes in the slave states; 55 per cent had voted for pro-Union candidates, mainly Bell with 593,000 votes. Anyway, the results when taken as a whole did not spell disaster for the South. The Southerners still controlled the Supreme Court and neither House of Congress had a Republican majority. Secession and civil war may have been brought closer, but there was nothing inevitable about either in November 1860.

Explain why the Republicans won the 1860 presidential election.

4.4 How did the election of Lincoln lead to the outbreak of war?

It is generally thought that Lincoln's election led to Southern Secession and that that led inevitably to war itself. Such an assessment will not, however, do. There were three phases to secession:

1. The decision of South Carolina to secede, which happened within weeks of Lincoln's election.

2. The decisions of six further slave states to join with South Carolina, which happened in the early weeks of 1861.

3. This led to the formation of the Confederacy in February 1861 and to the secession of a further four states in May/June 1861.

It was only in April 1861, six months after Lincoln's election, that the first shots of the Civil War were actually fired. During that six-month period there had been serious attempts at compromise, most significantly the Crittenden proposals, and much soul-searching from men on both sides of the conflict. America had dealt with crises like this before in 1850, 1819 and 1832, and most citizens assumed it would deal with it again. The purpose of this section is to see how events between Lincoln's election and the final secession led to the outbreak of fighting and then to all-out war. It is interesting to consider how much the conflict might, even at this stage, have been prevented.

The early secessions and formation of the Confederacy

The response of South Carolina was probably no surprise to anyone. The much-publicised threats to secede were quickly followed through. Within four days of Lincoln's election, the Legislature of South Carolina had voted unanimously to secede. This was confirmed, again unanimously, at a special convention held at Charleston in December. Thus, on 20 December 1860, South Carolina became the first state to leave the USA. That did not, of course, mean that any other would follow suit. The South Carolinians had already made their reputation for defiance in the Nullification Crisis in the 1830s. Then, South Carolina had been left to stand alone by the other southern states. It could easily have happened again. The South Carolinians were themselves aware of this. At the same time as they voted to secede, they appointed commissioners to lobby elsewhere and to prepare for a general convention of seceded states in the new year.

A debate now raged through the South. Through the winter of 1860–61, secessionists debated with **cooperationists** throughout the southern states. The pattern in all six seceding states was similar: in all but Texas elections were held for a convention to decide on whether to secede (Texas called a referendum to confirm a decision made by the Legislature). Even where the voting was close, as in Georgia for example, the conventions voted overwhelmingly for secession. Once the decision was taken, most southerners then pledged themselves to the decision. By the beginning of February 1861, Mississippi, Florida, Alabama, Georgia, Louisiana and Texas had all voted to join South Carolina in seceding. The seven rebel states met in Montgomery, Alabama on 4 February 1861 and declared their intention to form a new country, the Confederate States of America.

The Constitution, ratified by April, was modelled on the USA with more explicit protection of slavery and states' rights. The Stars and Bars were adopted, a new army and currency established, and Jefferson Davis was adopted as President (inaugurated on 18 February). Davis was a former Senator and cabinet member, as well as being a graduate of West Point (US military academy). His Vice-President, Alexander Stephens of Georgia, had been a leading anti-secessionist. From the start, the majority of Confederate leaders were anxious not to provoke the North. They sought a moderate reputation in the hope they might eventually entice the less enthusiastic Upper South states to join them. Thus, in his inauguration speech, Davis asked that the Confederacy be left alone. But Lincoln had no intention of doing that.

Attempts at compromise

Crises over the Union had been faced before, and the customary attempts at compromise now began again. Politicians had solved the problem in 1819 and 1850, surely they would do so again. Some historians have argued that this was still possible in 1861 and that it was the poor quality of the politicians at the time that allowed a crisis to escalate into war. This idea of 'blundering politicians' focuses on several figures, not least the President at the time, James Buchanan, whose inactivity in dealing with the rebels or taking a lead in finding compromise has been criticised both then and since. Lincoln, too, can be blamed. He would have nothing to do with the most serious attempt at compromise – the one led by Senator John Crittenden of Kentucky. Crittenden was in a strong position to find compromise. He was a slave-owning unionist from a border state and had sympathy with southern views whilst disapproving of secession. In December 1860, Congress met and Crittenden's proposals were put forward in a Senate which now excluded delegates from the states of the Lower South.

Cooperationsts: Those who supported a compromise solution with the northern states.

Jefferson Davis (1808–1889)
US politician; President of the short-lived Confederate States of America (1861–65). Served in US Army before becoming a cotton planter in Mississippi. Davis was leader of the Southern Democrats in the Senate from 1857. He was a defender of 'humane' slavery. In 1860, he issued a declaration in favour of secession from the USA. During the American Civil War, Davis showed strong leadership. He was imprisoned for two years after the War. Known for his fiery temper. His call for conscription in the South raised protests that he was a military dictator.

These Crittenden Proposals were clearly designed to reassure the South. They extended the Missouri Compromise line of 36 degree-30 to the Pacific, so allowing slavery below the line in all present territories plus those 'hereafter to be acquired'. This would give slave-owners protection in all southern territories while prohibiting slavery north of the line. It also meant that the possible expansion of the USA southwards into Mexico and Cuba could see slavery expanding as a force in the Union. A constitutional amendment was added, guaranteeing slavery where it existed, even in Washington DC, with federal compensation awarded to slave-holders if slaves escaped.

These proposals were flatly rejected by the Republicans, including Lincoln, and the amendments were defeated 25–23 in the Senate and 113–80 in the House of Representatives. It is hard to see how Lincoln could have supported such proposals given the platform he had been elected on, but it is clear that his outright opposition to them did nothing but bring the conflict closer. There were other attempts at reform. For example, in February 1861 a Peace Convention was called in Washington, but after three weeks' deliberations a compromise remarkably similar to Crittenden's proposals was defeated in Congress. One is probably forced to agree with historian David Potter when he wrote, 'given the momentum of secession and the fundamental set of Republicanism, it is probably safe to say that compromise was impossible from the start'.

Attitudes in the North

Northerners who had feared slavery expansion suddenly had a new issue to debate, secession. Some Northerners believed that the South was better left alone – let the Confederates go it alone and have a state free of the cancer of slavery. Most Southerners had expected the North to take this view too. But this was not the view of the President-elect, nor of the majority of people in the northern states. Northerners had seen the Union as perpetual – individual states had surrendered their sovereignty when they joined the Union. If states could simply secede whenever they felt like it, then the result would be **anarchy** and coherent government could never take place. The attitude of the 'Cincinnati News' is typical when they wrote:

Anarchy: Where nobody pays attention to any rules or laws. Anarchists advocate a society based upon free association and voluntary cooperation between groups and individuals.

> 'The doctrine of secession is anarchy. If the minority have the right to break up the Government at pleasure, because they have not had their own way, there is an end of all government.'

The majority might have agreed on their determination not to accept secession, but that did not mean they agreed on how they should now respond. Only a minority wanted an immediate dispatch of troops to the South. Most supported the deliberate inaction of both Buchanan and later Lincoln, who spent most of the weeks before and after his inauguration (on 4 March 1861) worrying about appointments rather than an impending war.

Most Northerners believed the South had over-reached itself, that once it became clear that the Upper South would not join them in their Confederacy they would return, tail between legs, to the union. It was probably that thinking which persuaded them not to take compromise solutions seriously. It was also that thinking which meant events were allowed to drift regarding federal property. Yet again, the mistaken perceptions of both sides were going to lead to an increase in rage. The South was serious about secession, just as the North was serious about not tolerating it. Neither side yet appreciated the intent of the other but, for the sake of saving time and of keeping the Upper South on side, neither said anything yet about it.

What happened at Fort Sumter?

Confederates: Supporters of the Confederate States of America, which were created in Montgomery, Alabama in February 1861.

Garrisons: Groups of soldiers whose job is to guard the town or building in which they live.

As the crisis deepened over the winter of 1860–61, most federal forts and arsenals that were based in the South were taken over by the **Confederates** without any trouble. The exceptions to this were Fort Pickens off the coast of Florida and Fort Sumter in Charleston Harbour. Both forts continued to have **garrisons** loyal to the Union. Fort Sumter became the focal point of tensions between North and South that eventually led to the first shots of the Civil War itself.

After December 1860, the garrison at Fort Sumter lost all contact with the federal government but its commander, Major Robert Anderson, was determined to defend federal property from the South Carolinians despite having fewer than 100 men. He withdrew from other federal fortifications in the harbour in order to concentrate on Fort Sumter. Initial attempts by President Buchanan to send supplies and reinforcements to Sumter led to a stand-off in January 1861. By March, Anderson was forced to send a message to Lincoln saying that he only had four to six weeks of supplies left. This was a critical moment. The Confederates could not allow the continuation of a northern-held fortress in the middle of one of their major ports. So they would not let reinforcements through. However, Lincoln knew that if he did not supply the fortress then he would look weak, only days into his Presidency. Yet a conflict with South Carolina might encourage the Upper South states to join with the Confederates, if they felt Lincoln was forcing the Union on the South.

Lincoln's Cabinet was divided. His generals advised withdrawal on the grounds that they could not hold the fort if South Carolina chose to become hostile. Lincoln dithered and changed his mind at least once, but by the end of March he had taken the fateful decision that he would re-provision (not reinforce) Forts Sumter and Pickens. On 4 April, Anderson was told by Lincoln to stay firm and on 9 April a naval expedition set out to relieve Fort Sumter. On 11 April, the Confederate Commander in Charleston, General Beauregard, acting under orders from Jefferson Davis, demanded Anderson's surrender. Anderson's refusal meant that, at 4.30 a.m., the two sides opened fire on one another and continued to do so for the following 33 hours. By the end of that time, Anderson was forced to surrender and he withdrew to Washington. However, the moment of truth had arrived. Although no one was killed in the exchanges at Fort Sumter, the period of tension had come to an end. The first shots of a four-year war had been fired.

How did the Upper South respond?

Both Lincoln and Davis issued calls to arms in the wake of the attack on Fort Sumter and both were overwhelmed with support and volunteers. However, immediate attention focused on what the Upper South would now do. Lincoln declared, on 19 April, that he was dealing with a rebellion and ordered an immediate blockade of the Southern rebel states. This put the Upper South on the spot. Slave states which had chosen, until that point, to remain in the Union, had to decide which side they would take. Most significantly, this applied to Virginia – the oldest state, possessing more industrial strength than the rest of the Confederacy combined. Most of the inhabitants of the Upper South preferred to remain in the Union themselves, but accepted the principle of the Calhoun Doctrine which said that their fellow Southerners had the right to secede. Now Lincoln was requiring them to take arms and support a war to force fellow southern states back into the Union. The debate in the Upper South took place reluctantly against a feeling that Lincoln had pushed them into an unnecessary corner.

The Upper South took stock. Four states – Virginia, North Carolina, Arkansas and Tennessee – now followed the Lower South into the Confederacy. The four remaining slave states stayed in the Union with varying degrees of enthusiasm. Delaware was always likely to support the Union, with only 2 per cent of its people holding slaves. The situation was more tense and uncertain in Maryland, Missouri and Kentucky. Kentucky tried for a time to remain neutral, while Missouri remained in the Union despite its pro-Confederate governor. Generally pro-Confederate, Maryland had voted for Breckinridge in 1860 and, on 19 April, riots had broken out in Baltimore when volunteer troops from Massachusetts had passed through (causing, incidentally, the first casualties of the Civil War when four soldiers and 12 civilians were killed).

Lincoln could not, however, afford to lose Maryland. Had he done so, he would have been forced to abandon Washington as a capital since it was between Virginia and Maryland. Working with the pro-Union Governor, Lincoln took drastic action, arresting potential rebels and suspending *habeas corpus*. By the summer, Maryland had been secured for the North. It is hard now to underestimate the importance of the decision of these states. Had the Confederacy remained the Lower South only, it is difficult to see how an effective war could have been waged, certainly over a sustained period of time. Equally, the decisions of Maryland, Kentucky and Missouri not to join the South deprived the Confederates of an extra 45 per cent white population and a massive 80 per cent increase in manufacturing capacity.

Why did the southern states secede?

There was no single motive behind the decision of the southern states to secede. It is important to distinguish between the motives of the Deep South, who seceded in the aftermath of Lincoln's election, and the Upper South who only seceded after the President had declared war. Several key issues can nonetheless be identified:

● The determination of South Carolina to leave the Union on the election of Lincoln but to ensure that this time they would not be left alone meant that South Carolinians actively canvassed the other southern states. Certainly, states were emboldened by the feeling that they were not alone and the Confederacy existed as a home to go to.

● A feeling that anti-slavery Northerners were beginning to dominate the Union was in many ways the main concern of the Deep South. It was not that Lincoln himself threatened slavery immediately (though many accepted his demonisation that had started with the debates against Lincoln), but the fact that a northern anti-slaver could be elected without any southern votes was an ominous sign for the future. The powers of a Republican president could be used against the South in other ways, such as in the appointment of Supreme Court judges and postmasters in the South.

● A confidence grew – encouraged by the 1857 crisis and King Cotton – that the South could survive alone, especially if it had control over its tariff levels. In some cases, southerners actually felt that their economy was being held back by northern economic concerns and they expected not only to survive but also to experience economic growth.

● The work of the 'fire-eaters' created a sense of momentum that carried a number of southerners along.

● The feeling that compromise had finally resolved sectional tensions in 1819 and 1850 meant that a number of moderates were slow to wake

1. Did President Lincoln's election make civil war inevitable?

2. Why did the states of the Upper South secede after the attack on Fort Sumter in April 1861?

up to the seriousness of intent of southern secessionists until it was too late.

● There was a genuine belief in the Calhoun Doctrine that particularly motivated the Upper South. Although they did not necessarily share the concerns about Lincoln that the Deep South felt, they were not prepared to fight to force the Deep South to return to the Union. They respected the right of those states to secede, though many in the Upper South hoped for a subsequent compromise to allow them to return.

4.5 What were the relative strengths of the sides on the eve of war?

Historians have tended to look at the formidable balance of resources between North and South in 1861 and conclude that the defeat of the South was almost inevitable from the start. Indeed, the historian Shelby Foote writes, in *The Civil War* (1991), of the North winning 'with one hand behind its back'. This was not, however, how contemporaries from either side, or abroad, saw things at the time. It was only as the Civil War drew on that the resource advantage of the North became clear.

What advantages was the South seen to have at the start?

The Confederacy was seen to have several advantages at the start:

● They expected to be able to rely on cotton exports – at an all-time high in 1860 – to sustain them. It was expected that those European

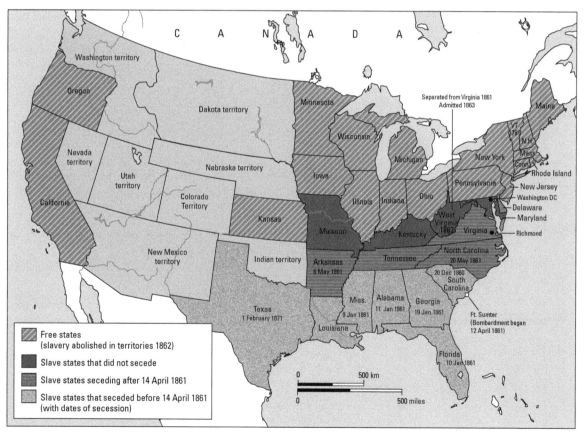

The United States on the eve of the Civil War

states that relied on cotton imports from the South, most significantly Britain, would be encouraged to recognise and support the Confederate Government.

- The nature of the Civil War was that the Union had to fight in the South in order to enforce federal authority, while the Confederates only had to defend their territory. Since the Confederacy was large (750,000 square miles), warfare favoured the defender.

- There were no obvious targets for the North to attack (except perhaps the capital, Richmond). This was a much greater task than that facing the South, who simply had to resist for long enough to convince the North to abandon their struggle.

- The South had a more obvious cause to fight for: they were defending their way of life, as they saw it. Almost all southerners, including those who had opposed secession, supported the fight against the North in 1861. Morale and determination were higher among ordinary southerners than in the North, where the cause of **federalism** was an abstract battlecry.

Federalism: Belief or support for a federal system of government (i.e. central government rather than state control).

- There was a feeling that the South and southern men were more suited to a military campaign. The assumption was that farmers, who were used to guns and the outdoors, would make better soldiers than factory workers. In addition, there was a strong military tradition in the South. Southerners dominated the military colleges and the higher ranks of the US Army. Many southerners had fought successfully in the recent war with Mexico.

- The North had only 44 per cent of its male population in military service in 1864, compared with 90 per cent of the white male population in the South.

- The slavery system also meant that a greater proportion of men from the South could fight without having such a detrimental effect on agricultural production.

In addition to these advantages, there were plenty of examples from military history of smaller, less well-resourced nations beating larger powers. Southerners could thus start the campaign in better heart than most later commentators gave them credit for (hindsight is a wonderful thing!). For the South the crucial thing was to induce war-weariness in the North as early as possible, so that pressure could be put on the northern leadership to abandon the campaign to coerce the southern states into the Union. Firm defence and resilience was what was needed, rather than any dramatic capture of major northern centres such as New York and Boston.

What advantages did the North have at the start?

There is, however, no doubting that the North had significant advantages over the South, especially in the longer term.

- The North had an overwhelming superiority of numbers. The population of the northern states was 22 million, compared with the southerners 9 million. The South was restricted further by their refusal to use slaves as soldiers. The superiority of numbers was not only a matter of troop numbers, it also meant that industrial and agricultural production would be able to sustain wartime levels more easily.

- The South had fewer major cities than the North (only New Orleans had a population greater than 50,000) and industry was confined to the mining area around the Appalachian mountains. By contrast, in 1860 the North produced 94 per cent of US pig iron and over 90 per cent of coal and firearms, as well as 80 per cent of the country's wheat. With twice as much railroad mileage too, the North could clearly arm, supply and transport its forces far more effectively than the Confederacy.

● The North also dominated at sea, both in terms of the navy and merchant navy. With the industrial imbalance, the South needed to import wheat and food but the northern blockade – even though it was never 100 per cent effective – severely limited such opportunities. Also, the South was unable to export its main product, cotton, which it needed in order to get foreign currency and foreign goods.

● Abraham Lincoln's political skill managed to keep three states – Maryland, Missouri and Kentucky – on the side of the Union, or at least out of the Confederate camp. This came about despite strong sentiment from large parts of these three slave states. (The allegiance of Delaware was always likely to be to the North and slavery had all but died out there.) A combination of firm action when needed and gentle treading at other times worked effectively in keeping all three states officially in the Union. This was important for resources (they would have greatly helped the Confederacy industrially), population balance (Missouri, in particular, had a large population of southern migrants) and geography. If Maryland had become part of the Confederacy then the Union capital in Washington DC would have been surrounded by enemy territory (see map opposite). Similarly, Kentucky and Missouri were critical to the campaigns out west. They acted as a buffer to any southern attempts to reach the Mid-West grain belt.

Most of the advantages that the North had in terms of resources would only become apparent as the Civil War went on. Although both sides set out in 1861 anticipating and planning a short campaign, it was the South that was most likely to suffer from the stalemate of 1861–62. Even though actual casualties in the early battles were, on the whole, worse for the North than the South, the Confederacy often lost a greater proportion of their available troops. Thus the apparent early victories of the South were often won at a greater cost in the long term. This imbalance between the two sides did not mean that the North was guaranteed victory, but it did dictate southern strategy, for Generals Lee and Davis were aware from the start that they needed to deliver quick blows that might destroy the morale of northern voters; hence the ill-fated attacks on Antietam (September 1862) and Gettysburg (July 1863). Lincoln, on the other hand, had to worry more about sustaining morale than victory in the field (though, of course, the two were linked). Both sides were well aware of attrition favouring the side with the greater numbers and resources.

1. What do you regard as the most important advantage the North had at the start of the Civil War? Explain your answer.

2. Given the advantages of the North over the South, how do you account for the long duration of the Civil War?

4.6 How did the two sides perform in the military campaigns?

Early Confederate successes

Both sides anticipated a quick war. Lincoln only requested men to enlist for three months when they signed up. It seemed that the decisive battles would take place in northern Virginia as the two capitals, Richmond and Washington, were only 98 miles apart. The aim of Lincoln and his advisers was to capture Richmond quickly and then force the Confederates to seek peace. The Confederates, however, were highly effective at preventing a Union breakthrough in the early years of the Civil War. They were able to make their own attacks on the North in September 1862.

Thomas 'Stonewall' Jackson (1824–1863)
Confederate general in the American Civil War. He acquired his nickname at the First Battle of Bull Run (21 July 1861), from the firmness with which his soldiers resisted the attack by northern troops. In 1862, Jackson organised the Shenandoah Valley campaign and assisted Robert E. Lee's invasion of Maryland. He also helped to defeat General Joseph Hooker's Union army at the Battle of Chancellorsville, Virginia (1863), but was fatally wounded by one of his soldiers in the confusion of battle.

Peninsula: A body of land surrounded on three sides by water.

The first major battle of the war, The First Battle of Manassas (Bull Run) on 21 July 1861, saw a Union army of 30,000 repulsed as they tried to march south to Richmond. They were forced to retreat back to Washington DC. It was at this battle that the southern officer Thomas 'Stonewall' Jackson earned his nickname for the brave way in which he and his troops held their ground 'like a stonewall'. Although the Confederates did not follow up the northern retreat with an attack on Washington, it was an important southern victory which showed Lincoln that he could not expect to force the South to return quickly to the Union.

Lincoln appointed George B. McClellan (at only 34) to head the Army of the Potomac for the planned attack on Richmond the following year, 1862. McClellan set about using the winter to restore morale and to create an effective and organised army of 150,000. He had learned his tactics from the Crimean War, and was determined to avoid full frontal assaults. He had learned sooner than most that modern warfare was increasingly favouring the defender. Determined to avoid a repeat of Bull Run, which he put down to over-confidence, McClellan's campaigning in 1862 ended up being over-cautious and indecisive. Urged on by Lincoln, he finally moved against Richmond in April 1862, when he decided to attack from the **peninsula** to the south of the city. With this in mind, McClellan ferried his troops down river to Fortress Monroe and laid siege to Yorktown.

Whilst McClellan was besieging Yorktown, the Confederates had time to reinforce and defend Richmond. By the time McClellan took Yorktown (which the Confederates had by then evacuated, happy to have delayed the Union attack) and began to move northwards up the peninsula, he had lost the initiative. By May 1862 he was within 20 miles of Richmond, but he preferred to wait for reinforcements despite outnumbering Confederate forces 2:1. The reinforcements, however, did not come for 'Stonewall' Jackson had been busy in the Shenandoah Valley with 18,000 men, diverting 60,000 Unionist soldiers in a series of battles.

When the Confederates began to counter-attack in June, under the new leader of the Confederate Army of North Virginia, General Robert E. Lee, McClellan decided he could not succeed. He retreated back down the peninsula. President Lincoln, frustrated at the lack of action, took the opportunity to replace McClellan with General John Pope.

Pope was, however, no more successful than McClellan. At the end of August 1862, he suffered a heavy defeat at the hands of Confederate generals Jackson and Longstreet in The Second Battle of Manassas (Bull Run). Lincoln, faced with little alternative, asked McClellan to resume command.

General Lee now decided to follow up his victories by taking the war into the North. He invaded Maryland with 40,000 troops early in

George B. McClellan (1826–1885)
Civil War general, commander-in-chief of Union forces (1861–62). He was first dismissed by President Lincoln after retreating from the planned attack on Richmond in May 1862. He was asked by Lincoln to resume command of Union forces after his successor, John Pope, suffered heavy defeats at the Second Battle of Bull Run. McClellan was dismissed for a second time by Lincoln after he delayed for five weeks in following up his victory over the Confederate General Lee at Antietam. McClellan was the Democrat Presidential candidate against Lincoln in 1864.

Robert E. Lee (1807–1870)
Confederate general in the American Civil War. Earlier he had served in the Mexican War and was responsible for suppressing John Brown's raid on Harper's Ferry in 1859 (see page 86). At the outbreak of the Civil War he joined the Confederate army of the South. In 1862, as commander of the army of North Virginia, he won the Seven Days' Battle, defending Richmond (Confederate capital) against General McClellan's Union forces. He also won victories at Fredricksburg and Chancellorsville (1863) and at Cold Harbor (1864). He was besieged in Petersburg (June 1864–April 1865) and surrendered to General Grant at Appomattax courthouse on 9 April.

September, leaving Jackson to capture the federal arsenal at Harper's Ferry with a smaller force. Lee hoped that by marching into Maryland he would take the fight out of Virginia (thus protecting the harvest there). He would be moving the fighting away from Richmond and could perhaps gain some support from Confederate sympathisers in Maryland. Lee was also aware that control of Maryland would threaten Washington DC. The people of the North were more likely to become demoralised if fighting was taking place on their own soil.

The Confederates were very confident but, unfortunately, Lee's battle plans fell into McClellan's hands. Discovering that Lee and Jackson were divided, McClellan blocked Lee's path at Antietam. Battle ensued, on 17 September 1862. The Battle of Antietam saw the highest casualties for a single day of the Civil War. At the end of it, neither side was a clear victor. Lee retreated into Virginia for the winter. So, in the sense that the South failed to meet their objectives, Lincoln was able to claim it as a northern victory. McClellan failed to follow up the victory by pursuing Lee, despite a 2 : 1 numerical advantage. President Lincoln, complaining that McClellan had 'the slows', replaced him again – this time with General Ambrose E. Burnside.

Burnside was more no successful than his predecessors. A further attempt on Richmond was stopped at the Battle of Fredericksburg in December 1862, when Lee easily outwitted Burnside. The Confederates suffered 4,000 casualties to the Union's 11,000. Lincoln's replacement for Burnside, the fiery Joseph Hooker, suffered an even greater disaster the following spring at the Battle of Chancellorsville. Lee, despite having to divide his troops and having fewer than half the numbers the North could rely on, inflicted a humiliating double defeat on the Unionists at Chancellorsville and Fredericksburg. Chancellorsville was probably Lee's greatest victory of the Civil War, but he lost a key commander when Jackson was fatally wounded. More importantly, it was clear to Lee (and to Jefferson Davis) that the imbalance of resources meant that the South could not keep on fighting indefinitely, even if they won the battles. At Chancellorsville, a significant Confederate victory and with fewer actual casualties, Lee lost 22 per cent of his men, compared with Hooker's 15 per cent.

Lee believed it was now essential to head north in order to try to inflict a devastating defeat on the North on their home territory. The hope was that this might convince enough people in the North to abandon their coercion of the South, or at least to force the Union to move troops over from the West, where the Confederates were not enjoying so much success. So, when Lee headed north in June 1863 to face the Army of the Potomac, now commanded by yet another general, George C. Meade, he was well aware of the significance of the battle he aimed to fight.

Gettysburg, Pennsylvania (1–3 July 1863)

If any battle can be seen as the turning point in the Civil War, then that fought at Gettysburg on 1–3 July 1863, is the one. Indeed, the combatants themselves recognised its importance. Lee, determined to force some movements in the war, commented after the first day that, 'I am going to whip them here, or they are going to whip me.'

The result of the battle hung in the balance and could easily have gone either way. It is one of the great 'what ifs' of military history. Gettysburg was a small town through which a number of main roads passed. It was here that the forward units of the Confederate Army encountered a small band of Unionists on 30 June. Both sides began pouring troops into the town and by the end of the first day of battle (1 July), the Confederates

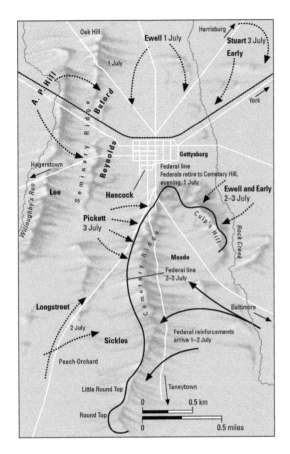

Battle of Gettysburg, 1–3 July
1863

seemed likely to secure a victory. They had taken the town and pushed Meade and his 85,000 troops on to a ridge (Cemetery Ridge) to the south.

The following day, Longstreet attacked the left flank of Meade's troops. He sustained heavy damage whilst taking the areas known as the Peach Orchard and Devil's Den. Crucially, Longstreet did not take a small hill known as Little Round Top. It was a chance moment and quick thinking on the part of a northern officer which saved the hill for the Union. From Little Round Top, the Unionist troops on Cemetery Hill would have been exposed to Confederate fire without having to launch a frontal assault.

By the end of day two, the situation had reached stalemate, with Meade's men having had a full day to dig in on the ridge and fortify their position. On 3 July, it was up to Lee to force events. He took the ill-fated decision to launch a direct attack on the centre of Unionist lines on Cemetery Ridge. After a lengthy artillery bombardment, in an attempt to weaken northern defences, the charge was led by General Pickett and his 15,000 men. The infamous 'Pickett's Charge' was to end in disaster, with 6,500 casualties in under an hour. The Confederates almost broke through, despite their appalling losses. General Lee, having lost 28,000 men in the three-day battle, was forced to return to Virginia. Any hopes of invading the North that year went with him.

In direct contrast to President Lincoln's tendency to remove his unsuccessful commander after each defeat, Jefferson Davis refused to accept Lee's resignation. 'To ask me to substitute you by someone in my judgement more fit to command ?... is to demand an impossibility', Davis wrote in response to Lee's letter. The Confederacy was helped by Meade's decision not to follow Lee into Virginia. That this was disastrous for the Confederacy was not in doubt, especially given the fall of Vicksburg in the West on the same day. Southern morale had taken a knock and Lee's aura of invincibility had been diminished. Further, it seemed that, while the South could hold off northern attacks in Virginia, the battles of Antietam and now Gettysburg suggested that the South could not deliver the knockout blow that might persuade the North to consider peace. It does not mean that a Confederate victory at Gettysburg would have guaranteed overall victory in the Civil War, but Confederate defeat made a victory seem much more remote. In confirming that the advantage lay with the defender, Gettysburg suggested that the Civil War would drag on for a few more months or years as each side tried to break the other's defences. The problem for the South was that the balance of resources did not favour them in a drawn-out war. Gettysburg meant that the American Civil War would not end in 1863, and a war that went beyond the winter was more likely to be won by the North.

The western theatre

Although much of the focus of the first two years of the Civil War was in Virginia, important developments were taking place further west, where Albert Sidney Johnston was in overall command of 40,000 Confederate forces defending a long and difficult border. Little movement took place until 1862, when Union troops launched an offensive to take some of the

Gunboats: Small ships that have several large guns fixed to them.

key river forts controlling the important waterway network that linked the Confederacy together. In the spring of 1862, 15,000 Union troops, under the command of General Ulysses S. Grant and supported by **gunboats**, captured Fort Henry and Fort Donelson. They gained control of the Cumberland and Tennessee rivers that flow eastwards into Tennessee. Confederate counter-attacks at Shiloh in April 1862 and in Kentucky in the summer and autumn had some success. However, Johnston was killed at Shiloh and Union reinforcements forced a Confederate retreat. In Kentucky, the new Confederate commander, General Braxton Bragg, was forced back into Tennessee because of supply problems.

In 1863, attention switched out west to the battle for the Mississippi port of Vicksburg, under siege by the Union since August of the previous year. Although the Union had captured the South's largest port, New Orleans, at the mouth of the Mississippi, in April 1862, Confederate control of Vicksburg prevented the Union from using the river. The Unionists were determined to capture a symbolic town that Davis referred to as 'the nailhead that held the South's two halves together'. Grant was charged with taking the town.

Ironclads: Ships of war cased with thick plates of iron or steel, as a defence against shot. See photo.

He succeeded in doing so on 4 July 1863, after a long and inspired campaign. The campaign involved crossing the Mississippi south of Vicksburg in **ironclads** that had sailed past the town in the night and then attacking two Confederate armies, marching 200 miles and fighting several battles before defeating Confederate armies in May 1863. Vicksburg then faced a serious and effective siege that came to an end with its surrender on 4 July, the day after the Battle of Gettysburg. The fall of Port Hudson five days later meant the Mississippi now became a 'Union highway' and the Confederacy was split in two.

Towards the end of 1863, fighting flared up again in Tennessee – this time in the east of the state, around the important railroad junction of Chattanooga. General Bragg, still commanding the western Confederate forces, had won a costly engagement at Chickamauga Creek in September 1863. The Unionists had been forced to retreat into Chattanooga itself. Bragg, however, refused to follow up the success with an attack on the main

Federal ironclad river gunboat

Union force and simply set up a siege that lasted several months, much to the anger of his officers. In November 1863, General Grant, fresh from his victory at Vicksburg and now appointed by Lincoln as Commander-in-Chief throughout the West, advanced quickly to Chattanooga. He destroyed the Confederate position in a stunning manoeuvre, forcing them to withdraw to Georgia. Davis now replaced Bragg, but the damage had been done. The South began 1864 looking very vulnerable.

1864: Grant takes charge

There had been three major defeats for the South in 1863, at least two of which – Gettysburg and Chattanooga – might well not have happened as they did. That counted for little in 1864, when the South found itself under attack from all sides. In March, Lincoln assembled a team that finally looked like an effective and proven command. Grant was now General-in-Chief of all Union armies, supported by Meade, who headed the Army of the Potomac, and Grant's close friend, William Sherman, who took control of the forces in the West.

Grant instructed Meade to pursue Lee wherever he went, while Sherman was to capture Atlanta (capital of Georgia) and then march into the heart of the Confederacy. At the same time, smaller campaigns were launched in Louisiana, the peninsula below Richmond – where McClellan had fought two years earlier – and in the Shenandoah Valley (the key to northern Virginia). These smaller campaigns had limited success and impact, but the major campaigns in Virginia and Georgia were crucial in 1864.

In Virginia, Meade and Grant were determined to draw Lee into open combat. Meanwhile, Lee sought the opposite: trying to keep the Union forces away from Richmond and drawing them into well-fortified positions, hoping to prolong the war. Lee was hoping that a prolonged campaign would encourage northern defeatism in time for the presidential elections in November, when the North might turn Lincoln out of office and seek a negotiated peace.

The consequence was a confusing and bloody series of battles throughout May and June. There were serious casualties on both sides, but especially the Unionists who sustained 50,000 casualties in the first month. By the end of July, the constant flanking of one another had settled down to a siege of Petersburg, an important railroad junction 20 miles south of Richmond. Although Grant had lost considerably more men than Lee, by the end of the 'Virginia campaign' he still had more men than Lee had started with. Lee, however, was seeing his numbers continually reduced. He found himself on the defensive by the end of the year. He could not hope for reinforcements from the Shenandoah Valley, because Union successes there in the autumn had secured the area for the Union.

Meanwhile, Sherman had moved into northern Georgia. By September, after a series of disputes and misjudgements within the Confederate defenders, Sherman had taken Atlanta. This was an important boost to northern morale in advance of Lincoln's campaign for re-election. In November, Sherman set out on his infamous 'March through Georgia'. He cut a 60-mile wide front through the state, destroying all in his path and doing damage worth $100 million to Georgia in the process. Sherman reached Savannah on the coast in December and set about planning to join up with Meade by marching north to Petersburg. The Confederate Army that had been defending Atlanta – under the young, brave but impetuous John Bell Hood – did not pursue Sherman. Instead, they attacked a Union army under General Thomas in Tennessee. The attack came to nothing and Thomas convincingly destroyed Hood's forces at the Battle of Nashville in December 1864.

Ulysses S. Grant (1822–1885)
18th President of the USA (1869–77), a Republican. Born Hiram Ulysses Grant. He was general-in-chief for the Union during the American Civil War. As President, he reformed the civil service and ratified the Treaty of Washington with the UK (1871). He carried through a liberal Reconstruction policy in the South. However, he failed to suppress extensive corruption within his own party and Cabinet, which tarnished the reputation of his second term.

William Tecumseh Sherman (1820–1891)
Union general in the American Civil War, renowned for smoking cigars. He had served in the Mexican War and then became a banker. Early in the Civil War, he served at the First Battle of Bull Run (1861) and at Shiloh (1862). He replaced General Grant as commander of the West (1864) and launched his 'Georgia campaign'. After capturing and burning Atlanta, he waged an economic campaign against the civilian population of Georgia and the Carolinas, laying waste to the countryside and driving the Confederates northwards. After the war, he was appointed commander of the army (1869–83).

The final months

With Lincoln triumphantly re-elected and the South demoralised after Sherman's march and under attack from all sides, northern victory seemed certain to come early on in 1865. The Confederacy was desperately short of men and resources. It resorted to desperate measures, offering at various times: a negotiated surrender, full emancipation and, in March 1865, the raising of slave regiments who could be offered freedom in return for fighting.

It was all in vain. Sherman marched north to Richmond, devastating South Carolina and capturing the last major southern ports on the way. Lee's lines defending Petersburg and Richmond were broken on 2 April. Lee headed westwards where he fought his last battle at Sayler's Creek on 6 April. On 9 April, Lee surrendered the Army of North Virginia to Grant at Appomattox. Within weeks, the final shots of the Civil War had been fired. Jefferson Davis initially fled from Richmond, urging the Confederacy to fight on, but there was no heart left in the Confederacy. Davis was captured on 10 May, with the last engagement of the war ending on 13 May in Texas.

The naval campaign

There may have been some doubt in 1861 as to the strongest army section militarily, but there was no question over the North's domination in naval terms. With a strong naval tradition, almost 300 ships in operation and more commissioned, the industrial capacity for quick manufacture and repair, and the majority of naval officers remaining loyal to the Union, the Confederacy could not have started at a greater disadvantage. Lincoln's strategy of blockading the South and the many inland waterways which allowed the easy movement of troops, meant that this, too, was a useful advantage to have. The Union's Secretary of the Navy, Gideon Welles, made good use of these advantages. This was seen most notably in the Peninsular Campaign of 1862 and the fall of Vicksburg in 1863.

The northern naval strategy had three elements to it:

● maintaining the blockade and capturing the southern sea ports

● using ships to transport troops and supplies

● controlling the inland waterways, particularly in the West.

Sabotage: The deliberate damaging or destruction of railroad lines, bridges etc., as a way of weakening the enemy.

The South had no navy to speak of, and could not hope to outbuild the North. So the Secretary of War for the Confederacy, Stephen Mallory, had to resort to tactics of **sabotage** and raids, rather than set-piece battles. This was not as defeatist an approach as it might sound. The North had 3,500 miles of coastline to patrol and Southern ships might well break through the blockade and inflict considerable damage, if they wished. Mallory made some major innovations in naval warfare so that, even if the North did have the better of it, the Confederates certainly kept the Unionists on their toes. Mallory's most important innovations were:

● The development of the 'ironclad' – a new vessel first used in March 1862 ('The Virginia'), but the North were quickly able to outproduce the South.

● Fast raiders, purchased in Britain by James Bullock to get round the neutrality laws. The most famous – 'The Alabama' and 'The Florida' – did inflict significant damage on Union shipping, sinking or damaging 200 merchant vessels.

● Torpedoes – which damaged or sank around 40 Union ships.

● The submarine – sank one boat in 1864, then sank itself.

It is hard to think what else Mallory might have done. Ultimately, the resource imbalance was unanswerable; the South never had more than 40 vessels in service at any one time. In all three areas – transport of troops, control of the inland waterways and sustaining the blockade – Northern naval dominance was a major factor in military success and planning.

How important were the military campaigns to the final outcome?

In recent years, historians have tended to neglect military factors. Instead, they have looked to economic, social and political issues to explain the outcome of the American Civil War, and wars generally. Although there were important domestic issues that had an impact on the war, the military campaigns do deserve serious study. For a start, there were moments when decisive battles, such as Gettysburg, the Peninsular Campaign and Antietam, might well have gone the other way. Also, it is clear that the prolonging of the war worked to the disadvantage of the less well-resourced South. Thus the military failure of Lee to break through in 1862 and 1863 is important. It is only by studying the battles that we can understand the difficulties General Lee faced. Similarly, the ability of the South to defend Richmond successfully in 1861–62 prevented a quick Union victory that might well have produced different consequences for the USA, if the greater slaughter of 1862–65 had not occurred.

It is also worth remembering that Lincoln was not only elected President in 1860 on a minority of the votes cast, but his re-election in 1864 was by no means certain. A Democratic President might well have been tempted to sign a negotiated peace. Confederate victories at Gettysburg, Vicksburg and Chattanooga could easily have encouraged defeatism in the North. Although many of the military problems facing the South were to do with inferior resources, there are plenty of examples in history of the better-resourced side being defeated. You only need to think of the Americans in Vietnam and the British in the War of Independence. It is thus significant that the tide really turned for the North with the appointment of Grant. Also, an early failure to break through by the South lengthened the Civil War and so diminished the chances of the Confederacy.

Raising and supplying troops
The North had a clear numerical advantage of troops. Around 2,000,000 northerners served in the armed forces during the War, compared with around 900,000 Confederates. Both sides originally relied on volunteers, and there were many of them in the early weeks. Initially, a number of volunteers were actually turned away. Local state militias were the main source of volunteers. After July 1862, Lincoln was able to call state militias into federal service for up to nine months.

Conscription: Making people in a particular country join the army, navy or air force. In America it worked like a form of lottery.

Draft: The practice of ordering people to serve in the armed forces, usually for a limited period of time. The term originated in America.

As it became clear that the Civil War was likely to drag on and was not going to be the romantic adventure that many early volunteers had expected, both the North and the South had to resort to **conscription**. The Confederacy passed the first **draft** law in April 1862 and the North followed in July 1863. The laws were unpopular and were resisted in both sections, most notably in New York, where the first draft selections caused riots in the summer of 1863, resulting in the deaths of several hundred people, especially blacks. The fact that rich people could avoid the draft by hiring a substitute or paying $300 was especially unpopular. Although conscription only accounted for around 10 per cent of the troops who fought in the Civil War, there were certainly a number of men who volunteered only when the threat of conscription was raised.

Both sides were initially reluctant to use black troops. General Lee had urged Davis to establish slave regiments, but it was only in the final, desperate weeks of March 1865 that the Confederacy agreed to such a measure, with the promise of freedom in return. In the North, there was also resistance to the idea of black troops. Even when they did use blacks it was in segregated regiments, usually in non-combat roles and, until 1864, for lower pay. There were some regiments before 1863, but the majority enlisted after the Emancipation Proclamation (see section 4.9) and at a time when whites were reluctant to volunteer. Of the 46,000 black men eligible to fight in the North, 33,000 enlisted. The rest of the black soldiers were slaves – about 100,000 from the Confederacy and a further 42,000 securing their freedom from the Union slave states of Kentucky, Missouri, Delaware and Maryland. By the end of the war, blacks were a major part of the Union army – around 180,000 had served.

War supply was less easy, especially for the South. In 1863, the South passed the Impressment Act, which allowed the seizure of goods in order to supply the troops. They were also helped by 'taxation-in-kind' that provided agricultural resources from the summer of 1863. Transportation was vitally important in supplying and moving troops. This was, in many ways, the first war in which railroads played a key part. The North had an advantage here for they not only had a larger railroad system but they could destroy the Southern network by tearing up rails in areas they controlled and they could more easily repair their own network.

The North was unable to blockade the South effectively, especially at first. Blockade-running was a highly profitable, if risky, venture that the Confederate Government became involved in by 1863. It required all blockade-runners to carry one-third of government cargo – that is, cotton exports and war supply imports. As a result, until the last weeks of the Civil War, the South secured the majority of its weapons from overseas.

Financing the war

Both governments adopted unprecedented policies to raise money. The South suffered particularly because of the decline in trade due to the northern blockade. It had to raise money centrally by demanding levies on individual states. Whilst both sides lacked full credit systems, the North was able to reform banking laws and to draw upon reasonable gold reserves, whereas in the South most capital was tied up in land and slaves.

The North passed a federal tax on incomes over $800 in August 1861. The Internal Revenue Act of 1862 saw significant taxation across the board. A similar policy was followed in the South where income tax and a 10 per cent tax 'in kind' was levied on agricultural produce after 1863 (i.e. agricultural goods rather than cash were handed over). Because each southern state was responsible for raising taxation for the federal government, a number of states did so reluctantly and inefficiently. Only 8 per cent of Confederate income was raised through taxation, compared with 20 per cent in the North.

The main method of raising funds for both sections was through borrowing. In the North around 70 per cent of the money raised for the war was borrowed ($2.6 billion), much in the form of war bonds bought by ordinary citizens hoping to establish a stake in northern victory. The Confederacy was able, initially, to raise money through loans and bonds secured on cotton. As the war went on and people became less convinced of a southern victory, loans became harder to raise and the last major loan was secured in January 1863.

In both North and South, the government issued paper money (**greenbacks**) that was not redeemable in gold or silver, so soon lost its value. The situation was bad in the North, where $450 million greenbacks were produced and where **inflation** ran at 80 per cent during the Civil War. In the South, where individual states also issued notes, inflation was rife. The

Greenbacks: American banknotes such as dollar bills.

Inflation: An increase, sustained over a period of time, in the general level of prices. It can be caused by an increase in the cost of raw materials which is then passed on to the consumer, or by a shortage of goods the demand for which pushes the prices up.

Confederate paper money bearing the likeness of Thomas 'Stonewall' Jackson.

shortage of goods and the ineffectiveness of other methods of raising money made this worse. Inflation destroyed the southern currency, with prices rising over 5,000 per cent during the Civil War. By 1865, the Confederate government was $800 million in debt, with state governments having run up equally unmanageable amounts.

Economics of war

Northerners in Congress took advantage of the absence of southern votes to pass various pieces of economic legislation that favoured the North. They had been struggling to get these through Congress in the years prior to the Civil War. Much of the legislation helped the expansion of northern industry after the war. Such acts included federal support for a transcontinental railroad, higher tariffs, the easing of immigration rules, improved banking laws and the 1862 Homestead Act. While most of the Acts needed some time before their full impact was felt, northern industry responded well to the demands of war placed upon it. There was:

- a significant increase in production of both agricultural and manufactured goods

- an expansion of communications and transport

- mechanisation that improved agricultural yields and industrial output.

Many speculators and investors could make considerable amounts out of wartime contracts. Although wages lagged behind prices, it was a time of general prosperity, especially as the need for soldiers helped to increase the demand for workers. Overall, economic growth was not as great as one might expect, but much of this was down to the decrease in population (not only war deaths but immigration also declined during the period) and to the loss of southern markets and capital. In areas of war demand, growth was dramatic. The inflationary impact of war finance helped companies to pay off debts and to invest in new techniques and machinery.

In the South, of course, it was a different story. The northern blockade, and the previous dependency on the northern states as a market and on northern transport for exporting meant that the South struggled to find a market for its agricultural goods, especially cotton. It therefore lacked the wherewithal to purchase necessary materials for war – a situation that got

Hoarding/riots/black marketeering:
These are all common in times of
shortages, especially when there is a
war going on. Shortages of food and
manufactured items may lead to riots
as people cannot get essential items.
Hoarding also occurs when items are
in short supply. By stockpiling, the
aim is to create a shortage, thereby
pushing up prices and thus making a
large profit for the hoarders when
they decide to sell. 'Black
marketeering' is the buying and
selling of goods illegally. Usually it is
conducted on a cash or barter basis.
Although the 'black market' generates
a large proportion of national income,
the fact that it is not recorded in any
accounting records means that no tax
is paid on the transaction. This makes
black marketeering attractive to those
buying and selling in the 'black
market'.

1. How important was Robert E.
Lee in the defence of the South
during the Civil War?

2. To what extent was Northern
victory due to its economic
strength?

worse as the fighting went on. Furthermore, whole areas of the South –
especially Virginia and Tennessee, and Georgia and South Carolina after
1864 – saw most of the fighting. These areas suffered the physical destruction that war brought. **Hoarding, riots and black marketeering** were rife,
especially given the inflation rate. The Confederate Government interfered
more directly in the southern economy than was the case in the North.
This caused some historians to talk of 'Confederate Socialism'. The
Confederate Government exercised considerable control over railroads,
communications and private industry, as well as encouraging planters to
shift from cotton to agricultural production. The longer the fighting went
on:

● the more the northern economy was stimulated and responded to the
demand positively;

● the more desperate the situation in the South became, so that, when
the end of the war came, many at home were grateful for peace in
whatever circumstances.

4.7 What opposition did the political leadership face during the Civil War?

Scapegoat: Someone is blamed
publicly for something that has
happened, although it may not be
their fault, just because other people
are angry about it and need to have
someone they can blame and punish.

Jefferson Davis faced criticism over his leadership from the start.
Historians have continued to criticise the way in which he governed and
led the Confederacy. Some of these claims have some validity, though there
is no doubt that a lot of colleagues and southern writers made Davis into
something of a scapegoat after the war. Similarly, Lincoln is remembered
today as the 'great emancipator', the man who won the war; but at the time
he faced criticism for his actions and decisions, and his re-election in 1864
was far from certain.

Davis did not work with colleagues easily and there was a high turnover
of personnel in his Cabinet. He had a number of disputes with his
commanders. He was not good at delegating and yet struggled to make
quick and effective decisions. Cabinet meetings in the Confederacy
dragged on and on. Davis was also accused of meddling in military affairs.
In his defence, he did have a military background. He was also firm in his
defence of General Lee, refusing to accept his resignation after Gettysburg.
This contrasts with Lincoln, who chopped and changed his top commanders throughout the first few years of the Civil War, before settling on
Grant in 1864. Lincoln, however, was a consummate manager of men. He
was not afraid to have in his Cabinet men with widely differing views who
had experience of government far ahead of himself. He got a lot out of
some very talented men. Lincoln had good working relations with
Congress. He also had a knack of knowing, for example, when he could
and when he could not try to abolish slavery.

Lincoln's other great advantage over Davis was his ability to make inspi-
rational speeches that captured the mood of the nation. He had great
self-confidence and an unswerving conviction that what he was doing was

right, and he was able to communicate this to the public and to the northern troops. Lincoln maintained unity in the North despite facing loyal but wary opposition. In the early years, he countered the growing defeatism that took hold as the war dragged on and the South inflicted embarrassing defeats. Davis, on the other hand, was not a great communicator. He did not build a national spirit of optimism and sacrifice which became necessary as the war turned against the South.

On the question of war powers and use of executive control, there is no doubt that Lincoln went much further than Davis. A number of contemporaries felt that Lincoln exceeded his powers, beyond a level that was constitutionally acceptable. On the other hand, some historians have criticised Davis for acting too cautiously. The historian David Donald, in *Lincoln* (1995), suggests that the South 'died of democracy' because Davis did not take a strong enough line against dissent and was too concerned with liberties. Davis made a virtue of this at the time, proclaiming in February 1862 that, by comparing himself with the Northern command, 'there has been no act on our part to impair personal liberty of the freedom of speech, of thought or of the press'.

Lincoln showed little concern for the civil liberties of individuals in the North during the Civil War. He supported the suspension of the writ of *habeas corpus* and agreed that anyone could be tried in a military court for preventing conscription or helping the enemy. A number of cases that ensued were highly suspect and many people suffered arbitrary arrest that Lincoln did little to oppose. In the early months, he took decisions before Congress met in July 1861 that included instituting the naval blockade, suspending basic freedoms of speech and association, removing *habeas corpus* in Maryland, raising troops and spending money on arms and supplies. Lincoln justified all this on the grounds of 'war powers' – a new phrase in America. It is clear that these actions played a significant role in saving the **border states** (see map on page 114) for the Union. Throughout the Civil War, Lincoln was not afraid to use direct powers if he felt they were necessary. He would worry about the clashes with Congress and the courts later.

It is possible to exaggerate the differences between North and South in terms of political control. After all, if Lincoln had been as tyrannical as his opponents claim, he would hardly have allowed the continued political debate that even saw him fighting for re-election in 1864. Similarly, Davis' concern for individual rights did not prevent him from supporting conscription when it came. However, it is fair to say that Lincoln did provide better and clearer leadership for the Union than Davis achieved for the Confederacy. This is not going as far as historian David Potter has in suggesting that if Davis and Lincoln had swapped roles, then the South might have won.

Border states: Slave states that stayed loyal to the Union during the Civil War. They were Missouri, Kentucky, Delaware and Maryland.

Internal opposition

Both Lincoln and Davis had to deal with critics on the home front during the Civil War. Some opposed the war altogether. Most southerners supported secession, or were at least happy to abide by the decision of the states to secede. However, a sizeable number of white southerners – around 90,000 – fought in the Union army. Western Virginia and eastern Tennessee, where slavery was not prevalent and economic conditions were closer to those in the North, showed substantial support for the Union. Indeed, West Virginia actually seceded from Virginia and became a free state of the Union in 1873. Support for war in the North was more solid in 1861. Douglas, the defeated northern Democratic candidate, called on all Democrats to rally round Lincoln. The President helped matters by promoting a number of Democrats to positions in the Administration and army, including McClellan (the commander of the Army of the Potomac). The few who opposed war initially were labelled 'Copperheads' by their opponents, and Republicans later tried to smear all Democrats with the label.

Even if northern Democrats were prepared to support the war, that did not mean they supported Lincoln's policies. Lincoln was attacked for his alleged abuses of presidential power and the Democrats were keen to criticise Republican economic policies, as well as more radical war measures like conscription and emancipation. In 1862, the Democrats enjoyed considerable success in the Congressional elections under the slogan 'The Constitution as it is: the Union as it was: the **Negroes** where they are'.

Negroes: People with black skin who came from Africa or whose ancestors came from Africa. In America, this term was used for slaves, which many people now find offensive.

Republicans had some success in discrediting the Democrats by claiming that they tacitly supported the Confederacy. In early 1863, with a series of defeats behind him, Lincoln had to take the arguments of leading peace Democrats seriously. His two greatest crises of internal opposition occurred in the summer of 1863.

Military tribunal: A court that usually deals with cases within the armed forces.

1. Lincoln supported General Burnside who had tried a leading peace Democrat, Clement Vallandingham, by **military tribunal**. As a civilian making speeches condemning the war and calling upon soldiers to desert, Vallandingham was clearly undermining the war effort. However, to try a civilian in a military court for making a speech was clearly taking things beyond the law. Although Lincoln backed Burnside, he set Vallandingham free afterwards but insisted he left the Union.

2. More serious for Lincoln were the anti-draft riots in New York in July 1863. Partially encouraged by the public opposition to the draft by the Democratic Governor, Horatio Seymour, over a hundred people were killed by a protesting mob. Lincoln acted swiftly, sending in 20,000 troops who shot rioters dead, where it was deemed necessary to restore order.

Lincoln's greatest personal test came in his campaign for re-election in November 1864. He had looked vulnerable at one point to a challenge from the more radical Republicans, who rallied round John Fremont (the Republican candidate in 1856). They wanted a stronger line on reconstructing the Union and handling the South than Lincoln favoured. However, the war began to turn in the North's favour again that autumn. Lincoln campaigned on a National Union platform in the hope of attracting War Democrat votes (i.e. Democrats who supported the Civil War; as opposed to peace Democrats who did not). This was made more likely by his choice of Andrew Johnson, a War Democrat from Tennessee, as his running-mate (vice-presidential candidate). The re-election of Lincoln looked more secure as a result.

The Democrats called for a negotiated peace and promised to preserve states' rights, although their candidate, the Union commander George McClellan, made it clear that he would keep fighting. The South saw the 1864 presidential election as their last hope of victory. They were hoping that the northern voters would be tired of the Civil War and would vote Lincoln out in the hope of getting some form of negotiated settlement. McClellan secured a respectable 45% of the vote, but Lincoln's victory on a platform of unconditional surrender and destruction of slavery paved the way for the final collapse of the Confederacy.

Jefferson Davis found that, as the war dragged on and looked less promising, so opposition increased. As in the North, opposition to the draft was the major cause of discontent in 1862–63. Opposition was widespread across the South, made worse by exemptions that favoured the rich and the planters. The extent to which class conflict followed can be exaggerated, but it does seem that at least some of the resentment stemmed from a perception that it was a 'rich man's war but a poor man's fight'. Small-scale farmers, in particular, found themselves heavily taxed and suffering inflation and shortage of goods. As the northern troops advanced, **refugees** moved into cities. These cities became a centres of discontent, with food riots in Atlanta and Richmond in 1863 and a growing number of strikes. Davis had to threaten striking workers with the draft.

Refugees: People who are forced to leave their country because there is a war or because of their political or religious beliefs.

More generally, Davis had to face the dilemma that the Confederacy had been formed on the principle of states' rights and so many of his fellow southerners resisted any attempts at creating a strong Confederate identity that would mean a lessening of state powers. Some state governors, such as Zebulon Vance in North Carolina and Joseph Brown in Georgia, protested at times against what they saw as the unnecessary centralisation of the Richmond government. Vance often prevented supplies reaching Confederate troops in north Virginia because he was concerned to maintain the defences of North Carolina. Brown opposed conscription and managed to prevent thousands of Georgians from fighting by granting exemptions.

1. Who do you think faced greater opposition during the Civil War: Abraham Lincoln or Jefferson Davis? Explain your answer.

2. Who was the more effective political leader: Lincoln or Davis? Give reasons for your answer.

Davis also faced opposition from the Confederate Congress where, although there was no official opposition, he found factions working against him, especially after 1863. He also lacked the support of his Vice-President, Alexander Stephens of Georgia, who described his President as 'weak and vacillating, timid, petulant, peevish, obstinate, but not firm'.

Although both leaders – Lincoln and Davis – could rely on the support of the majority of the people in their section, they both had to govern in the knowledge that such support had to be maintained with care. Davis had the added difficulty of having to maintain morale in the final two years when southern defeat looked increasingly likely.

4.8 How did foreign powers respond to the war?

The Confederacy was well aware that their best hopes of success lay in getting early recognition from major international powers, most importantly Britain. Recognition would not only establish international legitimacy, but it might also encourage some limited European involvement in the conflict, at least in helping to break the blockade. The Confederacy had reason to be hopeful too, for there were strong links between the southern states and the Lancashire cotton mills of northern England. The blockade might well threaten unemployment in the mill towns if their raw material supply dried up. It was also not lost on British policy-makers that if north America were divided into two separate states, Britain would be less likely to see a strong commercial rival emerge on the other side of the Atlantic.

Radicals: People who believe that there should be great and extreme changes in society.

Liberals: Moderates who favour gradual progress by the changing of laws, rather than by revolution.

The cause of states' rights was also taken up by a number of **radicals** in Britain who supported the nationalist claims of the southerners. On the other hand, a larger number of radicals and **liberals** were unwilling to back an uprising which was partly to do with preserving slavery. The British were aware that direct involvement in support of the South could easily lead to attacks on Canada or central American possessions. Although ties with the cotton-producing South were important, Britain also imported large amounts of grain from the North.

It was not surprising then that Britain chose to remain neutral during the American Civil War. Once Lincoln had issued the Emancipation Proclamation (see next section) and made slavery a main issue, that position became more fixed. Neutrality did not mean that Britain was not prepared to allow private trade between British military suppliers and Confederate agents. In fact, both sides made many military purchases in Europe. However, attempts at forcing British intervention by placing a voluntary embargo on cotton exports from the South failed, and probably made British politicians and industrialists look less favourably on the South.

There was a decent stockpile of supplies at the start of the American Civil War and, by the time the blockade had started to bite, Britain had found alternative supplies in India and Egypt. There was always a danger that Britain and the USA might find themselves at war accidentally. However, since neither side wanted that to happen, when the situation did look fragile – most notably over the Trent Affair in November 1861 – there was a flurry of diplomatic activity and face-saving compromises.

The French Government was instinctively more sympathetic to the Confederacy and would certainly have recognised the Richmond government if Britain had. Napoleon III had committed French troops to the Mexican War and hoped that he might get support from the Confederacy for increasing French involvement in Mexico in return for recognition. However, the French were not in a position to act alone and needed British naval support before getting involved in a fight with the Union.

Thus European involvement in the American Civil War was kept to a minimum, though the Confederacy in particular gained from Britain's liberal interpretation of neutrality when it came to providing weapons and commerce. British and French recognition of the Confederacy would have been a big boost to southern fortunes, but ironically such recognition was unlikely to come until Confederate victory seemed likely. One of the Confederacy's greatest political cards was never played.

Explain why Britain and/or France might have intervened in the Civil War.

4.9 What was the importance of the Emancipation Proclamation?

On 23 September 1862, Lincoln issued his Emancipation Proclamation. The proclamation stated that, as from 1 January 1863, any slaves in conquered enemy territory would be 'forever free'. Although this meant that slaves living in states that were loyal to the Union, or already conquered by it, did not get their freedom (something that earned the scorn of foreign commentators), most campaigners both for and against emancipation saw it as an important move. The Democrats opposed the proposals and made gains at the November 1862 elections when campaigning on the issue, while opponents of slavery saw it as an important first step. Lincoln won the support of prominent abolitionists who had been frustrated by his reluctance to move sooner. On 1 January 1863, Lincoln announced that the securing of freedom for all slaves in the Confederacy was a Union war aim.

Lincoln's motives in issuing the proclamation have been debated since the moment it occurred. He certainly felt that the time was right to add some ideological fervour to the war. He believed that commitment to the war cause in the North was sufficiently strong to survive the inevitable opposition that would come from the Democrats and some of the pro-Union border states. Lincoln was also forced into some kind of decision because of the course of events. As the North conquered areas in the South, the question of what to do with the slaves and their ambiguous position as human property was being resolved differently by different commanders. Lincoln himself was unhappy with slavery. Although he would not have split the Union to secure its abolition, it was unlikely that Lincoln would not take the opportunity to abolish slavery if it presented itself. He also felt that slavery was a lingering sore, having remarked that 'A House divided amongst itself cannot stand'. If slavery survived the war, then the Union would be condemned to new tensions later.

The consequences of the announcement and then the carrying out of the Emancipation Proclamation were significant.

Nationalism: The growth and spread of loyalty towards a nation, rather than to an individual ruler.

- Most importantly, Lincoln had raised the stakes of the Civil War. There could now be no compromise peace, for the South would not accept the northern war aim.

- It also made it more difficult for the South to secure foreign backing. While liberals in Europe were prepared to support a fight for **nationalism** and states' rights, they could not bring themselves to support a fight to maintain slavery.

1. Why did Lincoln choose September 1862 to issue the Emancipation Proclamation?

2. How did the Emancipation Proclamation help the northern war effort?

- A northern war aim was now adopted that was a simple rallying cry and put the Union on the high moral ground. Although there would be some people in the North who did not accept abolitionism, the new war aim certainly energised the soldiers in the field, as well as making Lincoln's position in the Republican Party stronger. Given his importance to northern victory, this was a great bonus.

- It helped to tip the population imbalance further in the North's favour by encouraging slaves to flee to the North. Black regiments now began to be accepted by northern troops, too.

4.10 Why did the North win the Civil War?
A CASE STUDY IN HISTORICAL INTERPRETATION

Historians are likely to argue for many years more about the relative importance of certain factors in the northern victory – and the extent to which the South could ever have anticipated victory. There are, though, several key areas which everyone accepts should be considered and which played some role in the eventual outcome. The emphasis put on one or the other may vary from writer to writer.

Superiority of numbers and resources

The idea that the South was condemned almost from the start given the advantages that the North had in resources and manpower was voiced as early as 19 April 1865 when Robert E. Lee reflected that: 'The Army of Northern Virginia has been compelled to yield to overwhelming numbers and resources.' This argument was certainly convincing, especially when you consider the extraordinary imbalance between the two sides. It is important, though, to look at current expectations which did not acknowledge Confederate defeat as inevitable. Remember also that resources alone have not determined the results of war in a number of other conflicts. Perhaps it is better to see resources as playing an increasingly important role as the fighting went on and developed into a **war of attrition**. Certainly by 1864 southern troops were being overwhelmed by sheer force of numbers, but it cannot explain why the South did not manage to make breakthroughs earlier in the war.

War of attrition: A conflict in which victory is gained by slowly wearing down the resources and resistance of the opposing power.

Political leadership

In a point by point comparison, it is probable that Lincoln would come out ahead of Davis as a wartime leader. He was more eloquent, more decisive, more inspiring. He managed his ministers better and was prepared to delegate wherever others were up to the job. There are also specific occasions when Lincoln played a crucial and cunning role, such as keeping the border states in the Union in 1861 and managing not to alienate opinion over the slavery issue. Instead, he managed to galvanise northern morale in 1862. Lincoln came to symbolise the northern war effort and the voters endorsed his total commitment to victory in 1864. Davis certainly made mistakes, but he did have the more difficult job to do and he had to manage colleagues who made his job harder, rather than easier. Both Administrations had good and bad ministers. However, it is probably fair to say that, on balance, Lincoln was better served, and he managed his ministers better.

Military actions and leadership

Initially, the war was fought better by the South. Robert E. Lee was recognised, both then and since, as one of the great commanders. Lincoln struggled to find his equal in the early years of the Civil War. However, it is clear that the appointment of Grant – first in overall command in the West and then, in 1864, to full command of all Union forces – finally brought an outstanding general into the Union war effort. There has been criticism of Lee for concentrating on Virginia and so losing the West early in the war, and for an attacking strategy at a time when war did not favour the attacker. This was demonstrated most clearly during Pickett's Charge at Gettysburg. However, it is hard to see how the Confederacy could have done anything but defend Richmond, and Lee proved a masterful commander in Virginia. His only major offensives were at Antietam and Gettysburg. These came when he was trying to force an end to the war by effecting a crushing defeat on the North in the North – a strategy hard to criticise, given the need to finish things quickly if the South was to have a hope of victory. If military acts did play a role, it is probably better to look at the effectiveness of northern tactics under Grant and Sherman. Here the concept of total war and the determination to take the fighting into the heart of the Confederacy did much to destroy southern morale in the later years.

Internal problems and strengths

The economy was better managed and finance more easily raised in the North than in the South. This was not just a question of the competence of the ministers involved, but also of the circumstances in which they operated. States' rights and a fear of provoking internal dissent made the Confederacy more timid than it needed to be in focusing the section on all-out victory. Lincoln was not without critics, but the economy and society saw things get better in the North, while the South had to cope with rampant inflation, growing shortages and, later, the consequences of destruction. Certainly, by the later years of the Civil War, southern morale had taken a beating and the Confederacy was beginning to collapse internally.

It is not easy to see any one factor as being solely, or even largely, responsible for northern victory, but it is useful to recognise the importance of different issues as different times in the conflict. For example, after Gettysburg it was unlikely the South would now win, but it was not until Lincoln's re-election in November 1864 that it became obvious that the North would not give up. Since the South only had to survive to win the conflict, it was really a matter of whether the North would give up the attempted coercion of the South that determined when the war would end and who would be the victor. Then the failure of the South to break through in 1862 and 1863, the determination of Lincoln and his confirmation as President in 1864 and the collapse of southern morale after that, all played their roles. Also, there remain doubts as to whether the South ever really possessed the resources and internal strengths to last out longer than the North.

1. What do you regard as the most important reason why the North won the Civil War? Explain your answer.

2. Why have historians argued about the reasons why the North won the Civil War?

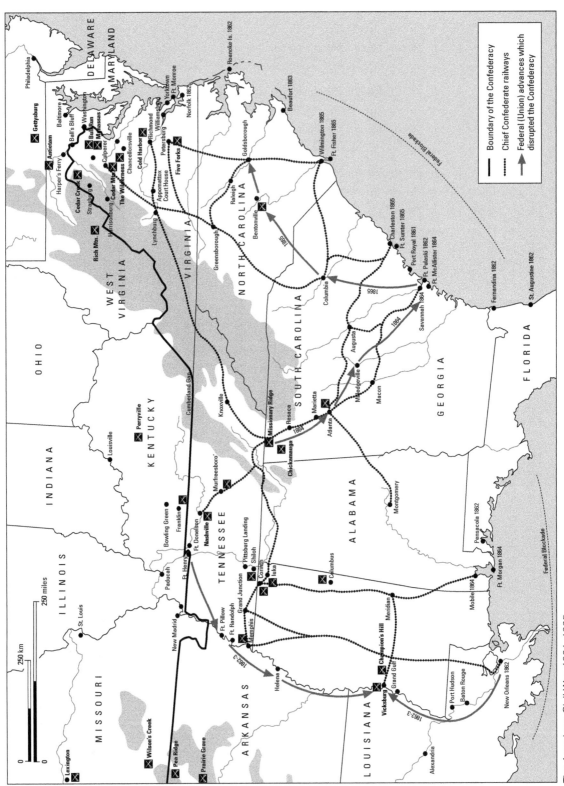

The American Civil War, 1861–1865

4.11 To what extent was the Civil War the 'first modern war'?

The American Civil War is almost equidistant in time between the battles of Waterloo (1815) and the Somme (1916–17). As such, the Civil War can be seen either as the last of the Napoleonic-style wars, or as the first of the modern era. Certainly, generals preparing for the carnage of the trenches in the First World War would have been well advised to study the battles of the American Civil War. Similarly, Wellington and Napoleon would have found much to remind them of their encounters. The truth is that the civil war in America bridges the gap between the two eras. A consideration of the civil war reveals several things.

Developments in military technology

These developments increasingly favoured the defender. From 1863, most infantry on both sides had rifle-muskets that could be loaded more quickly and were accurate at a greater distance. As a result, defending armies could fire several shots successively at an advancing army. The digging of trenches became commonplace as well, making it very difficult for an enemy to attack unless by surprise. This was especially so since opponents soon got wise to the likely attack on the flanks of a line and so defended these positions as effectively as elsewhere. The defender won almost all of the battles of the Civil War, until the final months. It did mean that, once the defender had won a battle, he could not easily follow up a victory. Consequently, war quickly developed into a process of wearing the opposition down.

Cavalry were rarely used on the Civil War battlefields as a charge by them stood little chance of success. More and more, the cavalry were used for reconnaissance and disruption of enemy supply lines.

Developments in tactics

Although, in the early stages of the Civil War, the traditional rules of etiquette were obeyed, later stages saw commanders such as Grant and Sherman taking their troops into the heart of enemy territory. They were

Union soldiers in camp at Harper's Ferry during 1862

not afraid to make civilians and their property legitimate targets. Sherman formulated the view that as war was terrible whatever the circumstances, it was best to bring it to as swift a conclusion as possible by making it as nasty but effective as was necessary. Although his 'March through Georgia' in 1864 and his attacks up the coast through the Carolinas in 1865 were not as destructive as much of 20th-century warfare, the deliberate aim of destroying civilian morale demonstrated a knowing cruelty that is a sign of the modern warfare. It is also recognition that, in an age of total warfare, all opponents – civil as well as military – are legitimate targets.

Increased importance of industrial supply

A third way in which the American Civil War can be seen as heralding modern developments is in the increased importance of industrial supply. As technology developed and weapons became more technically advanced, so it became more important to have an effective supply of iron, coal, **saltpetre** etc. Railroads and other forms of communication also assumed greater importance in ensuring that armies were kept in the field and were well supplied. Also, the growth of mass recruit armies, as opposed to the old professional bodies, made supply of food and uniforms all the more important. They also increased the civilian experience of war as families with no previous military experience could well find relatives and friends directly involved in the conflict.

For all the modern developments during the American Civil War, much fighting still took place on horseback or according to tactics learned during the Mexican Wars. However, there is no doubt that, with the benefit of hindsight, important trends in 20th-century warfare can be traced back to those conflicts. The idea of total war – one that involved home fronts as well as the military theatres – was clearly demonstrated between 1861 and 1865 in America.

Saltpetre: Potassium nitrate – a substance that is used in making gunpowder, matches and fertilisers.

---

1. What do you regard as the features of 'a modern war'?

2. Which aspects of the American Civil War make it 'a modern war'?

Source-based questions: Origins of the American Civil War

SOURCE A

(The non-slaveholding states) have assumed the right of deciding upon the propriety of our domestic institutions; and have denied the rights of property established in 15 of the States and recognised by the Constitution; they have denounced as sinful the institution of Slavery …. They have encouraged and assisted thousands of slaves to leave their homes; and those who have remained have been incited by emissaries, books and pictures, to servile insurrection …. A geographical line has been drawn across the Union, and all the States north of that line have united in the election of a man to the high office of President of the United States whose opinions and purposes are hostile to slavery.

24 December 1860, South Carolina defends its decision to secede in the Declaration of Causes of Secession.

SOURCE B

If I could save the Union without freeing any slave, I would do it; and if I could save it by freeing all the slaves, I would do it; and if I could save it by freeing some and leaving others alone, I would also do that. What I do about slavery and the colored race I do because I believe it helps to save this Union … I have here stated my purpose according to my view of official duty, and I intend no modification of my oft-expressed personal wish that all men everywhere could be free.

Letter from Lincoln to Horace Greeley's 'New York Tribune', 22 August 1862

SOURCE C

One-eighth of the whole population was colored slaves ... These slaves constituted a peculiar and powerful interest. All knew that this interest was somehow the cause of the war. To strengthen, perpetuate and extend this interest was the object for which the insurgents would rend the Union even by war, while the government claimed no right to do more than to restrict the territorial enlargement of it.

Abraham Lincoln speaking publicly in March 1865.

SOURCE D

[The Confederates fought] for the defence of an inherent, unalienable right to withdraw from a Union which they had, as sovereign communities, voluntarily entered ... The existence of African servitude was in no way the cause of the conflict, but only an incident.

Jefferson Davis, writing in his memoirs after the war.

1. Study Source A.

Explain what is being referred to in the highlighted phrases.

(a) 'denied the rights of property established in 15 of the States and recognised by the Constitution'

(b) 'assisted thousands of slaves to leave their homes'.

2. Using Source A, you need to be aware of the motives of the South Carolinians in publishing this declaration.

How far does it affect its reliability and usefulness?

3. Study Sources A and B.

How far do these two sources agree on what Lincoln's views regarding slavery were?

4. Does the fact that both sources B and C are public statements by Lincoln affect how far we can trust them as reflecting his views?

5. Study Source D.

(a) Is it possible that Davis would have written differently if this had been produced at the start of the War?

(b) How reliable are accounts written by eye-witnesses quite a long time after the events?

6. Study Sources C and D. How useful are these sources for understanding why the Civil War broke out?

7. Using the sources and the information in this chapter, do you agree with Lincoln's view in Source C that slavery was 'somehow the cause of the war'?

Further Reading

Texts designed for AS Level students

The Origins of the American Civil War 1846–1861 by Alan Farmer (Hodder and Stoughton, Access to History series, 1996)
The American Civil War 1861–1865 by Alan Farmer (Hodder and Stoughton, Access to History series, 1996)
A House Divided: Sectionalism and the Civil War, 1848 to 1865 by R. Sewell (John Hopkins University Press, 1988)

Texts for A2 and advanced study

Conflict and Compromise: The Political Economy of Slavery, Emancipation and the American Civil War by R. Ransom (Cambridge University Press, 1989)
The American Civil War by P. Parish (Holmes and Meir, 1975)
The Battle Cry of Freedom by J. McPherson (Penguin, 1988)

With Malice Toward None: a biography of Abraham Lincoln by S. Oates (Mentor, 1977)

Lincoln by D. Donald (Jonathan Cape Press, 1995)

The Origins of the American Civil War by Boyd and Hilton (Longman, Origins of Modern Wars series, 1998)

DVD

'The Civil War'– produced by Florentine Films, written and produced by Ken and Ric Burns (1990); divided into six one-hour episodes. Covers the causes but mainly the course of the American Civil War.

5 'The Gilded Age' to the First World War, 1865–1919

Key Issues

- How effectively did politicians deal with the problems facing America during industrialisation and expansion?

- Why did the American economy expand so quickly after 1865?

- How did the social and economic changes affect the lives of Americans, 1877–1914?

5.1 How did American society change in the period 1869–1896?

5.2 What were the key features of American politics, 1877–1896?

5.3 Who were the Populists and what did they believe?

5.4 What factors lay behind the economic expansion of the USA after 1865?

5.5 How did people respond to industrialisation?

5.6 What were the patterns of immigration during this period?

5.7 What was the impact of immigration on the USA?

5.8 What were the origins and aims of the Progressive movement?

5.9 What impact did Woodrow Wilson have on domestic affairs, 1913–1919?

Framework of Events

1876	Disputed Presidential election
1877	Compromise sees Rutherford Hayes accepted as President and end of Reconstruction period
1879	Rockefeller organises Standard Oil Trust
1880	Garfield is elected President
1881	Garfield assassinated; Arthur becomes President
1883	Pendleton (Civil Service reform) Act
1884	Cleveland is elected President
1886	American Federation of Labor (AFL) founded
1887	Cleveland vetoes Dependent Pensions Bill
	Interstate Commerce Act
1888	Harrison is elected President
1890	McKinley Tariff Act
	Sherman Anti-Trust Act
1892	Populist Party founded – Omaha Platform launched
	Ellis Island opened as a major immigrant clearance centre
	Cleveland is elected President for second time
1893	'Panic of 1893'
1894	Pullman Palace Car Company workers' strike
1896	McKinley is elected President, defeating Bryan, Democrat/Populist candidate
1898	Spanish–American War begins
1899	Treaty of Paris
1900	McKinley is re-elected President
1901	McKinley assassinated; Roosevelt becomes President
1902	Newlands Act
1903	Elkins Act
1904	Roosevelt is elected President
1905	Industrial Workers of the World (IWW) founded
1906	Hepburn, Meat Inspection and Pure Food and Drugs Acts

1907	More than 500,000 immigrants pass through Ellis Island
1908	Taft is elected President
1909	Payne–Aldrich Tariff
	Disputes between Ballinger and Pinchot
1910	Mann–Elkins Act
1911	Dissolution of Standard Oil Company ordered by Supreme Court
1912	Founding of Progressive Party
	Wilson is elected President after three-way battle with Taft and Roosevelt
1913	Underwood Tariff
	Federal Reserve Act
	Sixteenth and Seventeenth Amendments ratified
1914	Clayton Anti-Trust Act
1916	Federal Farm Loan, Keating–Owen, Adamson and Seamen's Acts
	Wilson is re-elected President
1917	Increased government control of the economy
	USA declares war on Germany
1919	Eighteenth Amendment is passed, introducing national prohibition.

Overview

THE end of the Civil War and victory for the Union in 1865 heralded a new age in American history. Before the Civil War, both northern and southern sections were predominantly agricultural, although the industry that there was was concentrated in the North and East. All this was to change in the following decades as America went through a process of industrialisation similar to that experienced in Britain, but at a much greater pace. By the end of the 19th century, the United States was the leading industrial power in the world. This chapter looks at the reasons for this economic transformation and expansion in the 'Reconstruction' period. It also looks at the wide-ranging effects that such dramatic and rapid change brought to American society and politics.

The rapid industrialisation was matched with significant urbanisation and the emergence of major urban centres such as New York, Chicago and Cleveland. Hundreds of thousands of immigrants flocked to these cities, not arriving from the traditional points of origin in western and northern Europe, but from Italy, Greece, Poland and Russia. These 'new immigrants' not only had a major impact on population growth in the USA (41 per cent of population growth in the 1880s was due to immigration), they also brought very different cultures and attitudes with them. Major cities quickly found themselves with Italian, Jewish and Polish quarters. These immigrants represented major challenges, as well as a source of cheap labour. Many met the hostility and fears of the native-born Americans who felt threatened and feared for the future of their protestant and individualistic Republic.

Politicians had to confront change that they could not keep up with. Initially, this was the 'Gilded Age', in which corruption and disconnection characterised the political system. In the cities, political bosses exercised ruthless and self-interested control, whilst nationally politicians often lined their own pocket and the two political parties offered little to choose between them. Slowly, reform came – sometimes from the politicians themselves, as in the Pendleton Act and the Sherman Anti-Trust Act – more often as a result of external pressure. Farmers and small-scale

Manhattan Island, New York.
1860s

1920s

2000s

businessmen in the West and the South increasingly felt isolated from the politicians in the East, who seemed to be in the pockets of the emerging 'big business' men, such as the self-made millionaires Rockefeller and Carnegie. Protest movements emerged which developed firstly into the Populist campaigns of the 1890s and later into the Progressive movement of the early 20th century. Although the Populists failed to win power nationally, they gained control of several states and cities. They formed the basis for the Progressive movement that saw major reforms in politics, economy and society in the first two decades of the 20th century, under Presidents Roosevelt, Taft and Wilson. Thus, in the 40 years between the end of Reconstruction and America's entry into the First World War, the country was transformed into a major economic power with a modern political system and a diverse and reformed society.

From the information contained in this chapter, what do you regard as the major feature of the Gilded Age in the period 1865 to 1919? Give reasons to support your answer.

5.1 How did American society change in the period 1869–1896?

During the period between the Civil War and the First World War, American society changed dramatically. The USA became a major industrial and international power during this period and through immigration, urbanisation and western expansion became the society we recognise today. However, the Presidents that governed during that period are far from household names today – few Americans would recall much, if anything, of Presidents Garfield and Arthur, Hayes and Harrison. During the period after Reconstruction, Congress provided the main focus for federal politics. The battle for control of Congress and the Presidency dominated party politics between the Democrats and Republicans. By the end of the period, third parties were increasingly challenging the stranglehold that the two main parties had on politics. Though the Republicans and Democrats saw off that challenge, by the 20th century the adoption of elements of progressive legislation by both parties showed a recognition that the politics of the 'Gilded Age' needed to come to an end.

How successful was the presidency of Grant, 1869–1877?

When the Republicans selected Ulysses Grant as their candidate for President in 1868, it was not because of his political record. Indeed he did

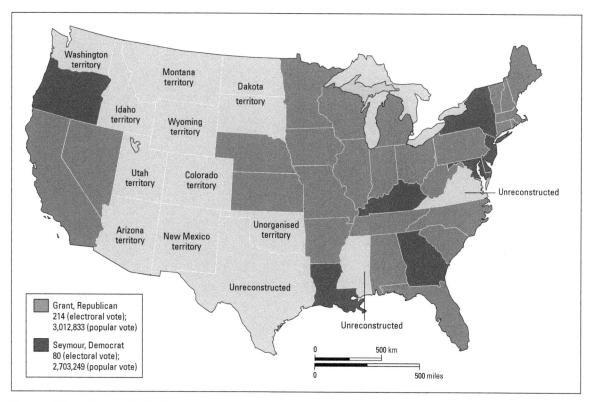

Map legend:
- Grant, Republican 214 (electoral vote); 3,012,833 (popular vote)
- Seymour, Democrat 80 (electoral vote); 2,703,249 (popular vote)

Presidential election results, 1868 – by states

not have one. He was chosen on the assumption that his war record would ensure that he was elected. Not only that, but the Radicals who dominated the party during the Reconstruction period saw in Grant someone who would be easy to influence. They also thought that Grant saw the role of President as essentially ceremonial and symbolic. Thus, his convincing victory in 1869 (winning 26 of the 34 states – see map) and re-election in 1872 gave Congress the opportunity to run the country essentially as it liked. Most of that time was spent on Reconstruction policy and later economic policies, while Grant surrounded himself with cronies, which did much to discredit the Presidency even further.

Reconstruction
The clashes that occurred under Lincoln and Johnson between the Presidency and Congress over the nature of Reconstruction policy and who was in charge, had been largely resolved by the time of Grant's election, and in favour of Congress. Thus Congress carried out the radical reconstruction favoured by men such as Thaddeus Stevens and Charles Sumner, with the support but minimal involvement of both the President and the Supreme Court. The mixture of **carpetbaggers**, **scallywags** and local blacks that dominated the Reconstruction governments of the South achieved mixed results, but their financial extravagance and corruption was little different from what was accepted elsewhere at the time. By 1870, all the former rebel states were back in the Union and the Fourteenth and Fifteenth Amendments to the US Constitution had been passed. When there appeared to be substantial white resistance to reconstruction, the federal government was initially prepared to get involved. It passed a series of Enforcement Acts, in 1870 and 1871, empowering the President to use military power to suppress southern violence and to use Congress to control federal elections.

This determination to enforce radical reconstruction gradually waned.

Carpetbaggers: Northerners who entered the Old South during Reconstruction (1865–1877) in order to exploit the area for profit.

Scallywags: Southern whites who cooperated with the federal occupation authorities in the Old South during the Reconstruction period.

Presidential election results, 1868–1900

Year	Candidate	Party	Votes	Electoral college
1868	**Grant**	Republican	3,013,421	214
	Seymour	Democratic	2,706,829	80
1872	**Grant**	Republican	3,596,745	286
	Greeley	Democratic	2,843,446	63*
1876	**Hayes**	Republican	4,036,572	185
	Tilden	Democratic	4,284,020	184
	Cooper	Greenback	81,737	
1880	**Garfield**	Republican	4,453,295	214
	Hancock	Democratic	4,414,082	155
	Weaver	Greenback-Labor	308,578	
	Dow	Prohibition	10,305	
1884	**Cleveland**	Democratic	4,879,507	219
	Blaine	Republican	4,850,298	182
	Butler	Greenback-Labor	175,370	
	St John	Prohibition	150,369	
1888	**Harrison**	Republican	5,447,129	233
	Cleveland	Democratic	5,537,857	168
	Fisk	Prohibition	249,506	
	Streeter	Union Labor	146,935	
1892	**Cleveland**	Democratic	5,555,426	277
	Harrison	Republican	5,182,690	145
	Weaver	People's	1,029,846	22
	Bidwell	Prohibition	264,133	
1896	**McKinley**	Republican	7,102,246	271
	Bryan	Democratic	6,492,559	176
	Palmer	National Democratic	133,148	
	Levering	Prohibition	132,007	
1900	**McKinley**	Republican	7,218,491	292
	Bryan	Democratic	6,356,734	155
	Wooley	Prohibition	208,914	

* Greeley died between the election and the meeting of the electoral college, so his votes were distributed between four other Democrats.

A summary of presidential actions

President	Dates in office	Main issues of presidency
Ulysses S. Grant	1869–77	Reconstruction
		Series of corruption scandals
Rutherford B. Hayes	1877–81	Ending of Reconstruction
		Clashes with Congress over currency reform
		Clashes with Conkling over appointments in New York
James A. Garfield	1881	Assassinated by frustrated office-seeker
Chester Arthur	1881–85	Civil Service Reform
Grover Cleveland	1885–89	Dawes Act 1887
		Inter-state Commerce Act 1887
		Clashes over vetoes of pension and pork-barrel bills
		Conflict with Congress over tariffs
Benjamin Harrison	1889–93	Billion Dollar Congress
		McKinley Tariff Act
		Dependent Pensions Act
		Sherman Anti-Trust Act
		Sherman Silver Purchase Act
Grover Cleveland	1893–97	'The Panic of 1893'
		Intervention in 1894 Pullman Strike
		Continued growth of Populists
William McKinley	1897–1901	Spanish–American War
		Development of an empire

Scandals in the Grant Administration

Gold scandal, 1869
Two friends of the President – Jay Gould and Jim Fisk – devised a scheme to corner the market in gold. By spreading rumours that the President would not allow the Government to sell its own gold and by buying up much of the remaining gold themselves, they forced the price of gold up before selling when its price was at its highest.

Credit Mobilier scandal
The Credit Mobilier company had been founded by the stockholders of the Union Pacific Railroad Company to divert profits from the Railroad Company to themselves. An investigation by Congress in 1873 revealed that shares had been distributed among various Congressmen, including Vice-President Schuyler Colfax, in order to influence railroad legislation and keep Congress out of any unhelpful investigations.

The 1873 salary grab
Congress voted major salary increases across the federal government, including a 50 per cent rise for Congressmen that was retrospective for two years. Public protest actually caused Congress to change its mind on the retrospective element, but the damage had been done to its reputation.

The Stanborn contracts of 1874
Secretary of the Treasury, William A. Richardson, was forced to resign after allowing a friend, John D. Stanborn, to claim exorbitant commissions for collecting unpaid revenues on Department taxes.

The Whiskey Ring
Grant's private secretary, General Orville Babcock, was part of a conspiracy in St Louis that saw a combination of officials and distillers defrauding the Government of millions in tax revenues on the sale of whiskey.

The Belknap Scandal of 1876
Secretary of War, William Belknap, was forced to resign in order to escape impeachment for accepting backhanders worth $25,000 for granting rights to sell supplies to Indian tribes.

By the mid-1870s, with the Supreme Court restricting the application of the Fourteenth Amendment and with the 1872 General Amnesty Act seeing Congress restore political privileges to thousands of former Confederates, there was little enthusiasm to pursue a vigorous policy ten years after the Civil War had ended. The 1876 election results were disputed, which led to a settlement that saw all federal troops withdrawn from the South in 1877 and the quick restoration of Democratic governments in the South.

Scandals and corruption
Although Grant was not personally corrupt, his time in office was marked by a series of scandals that undermined him, his office and the party to the extent that the term 'Grantism' emerged as an accepted word for corruption. By 1870, Senator James Grimes of Iowa was moved to describe the Republicans as 'the most corrupt and debauched political party that has ever existed'. Businessmen were able to buy off legislators and dominate political decision-making. There was virtually no civil service reform, much wasteful spending of government money and little achieved for it. Furthermore, the federal government set the standards for the rest of the country. The Reconstruction governments in the South were notoriously corrupt and gave the **Bourbons** the excuse they wanted to fight back. The political machine heavily controlled state government. At a local and city level, police would turn a blind eye to petty crime, such as gambling and prostitution, for a fee.

Bourbons: The white ruling class in the former Confederate states

1. What were the major issues that faced Grant as President?

2. Was the presidency of Ulysses Grant little more than a period of corrupt government? Explain your answer.

5.2 What were the key features of American politics, 1877–1896?

Politics was based on patronage, not principle

'The interests are in the main the interests of getting or keeping the patronage of government. Tenets and policies, points of political doctrine and points of political practice, have all but vanished. All has been lost, except office or the hope of it.'

Lord James Bryce's comments on the American Commonwealth in 1888 are appropriate for the whole period 1877–96. Elections were run ruthlessly, as a business, by the party bosses who organised local election machines. The most infamous of these was Tammany Hall, the New York City Democratic Party organisation. The party bosses were especially powerful in the cities where the large number of immigrants, the size of the electorate and the frequency of elections favoured party ticket voting. They were also helped by voting not being by secret ballot until 1890. Party bosses would instruct voters how to cast their votes, in return for help finding jobs, homes etc.

With the growth of the cities, there were many contracts to be handed out and many businesses found themselves depending on political supporters to get work. Many paid jobs, such as customs officials and post-masters, were in the gift of politicians from the President down. A change of party would lead to a whole-scale redistribution of jobs. The most notorious, the Democrats' Tweed Ring in New York, distributed 60,000 posts between 1869 and 1871, increasing city debts by $70 million in the process. Indeed, the assassin who killed President James Garfield in 1881 was a disgruntled office-seeker who shot the President as he was leaving Washington DC to escape the office-seekers who had plagued him since his election six months before. With little dividing the main parties politically, this may explain the relatively high turnout in elections during this period (80 per cent of the electorate voted in the 1888 presidential election, compared with only 55 per cent a hundred years later).

Lack of clear party divisions on the main issues

Although there were many issues that caused political debate during the period, the debate often took place within the two parties, rather than between them. Although the Republicans and Democrats tended to attract different types of supporters, it is best to see the two parties as coalitions rather than tightly organised and disciplined parties we are used to in today's politics. Wilson referred to the Democrats and Republicans as 'two empty bottles that differed only in their labels'. Indeed, on the main issues of the day – such as currency reform, big business, farming, civil service reform, immigration and the role of government – the area a Congressman came from was more likely to influence his vote than the party to which he belonged. Thus the Democratic President Grover Cleveland, coming from the east coast, was as opposed to cheap money policies as his Republican opponent in 1888, Benjamin Harrison. The Republican Chester Arthur spent much of his presidency reforming the civil service, in the teeth of the opposition of his previous Republican sponsor, Roscoe Conkling.

No party was able to dominate nationally during the period

The winning margin in all presidential elections fought between 1876 and 1892 was very close, less than 1 per cent in three of the five elections. In 1880, Garfield won the popular vote by only 9,000 votes out of nine million cast; whilst in 1888, Grover Cleveland actually got more votes than

Benjamin Harrison but lost in the electoral college. The political balance in Congress was also very close, with the Republicans tending to win in the Senate and the Democrats in the House of Representatives. On only one occasion between 1889 and 1891 did the same party (Republicans) control the presidency, Senate and House of Representatives. Because of this, party leaders found it hard to sustain a party programme. Inevitability, this led to compromise and **bipartisanship**. It also encouraged the development of **pork-barrel politics**, as Presidents and party leaders were forced to buy off supporters to get legislation through.

There was an absence of a strong presidency

Although generally decent and honest, few of the Presidents sought the powers or influence of Lincoln. The Presidency had been damaged during the Reconstruction period when Congress had established its predominance over Johnson during the impeachment trial – predominance confirmed by the Supreme Court. There was a general acceptance that the President's role was as a figurehead who presided over the **Administration** rather than being particularly proactive – an idea encouraged by Grant's deliberate lack of engagement from the major issues of the day. With real control being in the Congress, party officials were keen to find cooperative, friendly types as President who would be unlikely to upset too many people and would dispense the **patronage** as the parties hoped. Presidents did not always live up to this expectation. Chester Arthur played an important role in civil service reform, for example, but recent politics had tended to work against any President trying to increase his powers within the balances of the federal government.

How did the two main parties differ from one another?

There were only two national parties that had developed in, and survived, the Civil War and Reconstruction period: the Republicans and the Democrats. Parties existed most actively on a local level and only really acted nationally at election time, especially when it came to choosing a presidential candidate. The main role of the party organisations was to nominate candidates, raise funds, conduct election campaigns and, perhaps most importantly in this period, distribute patronage via government jobs and contracts. On many issues, there was little to distinguish one party from the other. The reasons for getting heavily involved in party politics were more to do with getting some of the spoils of office if your man won. It is, however, possible to see some pointers to party affiliation, even if the following suggestions are a serious generalisation and there are many regional exceptions.

The main issues in American politics, 1877–1896

Although the positions of the parties, personalities and electorate varied according to time and place, there were five major issues that occupied the federal government during the period 1877–1896. It is worth considering the issues involved in each of them, before assessing the attitudes and actions of the leading politicians.

The money issue – greenbacks, gold and silver
Since the 1790s, the United States had supported **bimetallism**. In 1834, a ratio of 1 : 16 in the value of gold to silver was agreed – that is, one ounce of gold would be worth 16 ounces of silver. The consequence of this was that silver was undervalued (i.e. it was actually worth more than the currency rates suggested, so silver ore would fetch more on the open market than the Mint would pay). This became worse as more gold was

Bipartisanship: Both parties having to put aside their differences for a while (e.g. in a war or over a piece of legislation on which they both agree).

Pork-barrel politics: Term to describe the way in which politicians went to Washington DC to gain benefits for their home state and district.

Administration: The presidential or executive branch of US government. The Administration consists of the President and his advisors, notably the secretaries of the various departments, such as Justice or Labor.

Patronage: Help and financial support given by someone to a person or a group.

Bimetallism: Using both gold and silver as currency.

discovered in California in 1848. As a result of this, instead of altering the ratio of gold to silver, silver was 'demonetised' in the 1873 Coinage Act, in other words it was no longer to be used as currency. At the same time, the price of silver began to fall and western silver miners immediately denounced the 'Crime of 1873'. They saw it as an east coast and gold miners' conspiracy. They demanded a repeal of the Coinage Act, so that silver could again be used. Unlimited circulation of silver would have had the consequence of putting more money into circulation (for there was a shortage of gold). This would, in turn, have had inflationary consequences (putting up prices). This was something that attracted farmers who were eager to get more money for the products that they sold internally. At the time they felt that keeping only gold kept prices down on internally produced goods, so they supported the silver miners. Others who supported inflationary measures were those who had to borrow money (often farmers) and exporters. An inflationary policy made money worth less over time and so made the cost of debts lower. Exporters would be able to sell their goods abroad more easily, as other countries would get more dollars for their own currencies and so be able to buy more with fewer pounds, francs or whatever.

This approach was opposed by those who called for an inflationary policy of sound money. They argued that increasing the amount of money in circulation would raise prices for ordinary consumers, undermine the value of pensions and savings, and make people less likely to invest in the American economy.

The debate not only took place in the arguments between gold and silver, but also between the use of coins and banknotes (known as greenbacks). It was not possible to follow an inflationary policy if all transactions had to take place in gold – for by definition you could only then have as much currency as you had gold. However, if you had banknotes, the notes did not cost as much to produce and a government could produce more of them if they wished to, making the dollar worth less. The 1875 Resumption Act made all greenbacks redeemable in gold, so that the Government could not do this. Thus campaigners for an inflationary policy could also campaign for the repeal of the 1875 Act, allowing for the printing of more notes.

The currency battle that was fought throughout this period was between those who supported 'sound money' policies and wanted to stick with gold and those who wanted to see inflationary measures that could either be brought about through the printing of more 'greenbacks' or by returning to bimetallism.

Corruption and civil service reform

Civil service: This consists of all the government departments that administer the affairs of the country and all the people who work in them.

Meritocracy: A social system in which people have power or prestige because of their abilities and intelligence, rather than because of their wealth or social status.

Most of the positions in the **civil service** were in the gift of the President (or the governors of states for that matter) and so tended to go to friends and supporters of the main political parties, regardless of whether they were the best people for the jobs. In 1881, the Civil Service Reform League was formed to campaign for an end to this patronage and the creation of a non-partisan civil service based on **meritocracy**, in which positions would be given on the basis of competitive examination rather than simply by presidential appointment. In this way, reformers hoped they could end corruption, the extravagance of the number of appointments and the size of salaries given, and the inefficiency and inadequacy of so many office holders.

This campaign was always likely to be difficult to convince politicians to support. It was all very well convincing politicians of the need for reform when they were out of government, if as soon as they were in government they were likely to want to reward their own supporters and suddenly be less interested in change. Nevertheless, improvements were gradually made during this period. It became especially significant when the assassination of President Garfield was seen as partly caused by the frustrations of office-seekers.

The tariff

This was one of the few issues that clearly separated the Republicans from the Democrats. There was also a regional and occupational distinction, with southerners and farmers tending to favour lowering tariffs, and easterners and industrialists favouring higher tariffs. Tariffs were used for two purposes: to raise government revenue and to protect American industry. Industrialists argued that American industry could not begin to compete with the more advanced industrial nations, especially Britain. So it was necessary to make American goods more attractive to American consumers by taxing foreign products coming into the country (i.e. tariffs). However, those who exported most of their items, especially farmers and cotton producers, felt that higher tariffs made their goods harder to sell abroad. This was both because of the likelihood that some countries would respond by taxing imports themselves, as well as because if Americans did not buy foreign goods then foreigners would not get the dollars they needed to buy American. It was also argued that tariffs added to the costs of imported goods in America and so allowed domestic producers to charge more, which meant farmers and consumers generally were out of pocket.

High tariffs throughout the period diminished the argument for tariffs as a money-raising measure, since the Government was regularly running a budget surplus. This meant that more money was going into the Treasury than was going out. Thus westerners and southerners increasingly came to see the government's tariff policy as one that discriminated in favour of industry over agriculture.

Pensions

One of the ways in which the Government dispensed of its ever-increasing surplus was through pensions. This was encouraged by the powerful **pressure group**, The Grand Army of the Republic, which represented war veterans. Pensions after the Civil War and from previous conflicts such as the Mexican Wars had generally been limited, both in the numbers claiming and the amounts claimed. However, the Arrears of Pensions Act of 1879 granted back-payment for disability connected with war service. Later the law was changed to allow pension payments for anyone unable to work and who had previously served in the army. By 1885, there were 350,000 names on the pension list and lawyers encouraged the number to grow. When the Bureau of Pensions did not award a pension to someone, lobbying of a representative usually led to a private pension bill being passed in Congress. In this way, the issue of pensions became crucial during the period and pensioners became an important pressure group, most closely identified with the Republicans as the 'party that saved the Union'.

Pressure group: An organisation that wishes to influence political decision-making but does not wish to gain political power.

Big business and regulation

The power of big business to dominate politicians became increasingly resented by individual producers and workers during this period. It was hard to counter given the financial support big business was able to give to secure the legislation and handbacks wanted. Increased pressure was put on governments to regulate some of the worst excesses of big business. This was initially on a local level and then developed upwards. On occasion, appeals were made to the courts – such as the '1877 Munn versus Illinois' ruling which said that states could regulate property in the interests of the public good where that property was operating in the public interest. This meant, for example, that they could prevent railroads from charging different prices to farmers and to large companies for the same journeys.

At other times, the federal government did take a lead with acts such as the Interstate Commerce Act of 1887 which created a regulatory body on railroads and the 1890 Sherman Anti-Trust Act which tried to limit the growth of large and powerful industrial **trusts**. Inevitably though, most politicians of both major parties depended on the support of big business and most of the legislation enacted lacked credibility.

Trusts: Groups of people that have control of, and invest, amounts of money, property etc. usually on behalf of other people.

How did the Presidents and Congresses deal with these issues?

The presidency of Rutherford Hayes, 1877–1881

Hayes was a modest and decent man, prouder of his Civil War record than anything he achieved as President. He himself said afterwards, 'I know my place was a very humble one – a place utterly unknown in history. But I am also glad to know that I was one of the good colonels.' Hayes' **White House** could not have been more different from that of Grant as he was determined to make the Republicans the 'party of morality'. There were morning prayers and nightly 'hymn sings'. Swearing, tobacco and alcohol went out with the corruption, with Mrs Hayes earning the nickname 'Lemonade Lucy' because of her insistence on strict teetotalism throughout the White House. Despite all this, Hayes could not escape the fact that his election in 1876 was marred by controversy. The Democrats never accepted a result that had required the disputed votes of three states to give Hayes a singe-vote victory in the electoral college. 'His Fraudulency' or 'Rutherfraud' Hayes had to accept from the start that his would be only a one-term Presidency.

Hayes remained faithful to the placation of the South as established in the 1877 Compromise. Troops were withdrawn from the remaining occupied states and Hayes appointed a Southern Democrat, David Key of Tennessee, to his Cabinet as Postmaster General. He was not going to abandon the Southern Republicans and blacks altogether though, and he **vetoed** Congressional attempts to repeal the Force Acts.

Hayes found himself in some conflict with Congress over appointments, immigration and currency reform. This indicated likely problems for some of his successors. Hayes found himself vetoing a bill designed to forbid Chinese immigration into California. He also vetoed the Bland–Allison Act of 1878 (although it was passed, amended) – an inflationary Act that tried to increase the amount of silver in circulation. Hayes thus associated himself firmly with those who supported currency stability and he also supported the Specie Act of 1879, which insisted that all greenbacks should be redeemed in gold after January 1879.

The most controversial aspects of Hayes' Presidency were his attempts to insist on a meritocratic system of appointments and his preference for civil service reform. Such policies were not easy to implement, for those who supported him in reaching the White House now expected their reward. In particular, he found himself in conflict with Senator Conkling of New York. Conkling was the powerful head of the **Stalwart faction** within the Republican Party and it was clear that the New York Customs House had been used by Conkling to reward Stalwarts with lucrative positions at the House. In 1877, Hayes dismissed two such officials, Chester Arthur and Alonzo Cornell. Hayes found himself in a massive struggle with Conkling. Although the President finally got his replacements through Congress, it was not without a real tussle and internal Republican bitterness. Hayes was scared off any further attempts at civil service reform.

Rutherford Birchard Hayes (1822–1893)
19th President of the USA (1877–81), a Republican. Major general on the Union side in the Civil War. During his presidency, federal troops were withdrawn from southern states (after the Reconstruction period) and the civil service was reformed. Noted for his honesty and integrity.

White House: Where the President of the USA resides when in office. It is in Washington DC and lives up to its name.

Vetoed: To become law a bill is passed through various stages in Congress and then signed by the President. The President can refuse to sign. This is called the veto.

Stalwart faction: A section within the Republican Party that supported President Grant, a radical policy towards the South and the spoils system.

**James A. Garfield
(1831–1881)**

20th President of the USA (1881), a Republican. Served in the Civil War with the Union forces. He held office for only four months before being assassinated in a Washington DC railway station by frustrated office-seeker, Charles Guiteau. His short term in office is marked by struggles within the Republican Party over influence and Cabinet posts.

**Chester A. Arthur
(1830–1886)**

21st President of the USA (1881–85), a Republican. Had never held an elected office until he was made Garfield's Vice-President in 1880. Became Garfield's successor when the President was shot by an angry office-seeker.

**James Gillespie Blaine
(1830–1893)**

A charismatic and loyal party man. Elected to the House of Representatives (1862), he became Speaker in 1868. He was unsuccessful in gaining the Republican presidential nominations (1876 and 1880). Served briefly as Garfield's Secretary of State. Gained the Republican presidential nomination in 1884, but was defeated by Grover Cleveland. During the Harrison Administration (1889–93), Blaine again served as Secretary of State.

Dogma: System of beliefs which is accepted as true and which people are expected to accept, without questioning it.

James Garfield and Chester Arthur, 1881–1885

Tensions within the Republican Party were evident when it came to choosing the candidates for the 1880 election. Roscoe Conkling and the Stalwarts, determined to avoid another Hayes, pushed for the return of the freer and more corrupt days of the early 1870s and for the adoption of Grant to run for a third term. A faction that rallied around Senator James Blaine of Maine opposed them. They were known as the Half-Breeds, because their more liberal Republicanism (favouring Hayes' conciliatory policy towards the South and civil service reform) seemed only half-hearted. With the Stalwarts pushing for Grant and the Half-Breeds for Blaine, the Republican Convention was deadlocked. On the 36th vote, the anti-Grant factions united behind Senator James Garfield, a less prominent Half-Breed, who promptly chose Chester Arthur as his running-mate as a sop to the Stalwarts.

In a bitter and contentious election campaign against Democrat General Winfield S. Hancock (Union commander at Gettysburg), Garfield triumphed by a majority of only 9,000 votes (though his victory in the electoral college was rather more convincing). Garfield immediately made it clear that he would favour his own Half-Breed faction. Blaine was the power behind the throne as Secretary of State, while appointments deliberately ignored the Stalwarts. Garfield even provoked the resignation of Conkling over his appointments to the New York Customs House – an action which, when Conkling failed to get the backing in New York he had expected, led to the Stalwart's leader retiring from politics altogether. His dealings with the Stalwarts were, however, to be his undoing. On 2 July 1881, Garfield was shot by a frustrated and unbalanced office-seeker, Charles Guiteau, who cried 'I am a Stalwart and Arthur is President now.' Guiteau was not quite right, for Garfield lingered on until September before dying of his wounds, but it meant that by the autumn the 'spoilsman's spoilsman' was in the White House with almost a full term to run.

Chester Arthur was quite different from his more austere predecessors. He threw out the sideboard presented to 'Lemonade Lucy' by the Women's Christian Temperance Union (it found its way into a saloon) and approached his unexpected task in a more relaxed and hospitable mood. However, the new President had never held an elected office until the Vice-Presidency, and it was only as a compromise that he had got that job. Closely associated with Conkling, he had been sacked by Hayes from the New York Customs House and virtually admitted his use of 'soap' in politics (i.e. 'you scrub my back and I'll scrub yours'). However, in office, Arthur was to be a disappointment to his former colleagues, so much so that Conkling found himself lamenting the end of the Hayes Administration. Arthur surprised almost everyone by the independence he showed, especially in his support for both civil service and tariff reform. In tariff reform he could not overcome the Republicans' unquestioning support for the **dogma** of high tariffs. The 'Mongrel Tariff' passed in 1883 was a measly reform worth a reduction of only 2 per cent, with some prices actually rising.

In tackling fraud and civil service reform, however, Arthur was far more successful. He supported the prosecution of former cronies in the Star Route Fraud cases. In 1882, he vetoed an $18 million river and harbour development bill because of its pork-barrel elements (though Congress overturned his veto). Most significantly, Arthur used the general public revulsion at the assassination of Garfield, at least partially because of the spoils system, to justify his cooperation with Congress and the Civil Service Reform League to pass the Pendleton Civil Service Act of 1883. He also appointed a reformer as its first chairman. Thus, the man sacked by

Hayes as a corrupt customs official, established as President the basis for a merit-driven civil service that by 1900 had 40 per cent of its posts listed as 'classified services'.

Arthur sought the Republican nomination for the 1884 election but, although he was popular enough with the public, his own party did not look kindly on someone who had blocked so many of their appointments and schemes. Instead they plumped for Conkling's old rival, James Blaine, as their candidate.

A Democrat in the White House – Grover Cleveland, 1885–1889

While most Republicans supported Blaine, a small but significant group objected to his association with the spoils system, especially over his involvement with an alleged scandal (The Mulligan Letters). It seemed that Blaine had accepted money for securing a land grant for an Arkansas railroad. This group, known as the Mugwumps, supported the Democratic candidate, Grover Cleveland. The Democrats had chosen well, for Cleveland had already established a reputation as an honest, practical opponent of the spoils system in his positions as Mayor of Buffalo and Governor of New York. As mayor, he had refused to accept 'pork-barrel bills', earning the title 'the veto mayor'. He also gained a good number of enemies in the process – something that seemed to do him no harm in the eyes of the ordinary voter: 'We love him for the enemies he has made,' wrote General Edward Bragg in 1884.

The election was another colourful one, with allegations about Blaine's financial **probity** being answered by the Republicans with rumours that Cleveland had fathered a child in his wilder bachelor days. In the end, the result was another close one, with Cleveland winning by a margin of 60,000 in the popular vote. There is no doubt that the Republicans were harmed by the Mugwumps' support for Cleveland. A late controversy in New York, where Catholic Irish took exception to the Republicans' claims that the Democrats were a party of 'rum, Romanism and rebellion', saw a late swing to the Democrats in this closely-fought state.

In office, Cleveland did bring to government the probity he promised. In the West, 81 million acres of public land were restored to the federal government after misappropriation by the 'cattle barons'. Various suits were brought against those interests that Cleveland saw as exploiting Indian lands and railroad deals. He vetoed 413 bills, more than twice that of all previous Presidents combined, believing government should be both honest and minimal. 'Though the people support the government, the government should not support the people,' he said when vetoing a bill, in 1887, to give $10,000 to relieve drought in Texas. Various Acts, passed in an unusual burst of bipartisanship, made government more efficient and balanced (see panel).

In spite of all that, those that anticipated significant civil service reform were to be disappointed. As the first Democratic politician to be elected since 1856, there were a lot of people expecting jobs and rewards from him. Although Cleveland extended the list of protected civil service jobs to 27,000, he essentially followed the party line and two-thirds of all federal office holders were Democrats by the time Cleveland left office.

The main issues occupying Cleveland when in office were concerned with pensions and tariffs. The cost to the government of pensions had grown rapidly throughout the period, so that by 1885 there were 350,000 names on the pensions' register and costs had risen to $80 million a year. Cleveland vetoed over 200 private pensions bills. The biggest clash with Congress came, however, in 1887 over the Dependent Pension Bill. This was passed by Congress but vetoed by Cleveland. In the Bill, the need to have been disabled 'in war' was removed and it became simply the case that anyone 'unable to

---

(Stephen) Grover Cleveland (1837–1908)

22nd and 24th President of the USA (1885–89 and 1893–97). A beer-drinking, 18—stone, 'ugly-honest' man from Buffalo. Mayor of Buffalo (1881) and Governor of New York. First Democratic President elected after the Civil War, and the only President to hold office in two non-consecutive terms. Within a year of taking office for the second time, four million were unemployed and the USA was virtually bankrupt. Cleveland attempted to check corruption in public life.

Probity: High standard of correct moral behaviour.

- The Tenure of Office Act, dating from Reconstruction days, was repealed in 1887.
- The Presidential Succession Act made it clearer who succeeded should the Vice-President also be incapacitated.
- The Electoral Count Act of 1887 helped to improve the procedure for disputed elections.
- The Interstate Commerce Act of 1887 created the first federal regulatory board with inter-state jurisdiction – a reform Cleveland only signed reluctantly – his instincts were for big business not big government, as we have seen.
- In 1889 the Agricultural Department was improved and upgraded.
- The Dawes Act of 1887 brought a solution (the success of which is dealt with elsewhere) to the question of Indian/Settler relations.

'Cleveland sweeping out the White House'. Grover Cleveland, acting on the orders of America herself, sweeps the dirt out of the White House.

Free trade: Agreements with trading partners by which each state accepted the products of the other without taxing them, confident that they would both benefit from the arrangement. The benefits of free trade were felt to be considerable: wider markets for domestic products, cheaper goods from elsewhere for the country's consumers, and possible stimulation of domestic industries through competition with strong foreign industries.

Benjamin Harrison (1833–1901)

23rd President of the USA (1889–93), a Republican. He called the first Pan-American Conference, which led to the establishment of the Pan-American Union, aimed at improving inter-American cooperation. It was also intended to develop commercial ties. This became the Organisation of American States in 1948.

---

work for any reason' qualified for a pension. The issue had not been resolved by the 1888 election and it gave the Republicans the opportunity to campaign on a promise to boost the finances of Union war veterans.

Initially, Cleveland had done little regarding tariffs, although it was a traditional Democratic issue to try and reduce them. At the end of 1887, he finally moved and proposed a reduction in tariffs that would reduce the average level from around 47 per cent to 40 per cent. The Bill was supported in the House of Representatives but floundered in the Senate. Like pensions, this was another issue that clearly separated the Democrats and Republicans when it came to the 1888 presidential election. Cleveland was not, in any sense, arguing for **free trade**. He was keen to point that out, stressing that he was not ideological about it: 'It is a condition which confronts us, not a theory.'

Thus the 1888 presidential election was the first since the Civil War with a clearly-defined issue dominating it: tariffs. The Democrats campaigned for Cleveland to be re-elected, relying on his record in office as a sound, efficient and honest President. The Republicans responded with Benjamin Harrison, grandson of a former President and a senator from Indiana. The campaign was hard-fought and dirty, with big business pouring substantial money into the Republican campaign to defend higher tariffs. There were rumours of bribery and personal scandals circulating throughout the campaign. The Republicans made a pitch for the veterans' votes with their promises on pensions and took the opportunity to remind voters of which side they had been on in the Civil War, over 20 years after its conclusion. In the end, Cleveland got the most votes but it was Harrison who carried the day, winning the key marginal states of Indiana and New York.

Benjamin Harrison and the 'Billion-dollar Congress', 1889–1893
On his election, Harrison rejoiced that 'Providence has given us the victory'. To which the Republican National Chairman privately responded to a journalist friend, 'Think of it. He ought to know that Providence hadn't a damn thing to do with it.' If he had not realised it initially, Harrison soon discovered how many promises had been made to get him to the White House. Although personally uncorrupt, he was soon lamenting: 'I could not name my own Cabinet. They had sold out every place to pay the election expenses.' The earnest and conservative President saw his Administration dominated by James Blaine, who returned as Secretary of State, Thomas Reed, the Speaker of the House and William McKinley, the powerful Chairman of the 'Ways and Means Committee' in the House. It soon became clear that Congress would be calling the shots.

With Republicans controlling both Houses of Congress and the Presidency – a rare moment in this period – they were determined to pass through a Republican agenda. They were helped significantly by Speaker Reed's rule changes, which he forced through the House to increase his own power and to minimise the impact of the Democrat minority. The Congress was quickly named the 'Billion-dollar Congress'. It was soon passing legislation to help its supporters, not least its big business paymasters.

In Harrison's first year, 31,000 of the 55,000 postmasters in the USA were replaced with Republican sympathisers. Over $1 billion was spent on pork-barrel measures to improve harbours, rivers and transport systems and in generous payments to bond-holders. The Dependent Pension Act of 1890 was similar to that vetoed by Cleveland in 1887 and saw the number of pensions rise from 490,000 in 1889 at a cost of $89 million to 966,000 and $175 million by 1893. The appointment of a leading veteran as the Pension Commissioner only served to further the generosity with which pensions were awarded. The most blatant sop to their supporters came in the Republicans' attitude to tariffs with the McKinley Tariff Act of 1890. The tariff reached new prohibitive heights of around 49.5 per cent by 1890. It allowed the President to put duties on goods kept on the free list if he felt it would pressurise them into a reciprocal tariff reduction. This time, the tariff was fixed so high that it did have an impact on prices. The perception that Republicans were favouring businessmen at the expense of consumers became widespread.

The Administration did pass some legislation that was more bipartisan in spirit. In 1890 the Sherman Anti-Trust Act marked the first attempt at limiting the powers of the Trusts, although it was only as effective as the courts and the President wanted it to be. In the same year, the Sherman Silver Purchase Act was passed which was, at least partially, inflationary. It pleased the silver miners in the West by committing the Treasury to buying 4.5 million ounces of silver a month, using notes redeemable with gold. This Act was passed in the hope of getting support for the Tariff Act and may also have been a response to the growing influence of the western states. This was best shown by the admission of six new states into the Union: North and South Dakota, Montana and Washington in 1889 and Idaho and Wyoming in 1890.

These more conciliatory measures were not enough, however, to save

1. In what ways was national politics corrupt in the period 1877–1896?

2. How far was the political system reformed between 1877–1896?

3. Explain why there was so much debate over tariffs and the currency in the period 1877–1896.

the Republicans from the voters' wrath. In the 1890 mid-term elections, the Republicans were dramatically turned out of the House, losing nearly half their seats, including McKinley's. Two years later, Cleveland was back as President, defeating Harrison in a rerun of 1888. Much of this was to do with successful Democratic attacks on the 'Billion-dollar Congress' and on the higher prices which were blamed on the high tariffs. There was also something of a Democratic revival as traditional supporters took exception to local Republican attempts at prohibition (six states went 'dry' in the 1880s) and anti-immigration policies – such as Wisconsin's law in 1889 which insisted that only English be used in schools in a state with large German and Scandinavian minorities. There was also something else going on in the early 1890s when rural discontent in the South and the West was beginning to make itself felt at the ballot box. In 1890, nine Congressmen were elected as 'Alliance-Populists'.

It is necessary now to look back and trace the development of a movement known as **Populism** that would dominate and determine the politics of the 1890s.

5.3 Who were the Populists and what did they believe?

Jefferson's vision of the yeoman farmers acting as the mainstream of the American Republic, his 'chosen people of God', had become somewhat tarnished by the later decades of the 19th century. The victory of the North in the Civil War, and the domination of the Republicans with their industrial and East Coast agenda since then, had made farmers and westerners feel marginalised by the political elites. Several movements emerged in the 1870s and 1880s to reflect the farmers' growing sense of isolation. This reached its peak in the 1890s when various strands of opinion were united, first in the Populist Party which won over one million votes in 1892 and carried four states, and later behind the populist Democratic candidate for President, William Jennings Bryan, in 1896.

The situation for western farmers was far from easy. Life was harsh and lonely on the frontier (see Chapter 3). Many were vulnerable to fluctuations in nature, such as the drop in rainfall levels between the mid-1880s and mid-1890s which caused extensive droughts, and the plagues of grasshoppers that frequently wreaked havoc on the plains. Things were made worse by the dramatic fall in prices that occurred during the period, as the table shows.

Price of crop per bushel

	1866	1893–1894
Wheat	$1.45	49c
Corn	75c	28c
Cotton	31c	6c

The fall in prices was primarily due to a significant increase in domestic production (with new acreage, agricultural and transport improvements and the natural response of farmers facing falling profits to produce more) and a major increase in overseas competition. There was a general global increase in production as new techniques were developed. The USA faced serious competition for their goods from Argentina, Canada, Australia and Russia, all of whom could transport agricultural goods further afield with improvements in refrigeration and canning. Although tariffs generally protected the American market, agriculture had relied on exports for a major part of its income (wheat producers exported around 40 per cent of production and cotton 70 per cent). American agriculture now faced markets closed or limited by cheap competition. Although many of these factors were beyond the control of federal government, inevitably farmers facing ruin looked for something or someone to blame. They soon found themselves attacking the system.

Tariffs were an obvious target. Even Cleveland's proposals to cut tariffs in 1887 would only have reduced average levels to 40 per cent. Farmers resented a situation in which they bought protected products manufactured in the USA and so kept at an artificially high price, while they were expected to sell unprotected agricultural products, both at home and abroad. They also faced the possibility that foreign markets would retaliate for their goods being taxed as they entered America by putting tariffs on American exports, often agricultural. The McKinley Tariff of 1890 was thus the last straw for many western farmers, who saw the government as significantly alien to their interests.

Railroad costs also caused resentment. Individual farmers were faced with higher charges than big business were, for using the same route. This was a consequence of the 'discriminatory system' by which railroad companies would negotiate special concessions for companies regularly using their lines or travelling on certain routes. It meant that travel between certain stretches of railroad, such as New York to Chicago or Baltimore, was significantly cheaper than in more rural areas where farmers found themselves charged two or three times as much. Naturally, farmers felt that they were paying disproportionately to the profits of the railroad companies.

The government's preference for a deflationary economic policy made the situation worse. Low commodity prices were encouraged and credit was tight, in an attempt to prevent significant inflation, with the consequence that money was expensive and interest rates high. Although much of this was to do with the governments, Republican and Democrat, an easier target for blame was the banks who charged high interest rates and considerable commission and service charges. Farmers often had to

Mortgaged: Land or property is used as a guarantee to a company in order to borrow money from them.

Crop-lien system: Ownership of the crops produced and sold is retained by the farmer until payment for the crops is received.

borrow and found much of their land **mortgaged** in the West or operating under the **crop-lien system** in the South. Failure to meet mortgages in the West saw farmers lose their land and become tenants or workers on the new bonanza farms that were springing up across the prairies. The currency issue was thus highly relevant to farmers who saw the continued determination to stick to gold and to avoid the inflationary implications of greenbacks or silver as another example of putting business interests in the East ahead of agricultural concerns in the South and West.

How do you account for the rise of Populism?

Despite these growing concerns, farmers did not immediately pose a serious political threat. Their physical isolation from one another, as well as a psychological sense of independence and 'rugged individualism', made farmers reluctant to come together, as workers tended to form unions. It was also difficult to focus on precisely what grievances farmers felt needed addressing and what it was within the powers of government – national and local. Nevertheless, there were early movements which began a tradition of rural protest and combination that eventually grew into the major political party that was the Populists.

The Granger Movement
Founded in 1867 by Oliver Kelly, the Granger Movement was initially a social and economic organisation that tried to create a sense of community among isolated farmers who could not tackle the problems that they faced alone. The National Grange of Patrons of Industry, as it was officially

Cartoon from 1873 entitled 'The Grange Awakening the Sleepers', showing a Granger attack on railroad practices.

Cartoon drawn for 'Harper's Weekly' in 1886 entitled 'The Senatorial Round-House'.

known, sought to promote farmer-owned cooperatives for buying and selling goods, so removing the middleman. The Granger Movement sponsored the creation of a whole host of companies and businesses owned cooperatively by farmers and run for farmers. By 1875, there were 800,000 members in 21,000 local parties (or lodges). Increasingly, the Granger Movement turned to political action to try and promote its members' interests. By 1873–74, there were Granger representatives in varying levels of control in 11 state legislatures, five of which passed so-called Granger Laws aimed at limiting the powers of railroad companies and big business generally in their state. Several cases went to court and the most famous ('Munn v Illinois' in 1877) marked the high point of Granger influence. As the economy began to improve in the later 1870s, membership tailed off. However, initial noises had been made to show that, when working together, the farmers could achieve something and a number of its members moved into the growing Greenback Party.

The Greenbacks

The Greenback Party had been established in 1875 and contested the 1876 presidential election. In 1878, they merged with the National Labor Reform Party to form the Greenback Labor Party and got more than a million votes and 14 representatives elected in 1878. Presidential candidate James Weaver secured 308,578 votes in the closely-fought 1880 election, though they had tailed off by 1884. The Greenback Party called for an inflationary economic policy that would, by printing paper money and increasing the amount of silver in circulation, make the dollar cheaper and so help farmers deal with their debts while improving their competitiveness when selling abroad.

The Farmers' Alliances

These alliances sprang up in the 1880s. They were a series of farmers' groups that had coalesced into three main areas by the end of the 1880s: the North-western Alliance in the Mid-West, the Southern Alliance and the

Colored Farmers' Alliance, all of which had a majority of about one million. The Southern Alliance, under the leadership of Dr Charles W. Macune, soon became the dominant organisation from which the others took a lead. In some ways, the alliances were similar to the Granger Movement of the 1870s, with attempts at cooperative movements and a strong sense of community. However, they also presented a clear political agenda. In 1899, the Northern and Southern alliances, though maintaining independence from one another, adopted similar programmes which included a graduated income tax, nationalisation of transport and communications, and free unlimited coinage of silver. They were thus reflecting the farmers' concerns over the previous decades for an inflationary monetary policy and checks on the discriminatory powers of big business. The movements were especially attracted to Macune's subtreasury plan, presented to but rejected by Congress in 1890.

Macune proposed that: the Treasury give loans at 80 per cent of the value of a farmer's stock; those crops be stored in a federal warehouse at 1 per cent interest; these loans be paid in legal-tender notes. The policy would combine several aims of the alliances – it would be inflationary, it would solve farmers' credit problems and it would allow farmers to choose when to resell their crops, letting them control market prices to some extent. Its rejection by Congress was hardly surprising, but it did galvanise many farmers into seeking their own political party as they felt that the rejection of the Macune Plan showed that they could not hope for their objectives to be met by the traditional parties.

Increasingly, farmers were calling for easier credit, inflationary fiscal policy and regulation of big business, especially railroads. They met some success in local politics. In the 1890 elections, Alliance candidates took control of the Legislatures of Kansas (where they also won the governorship) and Nebraska, and held the balance of power in South Dakota and Minnesota. In the South, the situation was more complex as many feared that if the Populists were to challenge the dominant Bourbon Democrat groups, they might split the white vote and let in black Republicans. This fear was not eased by the high profile of Tom Watson of Georgia, who urged the blacks and whites to fight together against the Bourbons. Most whites who might have been attracted to the Alliance movements did not share Watson's progressive views and preferred to try and influence Democratic politicians to accept some of the Alliance demands in return for their electoral support.

Thus, in 1890, we can detect four pro-Alliance governors and seven pro-Alliance Legislatures in the South. The experience of the Granger Movements, the Greenback Party and the Farmers' Alliances were important in raising issues and in encouraging farmers to see that they shared a common interest against the main parties dominated by eastern politicians and money. The basis for the emergence of the Populists had been set.

What was the importance of the 1892 and 1896 elections?

The Omaha Platform and the 1892 election
The Populists were formally created at a meeting in St Louis in February 1892, where a combination of Greenbackers, farmers' alliances, Knights of Labor and reform groups came together as the People's Party. They agreed to meet at Omaha on 4 July to adopt a platform and a presidential candidate for the November elections. At the July meeting, they selected James Weaver, a former Greenbacker and a respectable figure, as their presidential candidate and adopted what came to be known as the 'Omaha Platform', written by Ignatius Donnelly of Minnesota. The opening paragraphs illustrate the dramatic style and tone of the document:

'The conditions which surround us best justify our cooperation; we meet in the midst of a nation brought to the verge of moral, political and material ruin. Corruption dominates the ballot-box, the Legislatures, the Congress, and touches even the ermine of the bench [judges]. The people are demoralised; most of the States have been compelled to isolate the voters at the polling places to prevent universal intimidation or bribery. The newspapers are largely subsidised or muzzled, public opinion silenced, business prostrated, homes covered with mortgages, labor impoverished, and the land concentrating in the hands of capitalists.'

The platform combined the old concerns of Greenbackers and Farmers' Alliances with new attempts to secure rights for their 'fellow producers', the industrial workers. Thus the Populists were going one step beyond the previous pressure groups in trying to combine workers from the land and the country in one campaign against **capitalism** as represented by big business and big government. Not surprisingly, many eastern conservatives were terrified by, as they saw it, the wild excesses of the Populist platform and their colourful figures. Businessmen were keen to make their workers see that their future lay in a successful capitalist system. In the election of 1892 the Populists made little progress among the industrial workers of the East Coast. They also failed to make gains in the old Granger states of the Mid-West, where improvements in the economic situation made farmers less tempted by extremes and less likely to view the system as fundamentally against them.

Extreme parties tend to flourish in extreme circumstances. The South was not at this stage ready to abandon the Democrats either – the Democrats were in the process of dismantling the systems set up under Reconstruction and race remained the top priority for Southern Whites at this time, even the poorest. So, the Populists failed to make as much ground as they might have hoped, although Weaver did get more than a million votes and carried four western states – Colorado, Kansas, Nevada and Idaho.

Cleveland's Second Administration, 1893–1897

Cleveland's Second Administration was an unhappy one, dominated by the money issue. His actions as President confirmed to many that he was the tool of **Wall Street** and that there was little to choose between the Democrats and the Republicans when it came to the fundamental issues in politics. In the first year of the Administration, Cleveland had to deal with the 'Panic of 1893' – a serious depression caused by a drain on gold reserves which resulted in bankruptcies, closed banks and job losses. Cleveland's attitude remained *laissez faire* throughout, insisting that he could do little to promote recovery and that the recovery would be delayed if he succumbed to demands for public spending. Prudent financial measures to restore investors' confidence in the economy were what was needed, not financial irresponsibility through extra spending and an inflationary fiscal policy. Thus Cleveland repealed the Silver Purchase Act (though only with Republican support), negotiated a deal with J.P. Morgan's Syndicate for a $62 million loan, took out an injunction (against the Governor's wishes) to prevent a strike of the Pullman workers in 1894 and did little to change the tariff passed by McKinley back in 1890. The money issue became increasingly dominant in political debate, with the Republican leaders and the Democratic President clearly 'gold-bugs'. But there were 'free silver' factions in both parties and the Populists were pushing for inflationary policies too.

The 1896 Campaign

The Republicans made it quite clear where their views lay in the debate

Capitalism: A system of economics that allows private ownership of land, factories etc., rather than ownership by the government. People can get very rich and also become very poor. Most capitalist countries are also democracies.

Wall Street: The location of the New York Stock Exchange – a central market in a country for dealing in freely transferable stocks, shares and securities of all types.

'Gold-bugs': Those who supported the idea that the US currency should be based on gold.

when they chose William McKinley of Ohio – the man who had been most associated with the 1890 Tariff and a friend of big business – as their presidential candidate. They ran a typical Republican campaign with calls for a protective tariff, generous Union pensions, a deflationary economic policy and naval enlargement. The Democrats had a far more difficult time of it. At their Convention, there were lively debates between the gold-bugs, keen to support Cleveland's policies and actions, and the 'Silverites' who dominated the western and southern delegations. In the end, they adopted the brilliant orator, 36 year-old William Jennings Bryan of Nebraska as their candidate (causing a walkout by some of the pro-Cleveland easterners). They supported a platform that rejected the prudence of the Cleveland Administration and offered, for the first time since the 1860s, a genuine alternative to the Republican platform.

Elements of the Democratic Programme in 1896

- Free, unlimited coinage of gold and silver at 16:1.

- Lower tariffs so that their only function was to raise federal revenue and not as instruments of economic policy.

- Attacks on the use of injunctions in labour disputes.

- An enlargement of the powers of the Interstate Commerce Commission to prevent discriminatory abuses in transport.

Gold Standard: A monetary system under which national currencies have a fixed value in gold.

Egalitarian: A belief that all people are equal and should have the same rights and opportunities.

Bryan set the Convention alive with his famous 'Cross of Gold' speech, delivered after a series of speakers had defended Cleveland's Administration and suggested that maintaining the **Gold Standard** was critical. Bryan invoked the spirit of the Constitution and the Revolution, attacked heartless capitalism and reminded the Democrats of the **egalitarian** principles of Democrat hero Andrew Jackson. The delegates received his speech with rapturous applause. A sense of its power and vision can be gained from his final sentences:

> 'If they dare to come out in the open field and defend the Gold Standard as a good thing, we will fight them to the uttermost. Having behind us the producing masses of this nation and the world, supported by the commercial interests, the laboring interests and the toilers everywhere, we will answer their demand for a gold standard by saying to them: "You shall not press down upon the brow of labor this crown of thorns, you shall not crucify mankind upon a cross of gold." '

Nationalisation: Changing the ownership of a company or industry so that it is no longer private but owned by the state and controlled by the government.

The Populists, meeting in St Louis, now faced a dilemma. The Democrats had adopted the most popular policy, but not all the elements, of the Omaha Platform. If they supported the Democrats, then they would lose some parts of their programme, such as **nationalisation**, but if they put up their own candidate then the anti-gold-bug vote would be split and the Republicans would be likely to win easily. The period 1893–96 had seen some gains for them – for example, the Populists now controlled the legislature in South Carolina – but the big breakthrough had not occurred. Now they had the best chance ever of seeing one of their major policies adopted. However, in doing so they would lose their identity. In the end, they decided to compromise: they chose to support Bryan for President but put forward their own candidate, Tom Watson, for Vice-President.

The 1896 campaign was one of the most exciting, dramatic and polarised in American history. Bryan did not pretend that the battle was anything other than sectional, referring to the East as 'the enemy's country' and embarking on a whirlwind campaign that had him travelling 18,000

Demagoguery: The style of leadership where the leaders try to win support by appealing to people's emotions rather than by rational arguments.

William McKinley (1843–1901)
25th President of the United States (1897–1901). McKinley was a lawyer who entered politics as a Republican. He was a member of the House of Representatives from 1877 and Governor of Ohio from 1892. He was elected for two terms, but was shot and killed by an anarchist in 1901. It was under his presidency that the USA fought and won the Spanish–American War.

---

miles and making 600 speeches in 29 states. His revivalist, preachy style saw him contrasting the toiling masses against the evils of capitalist Wall Street and he certainly energised his supporters. However, whilst his style may have played well with his supporters, it horrified opponents who feared the radical **demagoguery** of both Bryan and Tom Watson. The 'New York Times' described Bryan as an 'irresponsible, irregulated, ignorant, prejudiced, pathetically honest and enthusiastic crank'.

McKinley deliberately played a restrained and traditional campaign and left the arguments to his close friend and politically shrewd campaign manager, Marcus Alonzo Hanna. The Republicans built up huge funds of $16 million from horrified industrialists. Hanna used committees to help galvanise the various groups in the East which they needed to win. Trade unionists, blacks, religious and ethnic groups all had their own campaign committees.

In the end, with the highest number of votes cast in US history, McKinley won 7,111,000 votes and 271 electoral college votes to Bryan's 6,509,000 and 176. As the map on page 142 shows, this does not reflect the full implications of the victory. McKinley won every state east of the Mississippi and north of the Ohio, while Bryan carried most of the South and the West. The Democrats and Populists had convinced their rural voters, but had failed to make inroads into the industrial workers in the East who had accepted Hanna's arguments that inflation would diminish their pay packets. Indeed, the Republicans did better among urban workers in 1896 than they had done in 1892. Some of the traditional farming states, such as Wisconsin and Iowa, also stayed Republican, where some improvements in the harvest diminished Bryan's apocalyptic warnings.

What, if anything, did the Populists achieve?

The 1896 election marked a high watermark for the Populists and their policies. McKinley's Administration adopted the traditional policies of sound money and of supporting the interests of business. The 1897 tariff was the highest ever and the 1900 Currency Act put the USA firmly on the Gold Standard. There followed a period of prosperity across the nation and new issues, such as imperialism (see Chapter 6) and progressivism (see section 5.8) dominated politics in a period that saw Republican Presidents for the next 16 years. Agricultural problems elsewhere helped US farmers regain the international market, while gold discoveries in Canada, Alaska and South Africa meant that the Gold Standard was not as deflationary as it had been before.

The 1900 election was a rerun of 1896 but its defining issue was imperialism, not silver, and Bryan had a new issue to get steamed up about. The Populists slowly lost their distinctive position and were subsumed into the larger parties, particularly the Democrats.

That is not to say that the Populists achieved nothing. One or other of the main political parties later adopted many of the reforms they proposed. The 1890s can be seen as having paved the way for the more significant reforms of the Progressive era that followed. The American political system, particularly with the electoral college, made it difficult for third parties to break through. However, the influence that the Populists had in changing the direction of the Democrats and in bringing to the fore issues that the two East Coast-dominated parties preferred to forget cannot be ignored. In many ways, the determination with which the Republicans and their East Coast supporters fought the 1892 and 1896 elections was a compliment to the Populists in recognising the seriousness of the threat they posed.

---

1. What do you regard as the most important reason for the rise of Populism? Explain your answer.

2. What changes did the Populists hope to make to politics and the economy?

3. To what extent was Populism a failure?

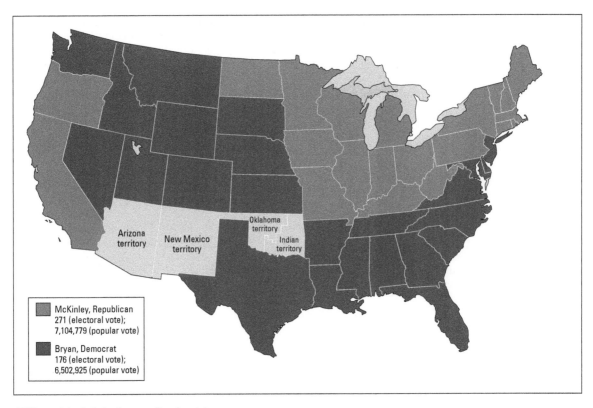

McKinley, Republican
271 (electoral vote);
7,104,779 (popular vote)

Bryan, Democrat
176 (electoral vote);
6,502,925 (popular vote)

1896 presidential election results – by states

5.4 What factors lay behind the economic expansion of the USA after 1865?

The period after the Civil War saw a major transformation of the American economy and society as massive industrialisation took place on an unprecedented scale. Although the Civil War is sometimes seen as a struggle between the industrial North and agricultural South, the North itself was still essentially an agricultural section in 1865. By 1900, though, the USA was producing 30 per cent of the world's manufactured goods and those employed in manufacturing, mining, construction and services had risen from four million to 18 million. The USA had also become the centre of industrial and commercial inventiveness. In the 1850s, there were an average of 2,000 patents granted each year; by the 1890s, that had reached a staggering 21,000. What lay behind this growth, and what were the consequences of it?

The Civil War

Increase in pig iron production in the USA	
1855–1860	17%
1860–1865	1%
1865–1870	100%

The Civil War inevitably played a key role in the economic expansion of the United States, but it would be wrong to see it as the key factor. Actually, economic growth during the American Civil War was lower than before or after, as the figures for pig iron production show. That does not mean the Civil War did not play a major role, but it is better to see the importance in terms of the significance of the Northern victory, rather than simply the stimulation of demand brought about by the needs of war.

The absence of the South in Congress meant that a number of Acts could be passed that had been held up because of sectional disagreements before that time. The Banking Acts established a system of credit that made it far easier for businessmen to get loans, while the inevitable inflation that the Civil War had caused (with demand outstripping supply in most industries) allowed industrialists to free themselves of debts. Acts such as the Homestead Act, the Land Grant College Act and the Transcontinental Railroad Act encouraged western expansion and the development of a national market and supply system. A federal bureau was established to encourage immigration and tariffs were increased to raise taxes, but it would also protect American industrial development. All these acts and policies were to establish the foundations for economic growth in the following decades.

As well as this, war-time savings and the needs of reconstruction meant that, in the immediate aftermath of war, there was likely to be an economic boom. The triumph of the North was seen as in some way responsible for the triumph of manufacture and industry and the War had rewarded successful entrepreneurs and encouraged innovation. These businessmen and industrialists went out into the post-war world emboldened, with government policies largely on their side and with the financial powers to invest for further success.

Factors causing the post-war economic growth

So many factors were at play that it is difficult to pinpoint which should be seen as the key ones, though historians have inevitably tried and examiners will want students to do the same (see diagram below).

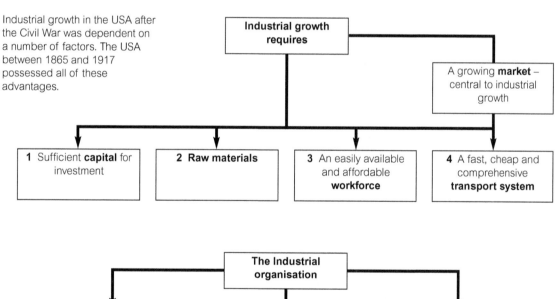

Industrial growth in the USA after the Civil War was dependent on a number of factors. The USA between 1865 and 1917 possessed all of these advantages.

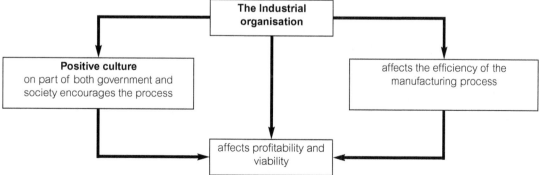

Capital

The availability of capital for investment had already improved before the Civil War with the growth of **corporations** chartered under state law. These allowed businesses to attract individual investors who would purchase shares in the companies and so provide them with start-up and investment capital. The War created an accumulation of capital as many people tended to save their earnings until the fighting was over, while the banking reforms encouraged investment. Also, a number of entrepreneurs had made significant profits out of the Civil War and were now looking to channel those profits into new economic enterprises.

Corporation: Large businesses or groups of companies which are all controlled and run together as single organisations.

Raw materials

The USA was almost self-sufficient in natural resources, especially following the expansion westwards. Huge deposits of coal, iron, lead, copper and timber were later supplemented by oil. Although natural resources alone were not sufficient to guarantee economic expansion – as the experience of states such as Russia and China in the same period show – and while developments in transport were also essential to be able to get access to these raw materials, an abundance of natural resources provided the raw materials for expansion. It is also significant that, because America possessed such resources within its borders, tariffs could be raised to protect industry without increasing the costs of raw materials (as would happen in countries that had to import some of them).

Workforce

A major increase in production could not occur without a similar increase in population, to provide a major source of labour as well as a growing market. The population increase of America during this period was significant.

Much, but not all, of this was due to a major increase in immigration – the details of which are explained in a later section. These immigrants tended to concentrate in the growing industrial centres of America, such as Chicago and New York. They provided an unending supply of cheap and eager labour, though it is important to remember that among them were also men and women of considerable skill who brought with them managerial and technological experience from the Old World.

Growth of population in the USA

Year	Population	% increase on previous decade
1860	31,443,321	35.6
1870	39,818,449	26.6
1880	50,155,783	26.0
1890	62,947,714	25.5

Industrial organisation

It is significant that the dominant economic organisation of the major industries was in large-scale enterprises often in the form of trusts or **holding companies**. Although this created some tensions politically (see below), in economic terms it allowed for coordination, sustained development and heavy investment in new technology that encouraged speedy growth.

Holding companies: Companies that own other companies that manufacture goods or produce services.

Market

Population growth, western expansion and improvements in transport and communications meant there was a massive continental market which provided internal demand for American goods. This could be protected from overseas competitors via tariffs because industry did not, at this stage, need to compete in the overseas market.

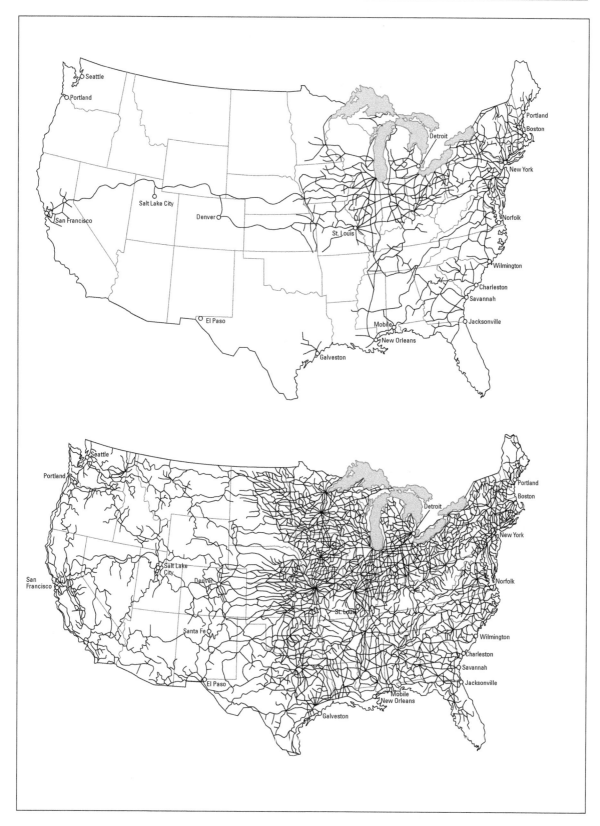

The network of railroads in the USA (top) in 1880; (bottom) in 1900.

Positive culture

Although it is hard to quantify, there were social and cultural attitudes that tended to favour economic enterprise and to look kindly on material achievement in the United States. These attitudes did not necessarily prevail in all European states, where dominant social groups often looked down on those whose wealth came from industry. This was helped by the triumph of the North in the Civil War and the consequent admiration for 'Yankee ingenuity'. This belief in hard work, thrift and individualism was taken up by immigrants who bought in to the American dream. They often accepted that hard work at the bottom of society might well one day see them, like Andrew Carnegie and John D. Rockefeller, as dollar millionaires. This support for entrepreneurship was also seen in the governments, at federal and local level, not only through specific acts, such as the support for tariffs and banking, but also through their instincts to favour management in labour disputes.

'Yankee ingenuity': The belief that people in the North-East USA had the ability to invent and develop industrial and manufacturing processes.

Transport and communications systems

Perhaps most central of all was the development of the transport system. This not only provided the links that allowed the creation of a national market and access to raw materials, but also the building of railroads was a stimulus to industrial development in itself. By 1890, the revenue from railroads was more than $1,000 million, double that of the federal government. Mileage of track had increased from 30,000 miles in 1860 to over 190,000 miles by 1900 (see map on page 145). By 1880, 90 per cent of all rolled steel manufactured in America was going to the railroads.

Railroads created a national market that allowed mass production to develop. This meant that industries such as steel manufacture could get access to both iron and coal – previously steel could only really be manufactured in areas which had easy access to both raw materials. Production costs were also substantially lowered with rail transport being something like 10 per cent of the cost of transportation by road. Railroads were also central in allowing the growth of cities, for major urban areas needed to be able to rely on fresh food being brought in from the surrounding farms.

1. What impact did the Civil War have on the economic growth of the USA?

2. Was the availability of abundant raw material the reason for the rapid growth of the US economy after 1865? Explain your answer.

As well as railroads, there were also important developments in communications: the telegraph in 1844 and the telephone in 1876. Such developments allowed large-scale management to spring up across the states. Companies could establish operations across the country and could coordinate industrial development, sales and purchases. These developments also led to wide-scale marketing and advertising across the West.

5.5 How did people respond to industrialisation?
A CASE STUDY IN HISTORICAL INTERPRETATION

Big business and the critics

One of the most interesting features of America's industrialisation was the rise of entrepreneurs, who dominated the organisation and development of certain industries and ended up controlling the majority of the industry in large-scale units. Men such as John D. Rockefeller, Andrew Carnegie and Cornelius Vanderbilt provoked controversy in their lifetimes, and have continued to do so ever since. Were they the 'robber barons' who ruthlessly exploited their workers and drove competitors over the edge? Or were they the key to American industrialisation and prosperity?

They certainly dominated the fields in which they operated. Carnegie reigned supreme over the US steel industry; Vanderbilt made his fortune in railroads; and Rockefeller controlled 90 per cent of US oil refining through

Andrew Carnegie (1835–1919)
Industrialist and **philanthropist** born in Scotland. Invested successfully in railroads, land and oil, before developing the Pittsburgh iron and steel industries – making the USA the world's leading producer. Having built up a vast industrial empire, Carnegie sold it off to the US Steel Trust in 1901. A New York music hall, which opened in 1891, was renamed the Carnegie Hall seven years later in honour of the contribution Andrew Carnegie had made to its construction.

William Henry Vanderbilt (1821–1885)
Financier and railroad promoter. Son of financier Cornelius Vanderbilt, he became the head of a railroad trust and was strongly opposed to government regulation of the industry. Vanderbilt was given control of the Staten Island Railroad in 1857; was named vice-president of the New York and Harlem Railroad in 1864 and acquired other railroad companies, before taking over as president of the New York Central Railroad in 1877. He is famous for his phrase, 'The public be damned'.

John D. Rockefeller (1839–1937)
Founder of Standard Oil (which had control of 90% of US refineries by 1882), making Rockefeller a millionaire. The activities of the Standard Oil Trust led to an outcry against monopolies (see below) and the passing of Sherman Anti-Trust Act 1890. Although the Trust was dissolved in 1892, it was refounded as a holding company in 1899. He founded the Rockefeller Foundation in 1913, to which his son, John Jnr, devoted his life.

Philanthropist: Person who freely gives money and other help to people who need it.

Vertical integration: Process whereby a businessman can get control of an industry. For instance, a brewer could buy barley and malt, as well as public houses. He then has complete control of the industry, from initial production through to sales.

Social Darwinism: 19th-century belief that people and societies operate in the same way as the animal kingdom, and that, as Charles Darwin argued, only those best fitted to their circumstances survive. The weak perish.

his Standard Oil Company of Ohio by 1879. Rockefeller developed the idea of a trust, whereby companies acquired by the main company could be held in trust so that what appeared to be independent companies were actually controlled and regulated by a central group of trustees. In this way, by 1882, Standard Oil controlled, through trusts, 77 oil companies which produced 90 per cent of all refined oil. Rockefeller could thus control the supply and price of oil across the USA. These business barons also developed the idea of **vertical integration** in order to ensure that, in Rockefeller's words, they need 'pay no one a profit'.

The methods employed by such men to acquire rival companies left much to be desired morally. They were widely attacked, especially by the competitors they drove out of business. These 'robber barons' did much, however, to stabilise the market for the products of these staple industries. For example, before Rockefeller the oil industry had been seriously undermined by gluts, followed by periods of scarcity. Companies using oil could never rely on a consistent price for their raw materials. Rockefeller could control this. Also, large-scale investment could go into developing new techniques and methods of production which made America highly competitive in the global market. Carnegie wrote his own justification, in *Gospel of Wealth* (1889), when he stated that: 'Not evil, but good, has come to the race from the accumulation of wealth by those who have the ability and energy that produces it.'

This philosophy, which was backed up by philosophers such as Herbert Spencer in England and William Sumner at Yale University, came to be known as **social Darwinism**, in which philosophers applied the laws of 'survival of the fittest' in nature to society at large. The great captains of industry (the 'naturally selected agents of society', in Sumner's words) were creating the wealth and jobs that benefited America and should be left to their own devices. This justification did have a catch, according to Carnegie, for the truly wealthy had a social responsibility to use their wealth for the public good. Carnegie was keen to use his money to promote the welfare of others. He did this not through handouts to the poor, which would encourage dependency and discourage a healthy work ethic, but rather through providing the means for self-improvement via institutions such as libraries, hospitals and public parks. 'The man who dies rich dies disgraced,' Carnegie added to his gospel.

Although the worship of big business and the 'rags-to-riches' stories were widespread, that did not mean there were no critics of this approach. By the 1880s, many were questioning the wisdom of unbridled capitalism.

Monopoly: A situation where the producer of particular goods or services controls the market, having eliminated all competitors.

- Some were afraid of the effective **monopoly** which many businessmen had and which would allow exploitation of consumers and workers by their ability to control prices and wages.

- Trade unionists felt it was harder to protect the interests of workers when there was a growing distance between manager and worker and an imbalance of power.

- Small-scale businessmen felt threatened by the undue influence their richer rivals had and by the deals they were able to strike with suppliers because of their greater purchasing power.

- Farmers resented the discriminatory practices that saw railroads charging individual farmers more to use their routes than they charged major companies which could negotiate bulk reductions.

- Many people felt that the emergence of powerful industrialists threatened the democratic institutions. Ironically, those same individuals who had used the opportunities the USA presented for upward mobility were now, by controlling the market and ruthlessly driving out competitors, undermining those opportunities for others.

Various journalists and political commentators began to attack the 'robber barons' and the culture of government *laissez-faire* that went with it. Political organisations sprang up, particularly in the West, which tried to limit the power of big business. (See section 5.3 above.) Henry George sold over two million copies of his book *Progress and Poverty* (published in 1882) that argued that industrial progress did not necessarily guarantee prosperity. For many, it brought quite the opposite. Henry Demarest Lloyd attacked Standard Oil in 1894 and called for public ownership of the major economic monopolies.

Some of these criticisms did lead to political action, initially at a local level and later nationally. The Granger Movement managed to pass various laws in some of the western states in the 1870s, which sought to restrict railroad companies by fixing maximum rates, forbidding discriminatory practices that saw different prices for different consumers, and establishing commissions to monitor and enforce the policies. When these were challenged in the courts, the Supreme Court intervened to confirm that, when private property was for public use, the states had the right to regulate public utilities ('Munn v Illinois', 1876). When state regulation still proved to be ineffective (largely because Congress continued to control matters of inter-state commerce, so action could only be taken against companies that operated within a state), the Interstate Commerce Act of 1887 was passed by Congress, albeit reluctantly. The Act prohibited pooling (a method by which individual companies worked together to control prices etc.), rebates for major consumers, discriminatory practices and higher charges for short hauls, and urged as well that all charges be 'reasonable and just'. Furthermore, it created an Interstate Commerce Commission of five members which had the powers to investigate railroad management.

Of course, commerce only dealt with transport and major industrial manufacturers continued with their monopoly practices. Where states tried to pass laws controlling trusts or combinations, many companies simply transferred their headquarters to less restrictive states. Some states deliberately encouraged this in order to attract industry. In 1890, the federal government bowed to pressure and passed the Sherman Anti-Trust Act. This declared that 'every contract, combination in the form of trust or otherwise, or conspiracy, in restraint of trade or commerce among the several states or with foreign nations, is illegal'. It allowed for suits to be brought by federal prosecutors, or individuals or firms who felt they had suffered by a trust. Those found guilty were liable to a $5,000 fine and a year in jail.

Although the Interstate Commerce Act and the Sherman Anti-Trust Act did bring some control to industry, the odds were still stacked firmly in favour of big business and little was done to enforce either Act effectively. The laws were loosely phrased, which allowed courts to interpret them very much as they wished. Most notoriously, in 1895 the Supreme Court ruled in 'United States versus E.C. Knight' that, despite the defendant controlling 98 per cent of the manufacture of refined sugar, he was not violating the terms of the Sherman Anti-Trust Act because manufacture was not trade. With this attitude in the courts, and no desire on the part of the government to take on the vested interests who poured money into the party organisations anyway, it is not surprising that there were only 36 suits brought under the Act between 1890 and 1901. None of these suits was against the really big corporations; and of the cases tried only 12 were won.

1. Why were the methods used by businessmen such as John D. Rockefeller criticised?

2. Why are there differing views on the impact of industrialisation on the USA?

5.6 What were the patterns of immigration during this period?

Between 1820 and 1900, around 20 million people arrived as immigrants into the United States, with by far the majority arriving in the final decades. Nine million arrived in the years 1900–10 alone, with a further six million the following decade. Between 1900 and 1910, 41 per cent of the increase in urban population was due directly to **immigration**. It is estimated that, in 1890, 80 per cent of New Yorkers had been born abroad. New York had twice the number of Irish that Dublin had, as many Germans as lived in Hamburg and more Italians than lived in Naples. Chicago had the largest population of Czechs living anywhere in the world and the third largest number of Poles, after Warsaw and Lodz. It was not only the case that immigration increased dramatically between 1880 and 1920, but also that immigrants came from different parts of the world. Thus in this period, the 'New Immigration' changed the pattern of immigration into the USA, both in scope and nature.

Before 1880, the vast majority of immigrants came from the north and west of Europe: Germans, British, Irish, French and Scandinavians made up over 80 per cent of immigrants in the 1860s, and most arrived in family groups with the intention of settling for good. This changed after 1880, when the majority came from southern and eastern Europe, were single men and often went back to Europe after a prolonged stay. The exception to this was Jewish immigration in which, facing **persecution** in Russia and eastern Europe and with no homeland to go to, most came to settle permanently in family groups. There is a problem establishing precisely where all these immigrants came from. Jews would be registered according to their country of birth. Poles were not listed separately between 1899 and 1918 and many of the Slavic groups coming from the Austro-Hungarian Empire, in particular, were labelled incorrectly as Germans or Austrians. One can say fairly confidently, however, that there was a major shift in immigration patterns during the period.

Immigration: The movement of foreign nationals attracted by the prosperity and stability of the country or region.

Persecution: A time when a group or people are treated cruelly and unfairly, especially because of their political or religious beliefs.

Why did people emigrate to the USA?

One would need to talk to immigrants to have a full idea of why they came. Also, each immigrant could tell a different story. However, most immigration can be seen as a combination of push and pull factors (i.e. there were reasons why they wanted to leave the countries in which they were born and lived, and there were specific reasons why, having decided to leave their homelands, it was the United States where they chose to settle).

Push factors (why people left their homelands)

● Socio-economic changes at home

Urbanisation: Making a country area more like a town, with more buildings, industry, business etc.

With most European populations rising and a significant growth in **urbanisation**, many traditional communities in eastern Europe and Russia were facing disruption to their traditional lifestyles. Although many left home to settle in the urban centres of America, not all did. A number found it easier to continue their traditional farming lifestyles out in the American West, or at least even if they did stay in the cities when they arrived they had planned otherwise. Even those who had always intended to settle in cities such as New York and Chicago found it easier to make such a dramatic decision to change their lifestyles if they were going to be changing anyway.

● Religious, political and racial persecution

Pan-Slavism: A doctrine that advocates the political union of all Slav peoples. This was widely viewed in other European states as a cover for the political ambitions of Russia.

Many groups who left Europe had been facing persecution at home. Jews faced severe and growing persecution at the end of the 19th century, particularly in Poland and Russia where a growth of nationalism and **pan-Slavism** saw an increase in physical attacks on Jewish villages and businesses, often with the support of the authorities. Some ethnic groups also faced persecution, such as the Armenians in Turkey, from where there was a dramatic increase in immigrants in the 1900s. Ethnic groups in multi-ethnic empires, especially the Austro-Hungarian Empire, felt they could sustain their cultural identity better elsewhere. There was also a growing intolerance in European capitals of anarchists and socialists, a number of whom chose to leave and plan their revolutions from afar.

● Economic problems

The most dramatic example of economic emigration is the Irish, who left in their thousands during the potato famine of the 1840s. Much emigration can be traced very specifically to moments of economic collapse in various European countries, particularly in southern Europe. For example, an outbreak of cholera and a collapse in the international fruit and wine market in the 1880s in southern Italy saw a sudden rise in Italian immi-

Immigrants catch their first glimpse of the Statue of Liberty as their ocean liner approaches New York harbour in 1915.

gration in the mid-1880s. Crop failure and a decline in the currant market may explain a major Greek exodus in 1907. Many of these immigrants were young men who went to the USA with the intention of returning. Many sent money back to their families in Europe or returned having made enough money to establish a business at home. It is interesting to note that 1,800,000 Hungarians were recorded as having entered America between 1880 and 1914, but in 1910 there were only 500,000 there – evidence indeed that the majority of immigrants returned home.

Pull factors (why people chose to settle in the USA)
● Economic opportunities

The most obvious reason why people settled in America was because of its reputation, largely justified, as a 'land of opportunity'. The economic expansion of the USA was both a cause and a consequence of mass immigration and the nature of the industrialisation meant that there was plenty of demand for unskilled labour, which the majority of immigrants represented. What appeared to be pitiable pay rates in America, seemed like small fortunes to the immigrants coming from severe poverty or **subsistence agriculture** in Europe and Russia.

Subsistence agriculture: This is the production of food solely for those that produce it and not for sale at market.

● Direct recruitment by American agents

A special bureau to encourage immigration had been established during the Civil War and many American companies sent agents to recruit cheap labour. This was known as contract labour – where workers had to agree to work for a company at a fixed price for a period of time – and was legal until 1885. Many of those arriving in America had had their passage paid for in advance and there was widespread advertising across Europe.

● America's spirit of toleration

At a time when most Europeans were denied the vote and when governments, particularly in the East, were highly authoritarian, the political freedom and liberties offered by the United States were highly attractive. Europeans would have been made aware of the Declaration of Independence that stated that 'all men are created equal', while the poem on the base of the Statue of Liberty called forth all those immigrants 'yearning to breathe free'. As in the case with economic opportunities, some of this may have been exaggerated, but compared with the political situation in Russia or Turkey, America really was a 'land of liberty'.

Sonnet written on 2 November 1883. It is inscribed on a plaque at the foot of the Statue of Liberty. The Statue of Liberty is the first thing that immigrants see as they sail into New York Harbour.

The 'New Colossus'

Not like the brazen giant of Greek fame,
With conquering limbs astride from land to land
Here at our sea-washed, sunset-gates shall stand
A mighty woman with a torch, whose flame
Is the imprisoned lightning, and her name
Mother of Exiles. From her beacon-hand
Glows world-wide welcome, her mild eyes command
The air-bridges harbour that twin-cities frame.

'Keep, ancient lands, your storied pomp!' cries she,
With silent lips. 'Give me your tired, your poor,
Your huddled masses yearning to breathe free,
The wretched refuse of your teeming shore;
Send these, the homeless, the tempest-tost to me,
I lift my lamp beside the golden door!'

By Emma Lazarus (1849–1887)

● Influence of relatives and friends

1. Draw a mind map and show on it the various reasons why people emigrated to the USA after 1865.

2. What do you regard as the main reason why people emigrated to the USA after 1865? Explain your answer.

Inevitably, many families followed early pioneers from their extended family or village. Indeed these cousins in the States would often pay the passage to be joined by their relatives or friends.

● Developments in transport

The transition from sail to steam allowed many more people to make the journey across the Atlantic. Also, railroads opened up the continent once immigrants arrived there. Indeed, many of the agents working to encourage immigration came from the railroad companies.

5.7 What was the impact of immigration on the USA?

The development of distinct ethnic neighbourhoods

Whatever their motives had been in moving to America, most immigrants on arrival did not get beyond the cities. Most lacked the capital to start up farming and were either attracted by the wages or quickly dragged into a system that saw influential figures from ethnic groups, often Italian or Greek, arrange the entire life for arriving immigrants, from housing to jobs and even the way they would vote. As a result, and because many were joining family or friends, certain nationalities were attracted to certain cities. Within cities, different neighbourhoods developed in one particular ethnic style. With everything else new, living in an ethnic neighbourhood also helped to provide some certainties and security at what could be a difficult time. Thus the Irish dominated Boston, Czechs and Poles flocked to Chicago, and the Italians took over Brooklyn, New York.

Economic impact

As the Government had clearly realised when it set up an immigration bureau in the Civil War to help fill the factories, the opportunities that immigration presented in providing a constant supply of cheap, unskilled labour were significant. Immigrants were desperate for work and often coming from a rural background, with little idea of employment law or working rights, they were easily exploited with contractors quickly signing up whole families and sending them off to various mid-West cities. Although a significant amount of urban growth was due to Americans moving from country to town, the largest factor in urban growth was immigration. In 1910, one-third of the population of the 12 largest cities in the USA was immigrant and a further third was composed of the children of immigrants. It is hard to imagine how the US economy could have grown in the way it did without this important supply of labour which was prepared to work for a rate most local workers would not accept. Inevitably, this led to some tensions between immigrants and local-born Americans who saw the immigrants as either threatening their job opportunities or depressing wage levels. There was strong working-class resentment of the new immigrants.

Political impact

The immigrants had had very little, if any, experience of politics in their previous lives and tended to vote in the same way in the cities in which they settled. Because they tended to live in ethnic neighbourhoods, they could easily dominate certain political districts and the local politicians exploited this. City bosses would provide a network of economic and social support

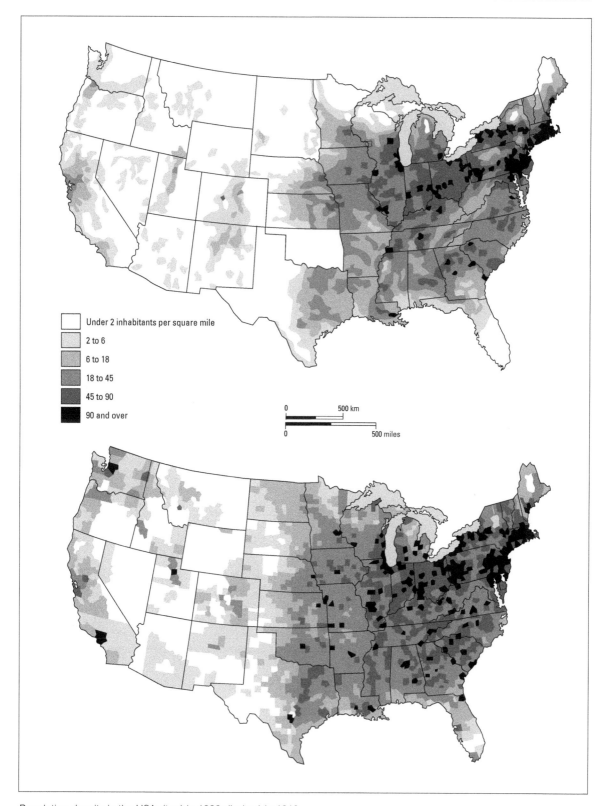

Population density in the USA: (top) in 1880; (below) in 1910.

Jeffersonian ideal: Belief that society should be made up of independent small-scale farms and businesses.

and in return could rely on the votes of these grateful immigrants. Naturally, this concerned many Americans who were wedded to the **Jeffersonian ideal** of the individual yeoman exercising his carefully considered right to vote and casting it wisely for the good of the whole.

Some concerns were also expressed that, as many of these new immigrants were Catholic, they owed their loyalties to the foreign Pope and the local priest, and were thus easily swayed and not always for patriotic reasons. The immigrants tended to be attracted to the Democratic Party, especially since the Republicans became increasingly associated with the Prohibition Movement which to some extent had racial overtones as the temperance reformers blamed much of the drink problems on the Catholic, German and Irish immigrants. As a consequence, the Democratic Party looked to immigrants in the northern cities to provide a balance to the continued domination of the Republican Party among native-born Americans in the North and East. The combination of white southerners, western farmers and urban immigrants was the coalition that helped the Democrats fight back, politically, in the decades after the Civil War.

Racial tension and discrimination

Perhaps inevitably, native-born Americans tended to use the immigrants as scapegoats to blame for the ills of society. By living in their own districts and making little attempt to integrate, the new immigrants made themselves easier targets than the old immigrants of north and west European extraction. Labour violence often erupted from immigrant slums, while the growth of anarchy and socialism among urban workers was blamed on European influences.

Immigration was seen as leading to a more corrupt and unpleasant society, less homogeneous and more violent. Although there were not the formal moves against immigrants that one saw in the 1850s, with the formation of the 'Know Nothings', and in the 'Red Scare' of the 1920s, there were outbreaks of violence and some discriminatory legislation was passed. Newspapers record stories of attacks on Greeks in Nebraska, Slavs in Utah and Chinese on the West Coast. In 1891, 11 Italians were lynched in New Orleans after a local jury acquitted them of murder. The reformation of the Ku Klux Klan in 1915 in Georgia was an ominous sign of what was to come. In 1887, the America Protective Association was formed with the aim of countering the impact of Catholics on public schools and immigrants in political life. The Asiatic Exclusion League was formed in 1905 to try and limit the numbers of Japanese who worked for lower wages. However, given the vast numbers of immigrants arriving in the USA in this period these examples are relatively few, especially when one looks at other periods of American history. It is a sign of how dramatically America was expanding and changing that the vast majority of immigrants seem to have settled quickly and effectively into the American nation.

1. Did the new immigrants have a greater impact on the economy or on politics? Explain your answer.

2. Did the new immigrants have a beneficial impact on the USA? Explain your answer.

5.8 What were the origins and aims of the Progressive movement?

Progressivism: An attitude to government that crossed political boundaries and was concerned with improving American politics and society in the light of the major upheaval that had transformed America since the Civil War.

Although there was a Progressive Party that contested the 1912 presidential election, Progressives were politicians and writers involved in both political parties, or neither. Who were the Progressives and what was **Progressivism**? Progressives looked on the 'Gilded Age' with distaste and were keen to end or reform the political corruption, monopolistic practices of the large firms and urban deprivation that had characterised the period. In many ways, they took on the role vacated by the Populists, although they were far more successful in bringing about changes, perhaps because they worked from within the existing political parties rather than challenging them from outside. This action took place at all levels in government, from President to city mayor. It included reforms such as limiting maximum working hours, improving working conditions and extending the franchise (vote). There was no specific programme that can be said to be progressive so what was done in its name of Progressivism varied according to the local circumstances. It is also important to remember that this did not mean that there was a sudden break with the old practices because for every progressive politician there was still one operating the old politics of graft and influence.

The Progressive movement was initially encouraged by a group of writers and journalists writing at the turn of the century. President Roosevelt christened them the 'muckrakers'. They used their books and articles to bring to the attention of the public various abuses in politics and business which stirred public opinion into demanding some regulation and change. Certain popular magazines, such as 'McClure's', 'Cosmopolitan' and 'Collier's' provided these writers with a forum for their disclosures, which were often presented in a sensationalist way.

Among the most influential were:

● Upton Sinclair, *The Jungle* (1906) – about conditions in Chicago's meat-packing industry.

● Lincoln Steffens, *Shame of the Cities* (1904) – about corruption in city governments across the USA.

● Frank Norris, *The Octopus* (1901) – attacking the Southern Pacific Railroad – and *The Pit* (1903) – attacking the Chicago grain market.

● Ida M. Tarbell, *History of the Standard Oil Company* (1904) – attacking monopolistic practices.

Although at times these 'muckrakers' claimed rather more significance for themselves than was justified, they played an important role in forcing the agenda of politicians or in providing moral and factual support for those who tried to pass some reform. Much of the work though was down to individual politicians appealing to the electorate over the heads of **vested interests**. They often acted from a genuine sense of justice and a feeling that, in industrialisation and urbanisation, America had somehow lost its way and had abandoned its guiding principles.

What did the Progressives achieve locally?

Progressivism tends to be viewed in the context of the achievements of three Presidents at federal level: Theodore Roosevelt, William Taft and Woodrow Wilson. Before looking at the work of these three men, it is important to consider the actions of politicians and activists at a local level where much of the early work was done and where reforms were pioneered.

Among the progressive governors and mayors, a small number stand out as men who became national figures and so promoted not only themselves but the ideas they were bringing to government. Perhaps the most influential of these was the Republican governor of Wisconsin, Robert M. La Follette, whose programme of reform both received national attention and became known as the 'Wisconsin Idea'. In particular, he took on the powerful vested interests in business, especially railroads, and politics. Other key progressive governors were the Republicans Charles Evans Hughes of New York and Hiram Johnson of California and Democrat Woodrow Wilson who gained a national name that would later help him secure the Presidency during his time as Governor of New Jersey. There were also a number of key

Vested interests: Strong reasons that someone has for acting in a particular way e.g. to protect their own money, power or reputation.

Robert M. La Follette (1855–1925)
He served as **district attorney** (1880–94) and as a member of the House of Representatives (1885–91). He was elected Governor of Wisconsin in 1900. As leader of the national progressive reform movement, he ran unsuccessfully for President in 1924.

District attorney: A lawyer in the USA who works for the state and who prosecutes people on its behalf. Often referred to as 'DA'.

figures at city level, most significantly Democrat Tom L. Johnson of Cleveland, Ohio, who was admired across the country for the work he did in cleaning up both the politics and social abuses of the city.

Much of the work of these men was concerned with breaking the powers of the political vested interests and trying to involve the people more directly in government action, whilst reforming the structure and administration of city government to make it more efficient and professional. The methods used varied and were tested and copied across the states. We will look briefly at some of these methods.

The initiative and the referendum

Both of these were first used in South Dakota in 1898 and allowed voters to have a direct say in proposing a particular law. Usually the support of around 10 per cent of the voters was required to sign a petition calling for a particular law, which was then submitted to the state legislature or to the people for approval. If passed, it became law.

The recall

This plan, first used in Los Angeles in 1903, allowed for the removal of an office-holder before his/her term ended if a sufficient proportion of the voters (usually around 25 per cent) was in favour and could start the process by a petition.

The direct primary

The party bosses had traditionally pre-selected the candidates for election well in advance and used the nominating conventions to great effect to impose their will and influence. The direct primary was first introduced by La Follette in Wisconsin in 1903. It was a preliminary election in which voters can nominate directly the candidate they would like to see run for their party in the general election that would follow.

Direct election of senators

Senators had not previously been elected directly, but had been nominated by their state legislatures – a practice that inevitably led to charges of influence and election-rigging. Gradually, more and more states introduced popular elections to determine who the voters wanted as their senatorial candidate, which the legislatures had little option but to accept. Eventually, the whole process became fully constitutional with the passage of the Seventeenth Amendment, a major progressive achievement, in 1913 (passed by Congress in 1911 but not ratified until 1913). This required the direct election of senators. It is a good example of a reform, eventually adopted at federal level, which had its origins in the actions of individual states.

The commission and city-manager plans

Pioneered by the city of Galveston, Texas, in 1900, the commission plan was a reorganisation of city government in which all the city functions were controlled by a small group of elected citizens (the commission), each of whom was responsible for one particular department, and which collectively made overall policy. All commissioners were, theoretically, equal with one serving as a ceremonial head, so diminishing the possibilities of one over-powerful figure dominating the city as mayor.

In some places, this developed further into the city-manager plan, pioneered in 1908 by Staunton, Virginia, and popularised by Dayton, Ohio, in 1914. In this plan, the elected commission acted more as a board of directors and appointed a non-political city manager who would hopefully have the skills and expertise to manage the city as a business rather than political fiefdom.

Although these plans did not work everywhere where they were tried, they marked an attempt to end the old days of the powerful city bosses who could easily act as a magnet for corruption. They showed early attempts at professionalising city management.

Female suffrage

The campaign for women's suffrage was also one taken up by a number of progressives. Various states gave the ballot to women before Congress passed the Nineteenth Amendment in 1919, which granted nationwide votes. Wyoming was the first state to do so, in 1890. This was followed by eight other states by 1913. All of them were in the West, reflecting the strength of the progressive movement there and the more egalitarian spirit of the frontier, where women were less likely to operate in separate spheres from men and were treated more as equals.

Welfare

Local progressives were not just concerned with political reforms. Several states and cities pioneered work in such areas as:

● slum clearance

● development of better services, such as educational and leisure facilities, in dealing with the urban growth

● improvements in employment legislation, especially for women and children, over issues such as hours and wages

● health and safety standards at work

● basic welfare for widows, orphans and the destitute.

How progressive were Presidents Roosevelt and Taft?

Although the work done at local level was significant, the man most associated with Progressivism was the Republican President from 1901–09 who dominated the political debate of his era – Theodore Roosevelt. He and his chosen successor, William H. Taft, used the position of President to bring about a number of progressive reforms in the federal government whilst simultaneously pursuing an aggressive foreign policy (see Chapter 6).

Roosevelt was not elected to office initially but became President when William McKinley was assassinated in September 1901. Many Republican leaders feared the young, dynamic Roosevelt. His progressive ideas did not sit comfortably with many of the **party elders**. Throughout his first Administration, Roosevelt feared that Mark Hanna – a leading industrialist and close friend of McKinley who had played a key role in getting his friend the nomination and was now the leading figure on the conservative wing of the Republicans – might stand against him for the nomination. Hanna died in 1904, Roosevelt easily secured the Republican nomination and was convincingly re-elected in 1904. He was thus able, over seven years, to bring to the Presidency a degree of progressivism that marked a considerable change from his Republican predecessors. Although some of the measures fell short of what many progressive campaigners had hoped

Theodore Roosevelt (1858–1919)
26th President of the USA (1901–09), a Republican. 'Teddy' or 'TR', as he was often known, was Assistant Secretary of the Navy (1897–98) and during the Spanish–American war he commanded a volunteer force of 'rough riders'. As McKinley's Vice-President he took over as President when McKinley was assassinated in 1901. At only 42, he was the youngest president. He already had a long record in public office, having been a Civil Service Commissioner, Police Commissioner and Governor of New York. When in office, he became more liberal. In 1906 he was awarded the Nobel Peace Prize for his part in ending the Russo–Japanese war. Writer of several historical works, including *The Naval War of 1812* (published in 1882) and *The Winning of the West* (1889–96). The 'teddy' bear was named after Theodore 'Teddy' Roosevelt.

Party elders: Senior members of a political party who have influence over policy.

William H. Taft (1857–1930)
27th President of the USA (1901–13), a Republican. Although his first interest was the judiciary, he accepted a post as governor of the Philippines and took responsibility for the construction of the Panama Canal (see page 174). He was Secretary of War (1904–08) in Theodore Roosevelt's Administration. His single term as President was noted for the struggles against the Progressives. As chief justice of the Supreme Court, Taft supported the minimum wage.

Roosevelt and Taft at the White House.

for, Roosevelt's energy and determination that his fellow citizens should take their civic responsibilities seriously helped to bolster the progressive cause. There were also several specific measures that he helped enact. In his State of the Union address in 1901, Roosevelt called for:

● more meritocracy in the civil service

● conservation of natural resources

● greater control of businesses and interstate transport by the federal government.

Although he reassured Republicans by initially keeping the Cabinet he inherited from McKinley, he was a dominant President who knew what he wanted.

The square deal

In order to give coherence and a philosophy to his policies, Roosevelt talked of a 'square deal' that would help all Americans – businessmen, farmers, consumers and workers. He got actively involved in a dispute involving the coal miners of eastern Pennsylvania, calling the mine owners and union leaders to the White House during a strike in 1902 and attempting mediation. When talks broke down and the mine owners refused to accept his proposals for an independent board of arbitration to resolve the issue, Roosevelt threatened to use federal troops to run the mines. He started putting private pressure on the mine owners. In the end, the employers agreed to submit to such a board and a decision was reached, in March 1903, that saw a 10 per cent wage increase and a nine-hour day, but no union recognition. Roosevelt's direct intervention was highly unusual but it paid off and became the basis of a settlement that lasted to the end of the First World War.

Roosevelt used his position to popularise the movement for better conservation of America's natural resources which were being threatened by the large-scale transfer of public land to private ownership, especially in the West. He put his authority behind the Newlands Act of 1902 which raised money from land sales to finance irrigation projects, and he gave strong support for the establishment and preservation of national parks – areas of outstanding natural beauty that could not be developed. He was behind the establishment of a national conservation commission in 1908 to oversee conservation in the West and to set aside 148 million acres of forest to protect timber reserves.

Roosevelt was not opposed to big business but he was keen to regulate to ensure fair competition and consumer-friendly practices. He supported the Pure Food and Drug Act of 1906 which outlawed the adulteration or false labelling of food and drugs as well as the Meat Inspection Act of 1908 that sought to improve conditions in the meat-processing industry, largely as a response to the 'muckraker' Upton Sinclair's research and writing. He also enforced more vigorously the terms of the 1890 Sherman Anti-Trust Act (see page 130) that had tended to be ignored by Cleveland and McKinley. Roosevelt established the Bureau of Corporations in 1903 which had the power to investigate allegations against trusts. He secured from Congress a special fund of $500,000 to allow the government to prosecute suits against companies. As a result, **24 indictments** were secured against the trusts during Roosevelt's presidency, twice as many as under previous administrations. He was also a prominent supporter of the successful case against the Northern Securities Company, a holding company that controlled stock in several railroad companies in the North and was found guilty of 'restraint of trade' by the Supreme Court in 1904. Roosevelt also encouraged legislation to strengthen the terms of the Interstate Commerce Act of 1877 through the Elkins Act of 1903 and the Hepburn Act of 1906 (see panel below).

Indictments: Official charges made against a person.

The Elkins Act 1903

● Secret rebates on railroads were confirmed as illegal, but now the recipient of the rebate could be prosecuted as well as the grantor.

● The agent of the railroad company was liable for any change in the published rates.

The Hepburn Act 1906

Strengthened the power of the Interstate Commerce Commission by:

● increasing its membership to seven (from five)

● giving it power to reduce rates deemed by it to be too high or discriminatory

● placing the burden of proof on the carrier rather than the Commission where there was legal challenge

● forbidding railroads to carry goods they had been involved in producing

● establishing a uniform system of accounting

● extending the authority of the Commission to pipelines, ferries and express companies.

Although the courts remained likely to favour big business, there was a growing tendency, supported by the Supreme Court, to uphold the Commission's judgements.

Much of Roosevelt's contribution to Progressivism was in encouraging reforms, although his commitment to conservation in particular was very real and significant. He chose not to stand again for President in 1908, though there was nothing to stop him from doing so. Instead, he supported William Taft, who easily won the Republican nomination and then beat the Democratic candidate, William Jennings Bryan, who was standing and losing for the third time.

Although Taft lacked the energy of Roosevelt (he weighed over 20 stone), he was more conciliatory than 'Teddy' Roosevelt. He remained committed to the progressive programme of his sponsor and he continued to encourage the prosecution of big business, the reservation of public lands and the extension of the merit system in the civil service.

- An eight-hour day was introduced for all employees on government contracts.

- The departments of Labor and Commerce were established in 1913 – the former to help workers secure decent working conditions and the latter to supervise America's commercial development.

- The Sixteenth Amendment was ratified in 1913, permitting the imposition of a graduated income tax.

- In 1910, the Mann–Elkins Act strengthened the powers of the Inter-state Commerce Commission still further, giving it authority to supervise telephone, telegraph and wireless companies, allowing it to institute its own legal proceedings and creating a new Commerce Court to speed up proceedings.

It was also during Taft's Presidency that two important suits took place against companies, using the anti-trust legislation. In 1911, the Standard Oil Company of New Jersey was dissolved for holding an illegal monopoly in oil refining. In the same year, the American Tobacco Company was ruled an illegal combination and forced to reorganise.

Taft was more cautious when it came to matters concerning tariffs, conservation and government procedure. In 1907, Roosevelt had argued that the tariff should be reduced and Taft indicated his support for this in the 1908 campaign. The tariff was at its highest level ever, at an average of 57 per cent in 1908, and was attracting considerable criticism, especially in the West, among workers and farmers who saw prices rising faster than wages. In 1909, there were long debates in Congress and eventually Taft intervened to encourage Congress to pass the compromise Payne–Aldrich Bill which reduced rates to a 40 per cent average. Although this did mark a reduction, it disappointed many progressive Republicans who had been arguing for a much greater reduction. They now feared Taft might be less amenable to their ideas than Roosevelt.

In conservation, Taft also upset many of Roosevelt's supporters by taking the side of his Secretary of Interior, Richard Ballinger, when he ruled that Roosevelt had taken too much power away from private inter-ests out West. The decision was to restore various lands to private ownership in Wyoming and Montana, as well as to open up parts of Alaska to private claims for coalmining areas. When Ballinger was criticised by Louis Glavis and Gifford Pinchot, federally employed conservationists promoted by Roosevelt, Taft dismissed them in 1909 and 1910 respec-tively. Pinchot, in particular, accused Taft of abandoning Roosevelt's commitment to conservation – an unfair exaggeration but one that stuck.

Then, in a series of struggles in 1910 between the conservative speaker in the House of Representatives, Joseph Cannon, and an alliance of Democrats and progressive Republicans, Taft found himself supporting Cannon who had not only identified himself as an opponent of progressive reforms, but had also lost the struggle to maintain his power over important House committees. It thus became clear that Taft did not have the support of the progressive Republicans and was losing his grip on the party in Congress.

1. What were the aims of the Progressives?

2. How successful were the Progressives in introducing reform by 1912?

Although Taft continued many of the policies associated with Roosevelt, and in many ways was more directly responsible for progressive legislation and actions, a number of progressive leaders began to feel that he was not as committed to the cause as they would have liked. They began to plot against him.

5.9 What impact did Woodrow Wilson have on domestic affairs, 1913–1919?

Woodrow Wilson (1856–1924)
28th President of the USA (1913–21), a Democrat. President of Princeton University (1902–10); Governor of New Jersey (1911–13). As President, he kept the USA out of the First World War until 1917, and in January 1918 issued his 'Fourteen Points' as a basis for a peace settlement. Awarded the Nobel Peace Prize in 1919 but was forced to retire from politics through illness.

What were the issues in the 1912 presidential election?

The 1912 election was a dramatic and unusual one in that the three candidates were all Progressives of a sort and all had been President at some point. It also marked the election of Woodrow Wilson, who was the only Democrat to be elected President between 1892 and 1932.

The Democrats
Woodrow Wilson, the liberal and progressive Governor of New Jersey, was selected as the Democratic candidate after 46 ballots, crucially winning the backing of William Jennings Bryan who changed his vote as he felt that Wilson offered the best hope of challenging the powers of big business. Wilson was far more liberal than either of the two previous progressive Presidents. Although he described himself as a 'progressive with the brakes on', he fought a campaign that called for a full attack on political and economic privilege. He made it clear that he saw the trusts and business monopoly as an evil that needed destroying. The Democrats also made their traditional pledges on tariffs, though Wilson went further than the previous Democratic President (Grover Cleveland) and called for a new tariff that would be used for revenue purposes only. This was a pledge that, in reality, meant a substantial reduction.

The Republicans
The Republicans selected Taft as their candidate for re-election but only after a hotly contested convention in which Theodore Roosevelt, after some hesitation, offered himself as candidate again. Roosevelt made it clear that he felt Taft had not sustained progressivism in office as much as he would have liked. It was clear from the way that delegates voted that Roosevelt was the more popular with the rank-and-file Republicans, but that Taft was the choice of the Republican leaders. So, with the party leaders controlling the convention and the majority of delegations, Taft emerged as Republican candidate. He fought the election promising much of the same, calling for a reduced but nonetheless protectionist tariff and for tougher regulation of the trusts.

The Progressives
Since January 1911, a number of Republican senators had formed the Progressive Republican League with the idea of ensuring that progressive ideas continue to influence Republican policy making. In particular, they called for nationwide political reforms, such as the direct election of sena-

tors, direct primaries and the use of the initiative, referendum and recall. Disappointed by the actions of Taft in government, encouraged by comments by Roosevelt and his supporters such as Pinchot and some of the muckraking journalists, the League decided, in October 1911, to field a presidential candidate. It adopted Senator Robert La Follette of Wisconsin who had won a name for himself and his Wisconsin Idea as an early progressive governor.

Although Roosevelt initially failed to support the plans of the Progressive League, his rejection by the Republicans at their convention led him to get involved with the Progressive Party which met in Chicago in August 1912. Although there to support La Follette many delegates felt that, in Roosevelt, they had someone who could win and he was nominated for President. The Progressives – known also as the 'Bull Moose' party because of Roosevelt's frequent use of the term (which means someone energetic) – thus found themselves splitting the Republican vote. The position taken by the Progressives on issues such as the tariff and trusts differed little from Taft's. In the end, a voter deciding between the Republicans and the Progressives was really faced with a choice of personalities and image rather than specific policy issues.

The split in the Republican Party gave the Democrats their first presidential victory since 1892, with Wilson winning 40 states and Taft trailing in a poor third, though the combined votes of Roosevelt and Taft outnumbered Wilson by over a million. Clearly, the results of 1912 were a consequence of Republican splits rather than of any popular enthusiasm for Wilson, although the Democrats did gain control of both the Senate and the House of Representatives. What is important about the 1912 election though is that it marked a clear victory for progressive policies. All three candidates clearly felt that in order to ensure victory they had to support political reform, lower tariffs and control of big business. In that sense, the election of 1912 marked the final confirmation that the 'Gilded Age' was well and truly behind Americans.

Results of the 1912 presidential election

		Popular vote	Electoral college
Woodrow Wilson	Democrat	6,296,547	435
Theodore Roosevelt	Progressive	4,118,571	88
William H. Taft	Republican	3,436,720	8
Eugene V. Debs	Socialist	900,672	0
Eugene W. Chafin	Prohibition	206,275	0

Woodrow Wilson campaign poster, 1912.

How progressive a president was Wilson?

In government, Wilson brought to a conclusion many of the reforms begun by Roosevelt and Taft. He was a passionate believer in justice and brought his liberal ideas to both domestic and foreign policy, although in foreign policy he struggled to stay true to his ideals in practice. In domestic affairs, he had more notable successes and played a proactive role in encouraging Congress to pass legislation he favoured. Most of the legislation passed was enacted in the early years of his Presidency, before the First World War came to preoccupy him.

The Administration supported several pieces of legislation to help farmers and workers:

● Smith–Lever Act (1914) – helped farmers learn new agricultural techniques by the introduction of home instruction.

- Federal Farm Loan Act (1916) – provided a federal farm loan bank in local districts so that farmers could get long-term mortgage loans at a lower rate than they would from commercial banks.

- Adamson Act (1916) – established an eight-hour day and overtime pay for railroad workers who were involved in interstate commerce (Congress could not get involved constitutionally in internal state employment law).

- Keating–Owen Act (1916) – banned articles produced by children under 14 from being traded or transported between states (although this was later deemed unconstitutional because it interfered with powers reserved by the states to regulate employment law).

- La Follette Seamen's Act (1915) – helped to improve safety, payment and conditions for sailors and merchant seamen.

Congress also produced a new anti-trust Act to supersede the inadequate Sherman Act of 1890 when it introduced the Clayton Anti-Trust Act of 1914. The Act contained certain provisions to help workers and farmers by making it clear that strikes, boycotts and **picketing** were not illegal under federal law (some courts had declared them so because they acted 'in restraint of trade') and limited the use of **injunctions** to prevent strikes. It also made it clear that agricultural and industrial trade unions were not classified as trusts. The Act clarified, too, several restrictions on business practice that had not been explicit in the Sherman Act, namely:

Picketing: The standing outside a factory or other place by a group of workers, especially trade union members, in order to protest about something. The intention is often to prevent people from going in or from leaving.

Injunctions: Instructions or orders that are given officially and formally by a court of law. They are often to stop something from happening, such as an injunction to prevent people striking.

- price discrimination in interstate trade

- major holding of one corporation's stock by another (aimed at limiting the powers of holding companies)

- directorates that interlocked in big businesses involved in interstate trade.

In addition, an Act of 1914 established the Federal Trade Commission – a board of five members with the power to oversee businesses involved in interstate trade by requiring the preparation of annual reports and by investigating practices such as advertising, labelling etc.

Wilson was also keen to bring a more effective banking and credit system to the USA. There had been problems in the USA where rigid credit and money supply systems had prevented easy cash flow when necessary, and Wilson was keen to ensure that money flowed more easily. He was helped by a report, in 1913, of the Pujo Committee that had looked into the financial power of a small group of bankers. It concluded that there was on Wall Street a 'money trust' that abused its control of money as much as big business did their industrial power. In 1913, Congress passed the Federal Reserve Act that created a nationwide system of credit administered by an independent Federal Reserve Board that regulated the rates of interest and currency circulation in 12 different districts of the USA. This not only brought currency under the central control of government, it also allowed the Board to create variations in the amount of currency flowing in different parts of the country so that some districts could have mildly inflationary policies whilst other areas maintained tight monetary control.

Not surprisingly, the Democrats used their control of both Houses of Congress and of the Presidency, to make a substantial reduction in the tariff. This was achieved in the Underwood Tariff of 1913, which included:

- a reduction of rates on almost 1,000 items

- an increase of rates on around 100 luxury items

- an increase in the number of free-items (not taxed at all) to include iron, wool and steel

- the introduction of a graduated income tax (to maintain federal revenues).

Wilson played a key role in getting the tariff reduction through Congress and in overcoming **lobbying** that sought to protect individual items.

Lobbying: A group of people try actively to persuade a government that a particular law should be changed or that a particular course of action should be taken.

Thus, Wilson's first term in office saw the completion of much of the progressive agenda of his Republican predecessors. Government became more efficient, business more regulated and the currency more flexible, whilst the interests of workers were protected as much as was possible at federal level, given the limitations on the power of the federal government by the Constitution. Although the Republicans, largely at Roosevelt's insistence when he turned down the chance to run as a Progressive again, reunited in the 1916 presidential election, Wilson managed to secure re-election and a popular **mandate** for his progressive domestic reforms.

Mandate: Political term for having the backing for a particular course of action as a result of an electoral win.

What impact did the First World War have on the Home Front in the USA?

Even before the USA formally entered the First World War, in April 1917, preparations had taken place. In August 1916, Congress had set up a Council of National Defense. In January 1917, the US Shipping Board was created to increase shipbuilding.

The biggest problem the USA faced was raising an army. Unlike most of the major European powers, the USA did not have conscription (compulsory military service). In April 1917, the Army numbered only 120,000 men. Under the Selective Service Act of May 1917, conscription was introduced. The Secretary of War, Newton Baker, efficiently organised the implementation of the Act. By the end of the war, in November 1918, 24 million men had been registered to join the armed forces and 3 million were called up to fight. In an unprecedented move, 11,000 women served in the navy during the First World War.

To ensure the US economy was prepared for world war, the War Industries Board was created in 1917 to organise purchases for the armed forces. From March 1918, Bernard Baruch ran the War Industries Board. To save fuel, a fuel administration was created.

On the agricultural front, a food administration was created in August 1917, under the leadership of Herbert Hoover. Hoover ensured food production was able not only to meet the requirements of the USA, but could also be shipped to Britain. He exhorted the US public not to waste food and he organised such public relations acts as 'Meatless Mondays' and 'Porkless Thursdays'.

One of the casualties of war was civil liberties. On 14 April 1917, President Wilson created the Committee on Public Information. Under the leadership of George Creel, this committee engaged in propaganda against Germany. Anti-German opposition aided the prohibition campaign because Germans dominated the US brewing industry.

The Espionage Act of June 1917 and the Sedition Act of May 1918 outlawed criticism of the war effort. Socialist leader and presidential candidate, Eugene Debs, was imprisoned under these laws. Also targeted was the extreme left-wing trade union organisation, the International Workers of the World – or 'Wobblies'. In total, over 1,500 people were imprisoned under the Acts.

These laws received support from the US Supreme Court in 1919 after the war. In 'Schenk versus the United States' the Court upheld the

1. Explain why Wilson won the 1912 presidential election.

2. How successful was Wilson in domestic affairs during his first term, 1913–1917?

3. How did the First World War affect life in America between 1917 and 1919?

conviction of a man for distributing anti-call-up pamphlets during the war.

By the end of the war, the role of the federal government in the lives of ordinary Americans had increased significantly. US involvement in the war had cost $35.5 billion: $24.3 billion in expenditure on the US war effort and $11.2 billion in loans to allied countries. In addition, the war provided the final push for the achievement of national prohibition. As millions of men went off to fight, most of their jobs were temporarily filled by women. Shortly after the war, Congress also introduced a constitutional amendment (Nineteenth Amendment) which finally gave women the vote.

Further Reading

Texts designed for AS Level students

The Enduring Vision, Volume 2 since 1865 by Paul Boyer and others (D.C. Heath and Co., 1995)

Texts for A2 and advanced study

The Limits of Liberty by Maldwyn Jones (Oxford University Press, 1995)
The Longman History of the United States by Hugh Brogan (Longman, Second edition 1999)
The Pivotal Decades, The US, 1900 to 1920 by John Milton Cooper Jr (W.W. Norton & Co., 1990)
Unity and Culture, The United States 1877 to 1900 by H. Wayne Morgan (Penguin, 1971)

6 US foreign policy, 1890–1919

Key Issues

- How far did US foreign policy change in the period 1890 to 1919?

- How important were US presidents in the conduct of foreign policy?

- Why did the USA emerge as one of the world's major powers by 1919?

6.1 Why were the 1890s a turning point in US foreign policy?
6.2 Historical interpretation: Why did the USA go to war with Spain in 1898?
6.3 How successful was Theodore Roosevelt's foreign policy?
6.4 How far had an 'American empire' been created by 1917?
6.5 Why did the USA become involved in the First World War?
6.6 How successful was Wilson's foreign policy 1917–1919?

Framework of Events

1898	Spanish–American War
	Annexation of Hawaii
1899	Boxer Rebellion breaks out in China
1902	Roosevelt Corollary
1906	Building of the Panama Canal starts
1907–1909	Voyage of the 'Great White Fleet'
1914	Start of First World War
	Panama Canal is opened
1915	Sinking of the 'Lusitania'
1917	American entry into First World War
1919	Paris Peace Conference

Overview

UP until the 1890s, the United States of America (USA) had largely kept out of the affairs of other countries. Its own inward expansion, followed by the Civil War and Reconstruction gave the USA little concern for foreign affairs. But this changed towards the end of the century. There was a growing body of opinion that the United States should take a fuller role in world affairs generally, and in those of Latin America in particular. Though there were as many arguments to counter this view, the two decades between 1890 and 1910 saw America take a more prominent role on the world stage, and even saw it acquire colonies of its own in the Caribbean and Pacific.

Over the turn of the century, Presidents Roosevelt and Taft consciously expanded America's role in the world. Theodore Roosevelt believed that the USA had a duty and a right to take a more prominent role in international affairs. Under his administration, the so-called 'Roosevelt Corollary' stated explicitly that the USA had the right to interfere in the affairs of the states of Latin America. Roosevelt also increased American involvement in the Far East – a policy continued by Taft with his encouragement of American financial investment in China.

Isolationism: A policy by which a state (e.g. the USA in the early 1930s) pursues its own domestic interests, in isolation from the wider considerations of international politics.

When war broke out in Europe in 1914, many felt it was an argument between the 'old powers' and was of no concern to the United States. However, once it affected American liberties – such as the freedom to travel and to trade – the President, Woodrow Wilson, became more concerned. German naval attacks eventually forced America into the War, where its role in providing extra equipment and a supply of fresh soldiers was instrumental in the final Allied victory. But the losses of the War and the disappointment of the peace conference made Americans cynical about playing a world role and they retreated into **isolationism**.

1. Write a sentence to explain the importance of each of the points in the mind map to US foreign policy in the period 1890 to 1919.

2. On balance, was US foreign policy a success or a failure in the years 1890 to 1919?

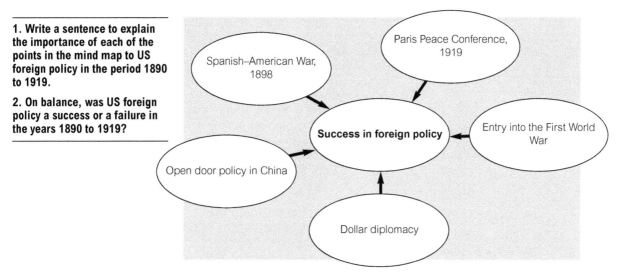

6.1 Why were the 1890s a turning point in US foreign policy?

Imperialism: The control of one country by another, usually by military and political occupation. It can also be by economic control.

Throughout much of the 19th century, when the European powers were extending their empires and embarking on the so-called 'scramble for Africa', the Americans stood above it all in an attitude of superiority. As a former colony, they condemned the **imperialism** of the Old World. Yet, in the last two decades of the century, America also embarked on colonial expansion in the Pacific and Caribbean, and interfered extensively in the affairs of Latin America.

The growth of imperialism

In the 1880s and 1890s, support for an imperialist foreign policy grew inside the USA for political, economic, social and even religious and racial reasons.

Since the 1840s, Americans had recognised the concept of 'Manifest Destiny', the idea that it was the destiny of the United States to dominate the northern half of the continent of America. This had encouraged the expansion westwards beyond the Mississippi and the Rockies. By the 1890s, the West had been settled and the British had made it clear that they had no intention of giving up Canada. Therefore, some argued that 'Manifest Destiny' could, and should, be extended to Latin America and even beyond. It was the duty of America to spread its civilisation. The United States had extended as far as it could across the continent, it was now time to look outwards for expansion.

This argument, unfortunately, had racial overtones. The Social Darwinism that became popular in Europe at the end of the 19th century (see page 143) also had supporters in the USA. American democracy and capitalism were clearly superior to the monarchies and the backward economies that existed in many parts of the world, so it was the duty of the USA to extend its power over these areas for their own good. Americans, in effect, were superior to other races and, therefore, were morally obliged to extend their influence in the world. This kind of thinking was famously illustrated by William McKinley when he referred to natives of the Philippines as America's 'little brown brothers' and talked of America's duty to 'uplift, civilise and Christianise' them, ignoring the fact that the vast majority of Filipinos were Roman Catholics. Yet it must also be said that in extending its 'civilisation' the USA did expand education, public health and democracy in many of the places it went to, and that many Christian missionaries acted out of a genuine desire to care for others.

However, there were also more practical political and economic motives for the support of imperialism, which were not much different from the justifications used by the European powers for their empires. America's industrial economy had grown rapidly in the 1870s and 1880s with gross national product (GNP) growing by 4 per cent annually but, by 1893, it was experiencing a downturn that began a four-year depression. There was a fear that the domestic market had been saturated, so overseas outlets had to be acquired. Asia, and China in particular, was seen as a potentially massive market for American goods. Also, overseas possessions would provide American manufacturers with access to cheap raw materials. Outward expansion would also relieve the labour tensions and unrest that had grown during the depression.

The USA was also concerned that, as European empires grew and extended further across the world, American power would be diminished. In effect, they were being left behind. Between 1875 and 1914, a quarter of the world was claimed as colonies by various powers: if the USA did not get into the imperial 'club' now it never would and the **balance of power** could shift against it.

Balance of power: The view that the important nations of the world should be roughly equal in terms of power and influence, otherwise there would be instability and war.

An influential book was Alfred Thayer Mahan's *The Influence of Sea Power on History* (published in 1890). In it, Mahan argued that the powerful nations of history had always been sea powers. With two coasts, the USA needed to become a major naval power and that required the acquisition of colonies as supply bases around the world. Mahan also argued for a canal connecting the Atlantic and Pacific Oceans, and emphasised the importance of the Caribbean in protecting that canal. The need for the USA to become a naval power was accepted and acted upon. By 1900, the US navy was the third largest in the world – after Britain and Germany. Clearly, the United States was increasingly seeing itself as a world power.

Arguments against imperialism

Although the voices in support of imperialism were getting louder in the 19th century, there was also a vocal and important minority arguing against it. In 1898, this minority formed the Anti-Imperialist League. Among its members were the writer Mark Twain, the steel magnate Andrew Carnegie and the lawyer and politician William Jennings Bryan.

As the historian Anders Stephanson points out, in *Manifest Destiny* (1995), the anti-imperialists had a range of arguments to counter the calls for expansion. When others talked of America's mission to civilise alien races, they pointed out that the USA did not have a record of treating its own minorities, such as African and Native Americans, particularly well. They argued that there were no massive new markets in Asia, that expansion would lead to further entanglements, possibly war, and that, unlike Britain, the USA had neither the manpower nor expertise to run an empire. They were, on the whole, correct. From a moral standpoint, the anti-imperialists argued that trying to dress up expansion as some kind of modification of 'Manifest Destiny' was deceitful and that it was nothing more than European-style imperialism. Far from enhancing America's position in the world it could weaken it because by acting like the other Great Powers the USA would lose its unique role as a powerful, democratic nation that respected the freedom of others. Above all, the anti-imperialists condemned those who forgot America's past: how could a colony that had fought a war for its freedom now enslave others?

Although the anti-imperialist movement had powerful friends and many supporters, it was moving against the tide of the era. Ultimately, it failed to prevent successive American administrations from building what was, in effect, an American empire.

The beginnings of expansion

European interference in the American continent had been condemned as far back as 1823 by the **Monroe Doctrine**, so when the British government fell into a border dispute with Venezuela over British Guiana in 1895, the Americans stepped in. The Americans urged **arbitration** of the dispute, which was accepted eventually and the matter settled. But Congress had granted President Cleveland the authority to use force if necessary. America had little direct interest in the dispute but it showed a renewed willingness to assert its authority on the continent.

Likewise in the Pacific, the Unites States found itself taking on a more active role as islands across the Ocean were viewed as vital links in maintaining and developing trade in Asia. For example, in 1889 a **joint protectorate** was established with Britain and Germany over the Samoan Islands.

The Hawaiian Islands had long been a destination for American missionaries and planters, and in 1887 the USA was granted exclusive use of Pearl Harbor (see map on page 178). In 1890, the island's right to export duty free sugar into the USA was abolished, leading to a fall in demand and a collapse of prices by 40 per cent. The Hawaiians and the plantation owners worried for their livelihoods and anti-foreign sentiment grew, led by the islands' Queen Liliuokalani. In 1893, American settlers and US marines toppled Queen Liliuokalani and set up a pro-American government, which requested annexation by the USA. President Cleveland was reluctant to do this, but in 1898 McKinley granted the request. This began a process which would culminate in Hawaii being granted full statehood in 1959.

It was clear that, in this decade, American attitudes to empire were changing significantly. The war with Spain was to see the United States taking on colonies in the Philippines and establishing what was, in effect, a colonial relationship with Cuba.

Monroe Doctrine: Statement made by President James Monroe in 1823 that the continent of America was independent and the European powers could not consider re-colonising it. An attack on these independent states could be viewed as an attack on the USA.

Arbitration: The judging of a dispute between nations or states by someone not involved, whose decision both sides agree to accept.

Joint protectorate: Where stronger nations agree to share the protection of a smaller, less powerful nation. This is usually done to keep out a rival power, rather than benefit the under-developed nation being 'looked after'.

1. What were the arguments for and against an American Empire in the period 1890–1896?

2. How far was American expansion in the period 1890–1896 governed by economic factors?

6.2 Why did the USA go to war with Spain in 1898?
A CASE STUDY IN HISTORICAL INTERPRETATION

Since 1492 when Columbus found the New World, large parts of America and the Caribbean had been settled by Spain. Between 1811 and 1830, the majority of Spanish colonies in South America had gained their independence, and the Cubans wanted theirs. Revolts against the Spanish broke out in 1868 and 1879; the third attempt, in 1895, was to be ultimately successful.

The revolt against Spanish rule began in 1895. In December, the Spanish dispatched 98,400 troops to crush the rebellion, joining the 63,000 already on the island. Although they were outnumbered, the rebels had many successes with the support of the ordinary people and by 1897 were declaring their independence. Initially, the Americans seemed keen to keep out of the conflict, but in February 1898 with the sinking of the 'Maine' they entered the war. Why did the Americans go to war? Was it the sinking of the 'Maine' or, as many claim, had the United States intended all along to replace Spanish control of Cuba with its own? In one sense, the Americans were simply putting the Monroe Doctrine into action and showing support for a fellow nation trying to win its freedom from a ruling kingdom thousands of miles away – just as they themselves had done a century before. But there were more complex motives for their action. Cuba roused the feelings of the nation and it had both strategic and economic importance to the USA.

'Yellow press': Style of journalism that was deliberately sensationalist so as to attract a mass readership.

When the war broke out, it was closely followed in the American press, notably the so-called '**yellow press**' of William Randolph Hearst and Joseph Pulitzer. These two men were locked in a circulation war over their respective newspapers, the 'New York Journal' and 'New York World'. They competed to tell the most sensational stories from the war, some of which were clearly untrue but all of which were ferociously anti-Spanish. Hearst's stories, in particular of the concentration camps of the 'butcher' General Weyler where as many as 200,000 died, provoked the Americans. In fact, there were atrocities on both sides, but the American people were genuinely outraged by the way the Spanish treated their rebel prisoners and the Cuban people. The historian Maldwyn Jones, in *The Limits of Liberty* (1995), sees this as an important factor and states that '[the] conflict was as much the product of idealism as a desire to assert American power'.

What ultimately pushed America into joining the war was the explosion in Havana harbour, in February 1898, which blew up and sank the 'USS Maine', killing 260 American sailors. Hearst immediately blamed Spain and urged the government into war with the battlecry 'Remember the Maine'. Investigations at the time blamed mines for sinking the ship, most probably laid by the Spanish. An investigation, in the 1970s, claimed that the explosion was most likely the result of sparks igniting ammunition in the hold and that it was simply an accident. Whatever the cause of the explosion, the effect was to push the United States towards war with Spain. Even then, McKinley took until 11 April to get approval from Congress to send troops to expel the Spaniards. He hoped for a negotiated settlement, but was unable to get Spain to agree to acceptable terms. McKinley didn't want war but knew the mood of the people was for intervention. The anti-Spanish hysteria had not been helped by the publication of a letter from the Spanish Ambassador in Washington, Dupuy de Lôme, criticising the President. In the end, with public opinion as it was and with the deaths of the sailors, McKinley had little choice but to declare war.

Congress debated Cuba for over a week. The anti-imperialists were

Teller Amendment: On 18 April 1898 a resolution for war with Spain was passed by Congress. This amendment to the resolution was intended to show that the USA had no desire to take over Cuba.

concerned to show that the USA had no intention of throwing the Spanish out and of taking over Cuba themselves. The **Teller Amendment** made this clear by stating that the United States believed that 'the people of the island of Cuba are, and of right ought to be, free and independent', and that 'the United States [rejects any] intention to exercise sovereignty, jurisdiction or control' over the island. This would seem to support Maldwyn Jones' view that the Spanish–American War was fought for noble motives. Although the Teller Amendment is good evidence of admirable intentions, the historian Louis Perez argues, in *The War of 1898* (1998), that it was passed in an atmosphere of pro-Cuban hysteria and masked America's real intention which was to take over the island.

Long before 1898, the Americans had shown an interest in acquiring Cuba. As early as 1854, they had offered to buy the island from Spain for $130 million. In 1881, the US Secretary of Defence, James G. Blaine wrote that 'If ever ceasing to be Spanish, Cuba must necessarily become part of America'. And in 1897, J.C. Breckenridge, Under-Secretary of War, wrote of Cuba: 'our policy must be to support the weaker against the stronger, until we have obtained the extermination of them both, in order to annex the Pearl of the Antilles [Cuba]'.

Cuba's strategic and economic position made it attractive to America. It controlled the Gulf of Mexico, the Caribbean and from there trade with South America. Also, if the Panama Canal were to be built, which seemed imminent in 1898, this would only increase Cuba's strategic importance. There were even those who argued that 'Manifest Destiny' extended to Cuba: just over 200 kilometres from the American coast it clearly should form part of the USA. The United States had $50 million invested in Cuba, primarily in sugar and tobacco, and 86 per cent of all Cuban exports went to the USA. If the Cubans were to become independent, this could damage American property and trade, whereas a Cuba under US control would create more markets and opportunities for American business. Blaine had talked about Cuba being 'part of the American commercial system'. It may be that it was the sinking of the 'Maine' which was the reason for war, or that the Americans genuinely wanted to help the Cuban people. Clearly, other motives also played their part, and the fact that America did take control of Cuba after the war would indicate that these factors were important.

How useful is this 1898 cartoon in explaining the causes of the Spanish–American War?

THE BIG TYPE WAR OF THE YELLOW KIDS.

Why did the USA win the War so easily?

The first American attack was in May 1898 in the Philippine Islands, which were a Spanish colony in the Pacific. The American navy, led by Commodore Dewey, attacked the Spanish fleet there, sinking ten ships and killing almost 400 sailors. On 13 August, they took the capital Manila.

In Cuba, too, there was a naval engagement at Santiago Bay where almost 500 Spanish sailors died when they tried to run the American blockade of the harbour. Earlier, in June, 17,000 troops had landed on Cuba itself. There were American victories at El Caney Hill and more famously at San Juan Hill where Theodore Roosevelt's 'Rough Riders' led the charge against the Spanish guns. In July, Santiago fell and on 12 August an **armistice** was signed. The historian Hugh Brogan, in *The Pelican History of the United States of America* (1985), calls it 'a short, businesslike affair' and Secretary of State John Hay called it 'a splendid little war'. But the United States had entered the war with Spain completely unprepared. The army at the time consisted of only 28,000 men and was dependent on local organisation, rather than on the federal government, for supplies and equipment. Needless to say, these were frequently inadequate. The United States lost 379 men in the fighting (100 of those at San Juan Hill) but lost another 5,000 to disease. It was as much due to luck and to the weariness of the Spanish that they won.

Under the Treaty of Paris, the USA acquired the Philippines, Guam and Puerto Rico. Cuba was recognised as independent, but American troops stayed on the island for another four years and an American 'governor' was put in charge. The justification was that Cuba needed help with establishing stability after the war, and with writing its constitution. As a nation that had been through a similar process of fighting for independence and setting up a new state with a new constitution, American advice might have been helpful.

Armistice: Agreement between countries who are at war with one another to stop fighting for a time and to discuss ways of making a peaceful settlement.

What does this map show about the important role played by the navy in winning the war?

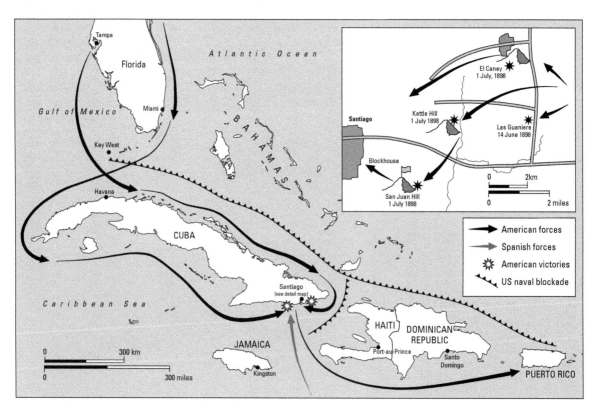

The Spanish–American War in Cuba, 1898

The real reason, suggested by the Platt Amendment 1901, was to maintain some element of control over Cuba. This amendment to the Cuban constitution gave the United States the right to intervene to maintain the independence and stability of Cuba, and it asserted that Cuba could not make treaties that would impair that independence. It was America who would decide what did and did not impair Cuban independence. The constitution also granted the USA the right to maintain a base at Guantánamo Bay. American troops were withdrawn from the island in 1902 and a new government was set up and run by Cubans. America had, and indeed still has, the base at Guantánamo, and US companies continued to dominate the Cuban economy until the revolution led by Fidel Castro in 1958. Clearly, whether or not the USA had fought the war to guarantee Cuban freedom from Spain, the Treaty of Paris gave America a large say in Cuban affairs.

1. How did the USA defeat the Spanish in Cuba?

2. Why, and how far, do historians differ in their explanations of American reasons for going to war with Spain in 1898?

6.3 How successful was Theodore Roosevelt's foreign policy?

When President McKinley was shot in 1901, his Vice-President, Theodore Roosevelt (TR), became the youngest president of the United States. At only 42, he already had a long record in public office. He was Assistant Secretary of the Navy when the Spanish–American War broke out and he resigned his post to join the cavalry, being nominated for the Congressional Medal of Honour for the Battle at San Juan Hill. It was Theodore Roosevelt who finally seemed to move America onto the world stage to take its place as one of the Great Powers.

'Teddy' Roosevelt served as President from 1901 to 1909, being elected in his own right in 1904. His Administration was marked by an era of progressive reform (see Chapter 5). To an extent this concern for domestic reform meant that the public and Congress would not always support his actions. It also meant that he was left to get on with the business of running foreign affairs very much in his own way. His skill in international relations is frequently contrasted with Woodrow Wilson's. Where Wilson was naïve, TR understood when to threaten force and when to act behind the scenes; where Wilson believed in self-determination and the rights of all nations, TR believed the world was divided into the civilised and the barbaric. It was the duty of the civilised, Christian nations – such as the USA – to help those countries that were backward and lawless, even if that meant using force. This view of the world as two halves also had a racial component since the civilised nations were, on the whole, white, western and Christian. The Japanese, as an orderly and industrial nation, were also included in TR's definition of 'civilised'. Roosevelt hoped that the Japanese would exert an orderly influence in the eastern hemisphere as America did in the western hemisphere.

TR also believed that an active foreign policy would be good for the nation. Like many men of his time, he worried about the lazy nature of modern society. He saw virtue in the hardship of struggle and war. Of his own experiences in Cuba, he said: 'It makes me feel as though I could now leave something to my children which will serve as an apology for my having existed.' With these views it was likely that Theodore Roosevelt would pursue an active foreign policy.

The Panama Canal

As Alfred Thayer Mahan pointed out in *The Influence of Sea Power on History* (1890), the USA was unusual among the Great Powers in being both a Pacific and Atlantic power. As a result of the Spanish–American

War, the United States became a Caribbean power with its temporary acquisition of Cuba. This brought the long-discussed plans for a canal through the Isthmus of Panama much higher up the political agenda.

Ferdinand de Lesseps, the man who built the Suez Canal, had obtained a lease on Panama from the Colombian government but had gone bankrupt trying to get the canal built. In 1889, he offered the canal project to the American government for $109 million, but was refused, partly because the price was too high and partly because the British had an equal interest in the area under a treaty of 1850. Both of these problems were overcome. The Hay–Paunceforte Treaty of 1901 gave the Americans exclusive control over the proposed area and, when de Lesseps lowered his price to $40 million, the agreement went forward. A 99-year lease was agreed with the Colombian government in 1903, but the Colombians then delayed, wanting to negotiate new terms once the agreement made with de Lesseps ran out the following year. The American government was not prepared to wait and so end up with less favourable terms. In November, a Panamanian revolution broke out against Colombian rule. In fact, the 'revolution' had been organised by an employee of the Canal Company, Philippe Bunau-Varilla, helped and supported by the Americans. Roosevelt sent the cruiser 'Nashville' to prevent the Colombians from re-taking control of Panama. The Americans recognised the rebel government and then negotiated with them for control of a strip, 10 miles wide, across the Isthmus of Panama. The USA was granted

What does this map show about the strategic importance of the Panama Canal?

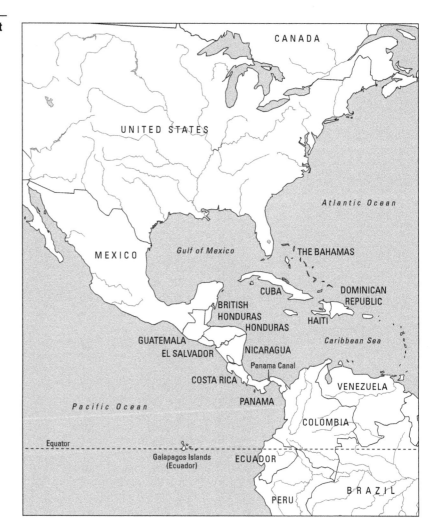

The Panama Canal

control of the Canal Zone forever for the price of $10 million and $1/4 million rent per year. Work began in 1907 and, in 1914, the Canal opened to traffic.

Roosevelt boasted that he had taken the Canal Zone while Congress talked. There was much support for his methods within the United States, since there had been previous attempts by Panamanians to gain their independence from Colombia. In Latin America, however, the methods he had used caused dismay and much mistrust. This was not to be the last time that the United States would encourage trouble in Latin America for its own ends.

Theodore Roosevelt acted decisively in foreign affairs. Under the Constitution, the President has control of foreign policy, but McKinley had ensured that he had congressional approval before going to war with Spain. Roosevelt acted much more on his own initiative. He acquired the Panama Canal for the United States without much reference to Congress. As America's role in the world grew, so did the importance of foreign policy: and as the President controls foreign policy this meant a growth in the power of the presidential office.

The Roosevelt Corollary

With the USA now having a much greater interest in Latin American affairs through its possessions in Cuba and Panama, Roosevelt felt that its right to intervene in order to maintain stability in the area and to protect US interests must be upheld. The crisis came in 1902 when the government of Venezuela defaulted on debts to Europe. A combined fleet from Britain, Germany and Italy blockaded the Venezuelan coast. The USA feared that the Europeans would use this excuse to take bases or to land in the area – a fear heightened when the Germans began to bombard Venezuelan ports. Any attempt by the Europeans to establish themselves in Latin America would be a clear violation of the Monroe Doctrine. But TR went further and issued an amendment to the Doctrine, which became known as the 'Roosevelt Corollary'.

In the Roosevelt Corollary he stated that to preserve order the United States had the right to intervene in the affairs of other countries on the continent in cases of 'chronic wrongdoing or impotence'. What exactly constituted 'wrongdoing' was for the Americans to decide. It was used to justify their taking over the finances of the Dominican Republic in 1905, when it defaulted on its debt. 'Wrongdoing' was also used to explain military intervention some years later, in Nicaragua in 1912 and Haiti in 1918.

Far from being an isolationist power, America was now declaring to the world that the Western Hemisphere was its sphere of influence. Yet it would be misleading to equate this simply with European empire-building. It cannot be denied that the United States was interfering in the internal affairs of sovereign nations for its own ends, but Roosevelt thought it was crucial to maintain stability in Latin America. If some level of stability were not maintained, the European powers themselves might seek to interfere. Although US marines remained in the Dominican Republic until 1924, and in Nicaragua and Haiti for a further decade, when they left it was because the American government withdrew them. In many of Europe's colonies, imperial forces were only withdrawn after long and bloody fights for independence. Although the USA might interfere, TR had successfully preserved Latin American independence from Europe, and in several cases American involvement did improve financial stability.

Japan

Under President Roosevelt, American interest and involvement in the Far East continued to grow. The Russo–Japanese War of 1904–05, it was feared, would create instability in the area. But the swiftness and ease of the Japanese victory, rather than calming American fears, increased them as they saw the balance of power in the Far East shifting in Japan's favour. Roosevelt worked hard to bring the two powers together to establish peace. Under the Treaty of Portsmouth in 1905, Japan gained Korea, South Sakhalin and the southern part of Manchuria. In spite of Roosevelt gaining the Nobel Peace Prize for his mediation of the treaty, Japanese–American relations worsened. America feared the growth in Japanese power in the Far East, while Japan resented American racism as schools in San Francisco proposed to **segregate** Japanese children.

Segregate: To keep apart usually because of race, sex or religion. In this instance, Japanese students in schools in San Francisco were deliberately separated from other children because of their ethnic origins.

To ease relations, Roosevelt got the school boards to back down. Then, in 1907, he sent the 'Great White Fleet' on a tour of Pacific ports to underline America's interest in the area. The fleet received an invitation and friendly welcome to Japan. This was followed by the 1908 Root–Takahira Agreement recognising the status quo in the Far East and Pacific. The potential breakdown had been averted but its signs for the future were ominous. Japanese power in the Pacific was growing and its own needs for new markets were pushing it to expand, while at the same time America's needs drew it into a more active world role and expansion in the Far East. With the defeat of Russia and the decay of China, there was little to check Japanese ambitions. The foundations for Pearl Harbor were being laid. In the short term, TR had vastly improved relations in the area and, in his own words, performed 'an important service … to peace.'

'In office Roosevelt actually performed on the whole with consummate skill and prudence in the foreign arena,' wrote Anders Stephanson in *Manifest Destiny* (1995). Roosevelt had expanded American power considerably in Latin America, through the Roosevelt Corollary and through the building of the Panama Canal. He had helped bring peace to the Far East, and through the two-year voyage of the 'Great White Fleet' he had signalled America's power and presence to the world. Most of this had been achieved through diplomacy. Though he was not averse to threatening force when necessary, TR largely kept America out of conflict. If his aim had been to increase the influence and role of the Americans in world affairs, he had undoubtedly been successful.

1. What was the purpose of the 'Great White Fleet' voyage?

2. How far would you agree that in foreign policy Theodore Roosevelt performed with 'skill and prudence'?

6.4 How far had an 'American Empire' been created by 1917?

Both before and after Theodore Roosevelt, American power in the world had been expanding. Under McKinley, Taft and Wilson, the involvement of the United States in world affairs grew. Their methods and motives might have differed, but the effect was the same. By 1917, the USA had interests around the globe.

Why did the USA get more involved in China?

American politicians and businessmen alike eyed China with avarice. With 3.5 billion square miles and a population three times the size of the USA, the potential markets for American trade were huge. The crumbling political system within China had allowed the European powers to dominate China's politics, and successive American administrations feared that they might be squeezed out. To prevent this, McKinley's Secretary of State, John Hay, sent a note to the European capitals asking for an **'open door'** policy with regard to trade in China. In fact, the European powers virtually ignored the letter, but Hay announced that they had accepted it. The historian Alan Brinkley, in *The Unfinished Nation* (1993), points out how the

'Open door': The idea that all nations should have free and equal access to trade with China.

USA was building an informal empire rather than directly colonising areas, as Europe had done. America used its economic power to extend its influence not its military might. The rivalries between the Europeans themselves meant they could not make any attempt to prevent American penetration into Chinese affairs.

However, foreign involvement led to military involvement. In June 1899, the Society of the Harmonious Righteous Fists (often referred to as 'Boxers' by western journalists) began a revolt against foreign domination of China. They murdered several hundred Europeans and Chinese who had converted to Christianity. By 1899, they had surrounded the diplomatic residential section of Peking. A year later, a multi-national force was sent to crush this so-called 'Boxer Rebellion' and the USA contributed 2,500 troops. When the revolt was over, Hay once again committed America to the open door policy in China. The other powers now accepted this and the area was kept open to American trade.

The importance of free trade to American expansion and influence in the world can be seen running from the open door policy through Wilson's Fourteen Points (see page 185) and even to the anti-globalisation protests against McDonald's in the 1990s. In fact, under William Taft the idea of using American financial and economic power as a way of gaining influence became overt and was known as 'dollar diplomacy'. Railway workers and bankers, for example, were encouraged to invest in areas like Manchuria and Latin America. US external investment increased sevenfold between 1860 and 1914.

The Philippines, 1898–1901

Emilio Aguinaldo (1869–1964)
Politician and soldier. Fought against the Spanish in 1896 and then led the fight for Philippine independence against the USA.

Further eastwards, as a result of the Spanish–American War, the USA had also gained the Philippines. It was initially seen as a stepping stone to the Far East, but quickly became a liability. Having had no say in their transfer from Spanish to American control, the Filipinos revolted demanding independence. They were led by Emilio Aguinaldo. It took three years and 70,000 soldiers to crush the rebellion and to capture Aguinaldo. Some 4,300 Americans died and the American treatment of their 'little brown brothers' was no better than the treatment the Spanish had handed out to the Cubans, and which had been so widely condemned in the United States. In many ways, the frustration of the soldiers fighting a **guerrilla war** so far from home, leading to anger, frustration and subsequent atrocities, more resembles Vietnam than Cuba. There were killings of prisoners-of-war (POWs), executions and destruction of crops. It is estimated between 20,000 and 50,000 Filipinos died in the three-year war. Although the Filipinos often refer to their colonial past as '200 years in a convent followed by 50 years in a whorehouse', American rule brought significant improvements with the building of schools, hospitals, roads, sewage systems etc. An American governor-general governed the islands, but there was also an elected assembly and the promise of self-rule. There was never the support for annexation, either within the islands or in the USA, that there was in Cuba or Hawaii. Independence was eventually gained shortly after the end of the Second World War.

Guerrilla war: A plan of campaign fought against a regular army by small bands of armed men and women.

Mexico

Woodrow Wilson was very critical of policies such as 'dollar diplomacy' and the interference of the United States in other countries, yet he too sent American troops into Latin America. It was Wilson who sent the marines into Haiti and increased control over the Dominican Republic, and in Mexico he involved the USA in a civil war.

Francisco Indalecio Madero (1873–1913)
Revolutionary and reformer. Overthrew the government of President Díaz. Madero was President of Mexico from 1911.

Victoriano Huerta (1854–1916)
Military and political leader. Toppled Madero's government but was forced from office because of his oppressive rule.

Venustiano Carranza (1859–1920)
Politician and rival of Huerta. President of Mexico, 1914–1920. Introduced new constitution in 1917.

Constitutionalist: Person who organises or governs a country according to a constitution.

Francisco 'Pancho' Villa (1877–1923)
Mexican revolutionary. The son of a peasant, he became a military commander in the 1910 revolution. His actions brought American involvement in Mexico, but after their withdrawal he continued to oppose Carranza until 1920. Villa was assassinated in 1923.

How far could the USA, by 1914, be regarded as a Pacific power?

In 1913, the government of Francisco Madero was toppled by Victoriano Huerta and Madero was murdered. Wilson referred to Huerta's men as 'butchers' and refused to recognise them. Instead, he sent arms and support to **constitutionalist** rebels led by Venustiano Carranza. Seven thousand soldiers were sent to the port of Vera Cruz to prevent Huerta getting his own arms supplies from the Germans. The tactic appeared to have been successful. Huerta's government fell and Carranza took power.

Yet Woodrow Wilson's support for Carranza had been half-hearted. At the same time, the Americans had been hinting that they would support the soldiers led by the nationalist 'Pancho' Villa. When the Americans recognised the Carranza government, Villa was furious and launched two raids over the border killing 35 American citizens. Thousands of US soldiers were sent to hunt him down, unsuccessfully. But the danger of America getting bogged down in the confused and violent politics of

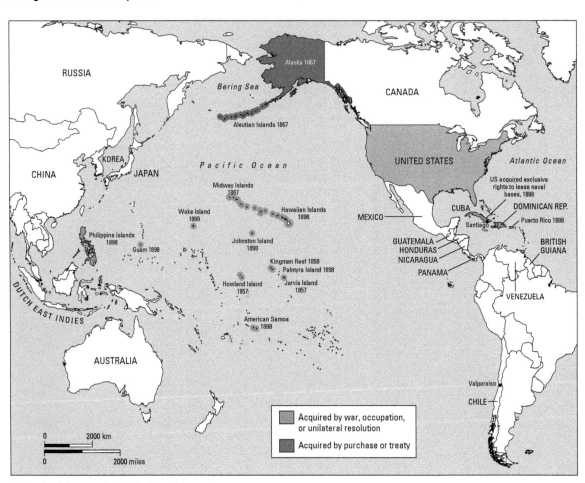

US territorial expansion in the late 19th century

Mexico was clear. With the war in Europe increasingly taking his attention, Wilson negotiated with Carranza. A new constitution was issued and American troops withdrew.

As several writers show, for all he said about self-determination Wilson was as prepared as Roosevelt or McKinley to use troops to protect what he believed to be America's interests. He might disapprove of the Roosevelt Corollary but when American security or business interests, or even his own views on what constituted a democratic government, demanded it he acted in accordance with its principles.

From the Philippines to Mexico, it is clear that in the two decades before the First World War America had changed its attitude to the outside world. It had gained possessions in Hawaii, Guam, the Philippines, Samoa, the Virgin Islands, Puerto Rico and several other Pacific islands, and had been directly involved in the affairs of Cuba, Mexico, China, Nicaragua, Haiti and several other Latin American countries. Yet the United States could not be said to be an imperial power in the way that Britain or France was. There was no colonial office set up at home, no civil service trained to run the 'colonies', no attempt to make their new possessions part of an American Empire ruled by Washington. Americans were still suspicious of colonialism and while there was support for a more active foreign policy, there was also a strong desire for the USA simply to look after its own economic and strategic interests and not become involved in empire-building. Yet there is a contradiction here. Looking after American interests required involvement in foreign affairs, and though America did not control vast areas of the world like Britain, it did take over some areas as its own, such as Hawaii. It also used its economic power to control the affairs of other areas, such as Cuba. America's colonial past, and its desire to play a part in the world fitting its status, meant that its attitude towards empire was contradictory. This contradiction can be seen in American foreign policy through both world wars and into the Cold War and beyond.

1. Why was influence in China considered important?

2. How far was American expansion between 1896 and 1914 a result of the Spanish–American war?

6.5 Why did the USA become involved in the First World War?

In August 1914, war broke out in Europe between Britain, France and Russia on one side, and Germany and Austria-Hungary on the other. Over the next three years the war spread, dragging in many of the other European nations. Even the Japanese joined the war, on 23 August 1914. The war would last four years and cost the lives of 18 million people.

The eight million Americans of German descent were sympathetic to the so-called Central Powers. Irish-Americans were also sympathetic due to their resentment of British rule in Ireland, as were many Jews and Poles who had fled to America to escape Russian persecution. But support for the Allies was stronger. Ties of language, culture and history meant that the majority of Americans supported Britain. There was also a long friendship with France going back to the War of Independence. With the exception of autocratic Russia, the Allied Powers were seen as the decent and democratic nations defending Europe from the unprovoked aggression of the **militaristic** Germans. This attitude was encouraged by very effective British propaganda which emphasised German 'atrocities', particularly against the defenceless Belgians.

Militaristic: Aggressive, heavily relying on military force.

There were some in America who thought that the United States should take part in the War. Ex-president Theodore Roosevelt thought staying out was cowardly. Others, including some in the Administration, felt that America needed to be prepared to defend democracy. They formed groups such as the National Security League. President Wilson himself was appalled by the German attack on neutral Belgium. However, he felt, as the vast majority of Americans did, that the war was a European affair and they did not want to be dragged into it. Wilson urged the people to be neutral in thought and deed, to show by example that Americans were somehow 'better', that there were other ways to resolve issues. The American public might be sympathetic to the Allied cause, but it was not their fight and, above all, they wanted to keep out of it.

Being neutral, however, proved more difficult than the Americans had imagined. They had an economic involvement in the War long before their military involvement. The First World War created a boom in American industry and agriculture with sales of goods and supplies to both sides. Money was loaned to enable the Europeans to pay for the goods they bought. By 1917, the USA had loaned over $2 billion to the Allies and $27 million to the Germans. Understandably, the Germans complained that this was hardly neutrality, but even before the War the United States had done a great deal more trade with Britain than with Germany. This led some to believe that America got involved in the war for financial reasons. Clearly, an Allied victory was preferable in order to protect American investment and it was probably a contributory factor to the decision to enter the War in 1917. Public opinion and American security also favoured an Allied victory and may have affected the Senate's decision. But it was the war at sea that was the ultimate cause of US entry into the First World War.

Early on in the war, Britain had used its naval strength to blockade the German coast and to stop and search vessels believed to be taking goods to the Central Powers. Some shipping lanes were also mined. America protested when its own ships were stopped or goods seized, but for Britain the blockade was an effective weapon. By 1915, the blockade was already causing shortages in Germany.

The Germans responded with submarine warfare to try and sink British ships and starve Britain into surrender. In February 1915, they announced that Allied ships would be sunk without warning. Though this made sense militarily, it went against accepted 'rules' of warfare. In the USA, it was seen as barbaric and as an infringement of the freedom of the seas. The American government protested. Some proposed banning US citizens from travelling on Allied vessels, but Wilson felt that this limited American freedoms. Then, on 7 May, the Germans sank the British passenger liner the 'Lusitania'. Of the 1,200 who died on the ship, 128 were Americans. In fact, the ship had been carrying ammunition. The Germans knew that Britain used liners for that purpose and saw the ship as a fair target, but public opinion in America was incensed. When two more Americans were killed on the 'Arabic' in August, the Germans seemed to back off in the face of American anger. In 1916, more Americans were hurt when the 'Sussex' was sunk. Wilson made it clear to Germany that if they continued to endanger American lives there would be serious consequences. The Germans were anxious to keep the Americans out of the War and they abandoned the U-boat (German submarine) campaign.

The crisis seemed to have been averted and Wilson went to the polls in 1916 on the slogan of having kept America out of the war. He won by a narrow victory of 277 electoral college votes to 254. Throughout 1916, Wilson had worked to avoid war. He proposed a peace conference to Edward Grey, the British Foreign Secretary, indicating that, if the Allies accepted the conference and the Germans did not, the USA might join the war against Germany. It came to nothing, as neither side really believed America would join. It is doubtful if Wilson could have carried Congress with him had he proposed it seriously. He knew that the public still did not want war.

Wilson also realised that, should war come, America needed to be more prepared than it was. He asked Congress for an increased army and navy. The army was increased to over 200,000 men and the National Guard to 400,000. (Just how unprepared America was is illustrated by the fact that General Haig was able to field 200,000 British soldiers at the Battle of the Somme alone.) A massive naval building programme was also embarked on which would soon see the American navy as one of the two most powerful in the world. This build-up caused criticism, with accusations that Wilson was getting America ready to join the War. Wilson did not want war, but as President, and Commander-in-Chief, he knew that he had to be ready if it came.

By the 'turnip winter' of 1916–1917, Germans were suffering severe hardship and hunger due to the British blockade. In January, in an effort to end the war, they announced the resumption of unrestricted U-boat warfare. After the agreement over the 'Sussex', the Germans knew they were risking bringing the United States into the conflict, but they felt they had to take the risk. They gambled that the Americans might not fight, or that if they did it would take too long for them to mobilise, by which time the Germans would have won. In both of these, they were wrong.

Although the January announcement led to a break in diplomatic relations, Congress was not yet ready to declare war. They even refused Wilson's request to have American merchant ships armed. Two events strengthened Wilson's hand. Firstly, the February Revolution in Russia ended the **autocracy** and brought in a Provisional Government promising democratic reforms. This meant that the Allied cause could now be seen as thoroughly democratic. Secondly, the British presented the Americans with a copy of the 'Zimmerman Telegram'. The British had intercepted the telegram from the German Foreign Minister, Arthur Zimmerman, to the German ambassador in Mexico. It suggested to the Mexican government that if they joined the war against the USA, Germany would ensure that in the end they got back New Mexico, Texas and Arizona, which they had lost to America in the 1840s. This was a violation of the Monroe Doctrine and put America and Germany on a collision course. The further loss of American lives at sea, in February and March of 1917, finally turned public opinion. Although there were a few Mid-Western Congressmen and Senators who held out, when Wilson asked Congress for a declaration of war in April it was granted by 82–6 votes in the Senate and 373–50 in the House of Representatives. He promised to make the world 'safe for democracy', and on 6 April the United States declared war on Germany.

Autocracy: Political system in which the ruler has total power and is answerable to no one.

1. In what ways did the United States have an interest in the outcome of the First World War before 1917?

2. 'It was the U-boat campaign of 1917 which brought America into the First World War.' How far would you agree with this view?

6.6 How successful was Wilson's foreign policy 1917–1919?

America and the First World War

When America declared war, it was expected that its contribution would be primarily economic, but by 1917 the Allied forces were exhausted and their economies in collapse. In the first few months of the year, almost two million tons of shipping had been lost, 340,000 British soldiers had been killed or wounded in the mud of Passchendaele and the French Army was in mutiny. Americans had not been prepared by Wilson for the necessity of sending their young men to fight in Europe, but American troops were vital to the war effort.

The Selective Services Act introduced conscription in May 1917. Initially, men aged 21–30 were called up, though this was later extended to men aged 18–45. During the course of the War, 3.5 million men were drafted, with an additional 1.5 million who volunteered, including

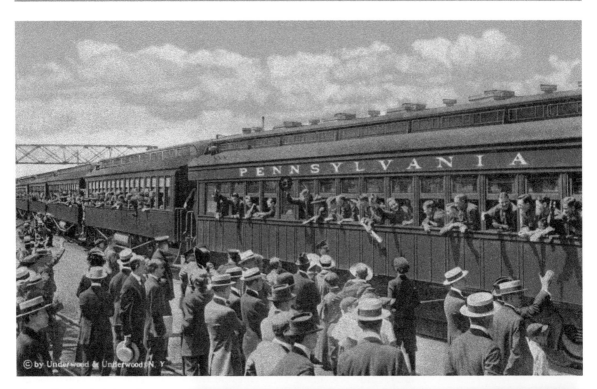

Above: Postcard of departing troops, 1917.

Right: Red Cross workers bring gifts to soldiers leaving for World War I at a railroad station.

Do these pictures tell us anything about attitudes to the War?

260,000 African-Americans. Over half of these men eventually served on the Western Front, and over 100,000 would give their lives to the War.

Training and equipping these men took time and, by March 1918, only 84,000 American soldiers had arrived in Europe. When they arrived in Europe the American soldiers wore British helmets, as America was not producing its own. A War Industries Board was set up to organise supplies and raw materials. Wilson put financier Bernard Baruch in charge, and although there continued to be many inefficiencies and mistakes it was soon supplying the needs of the military. It taught a useful lesson, for those

General John Joseph Pershing (1860–1948)
American army officer. Commanded soldiers in the Mexican War and led American Expeditionary Force in the First World War.

Vladimir Illyich Ulyanov, 'Lenin' (1870–1924)
Russian revolutionary and leader of the Bolshevik or Communist Party. Along with Leon Trotsky, he organised the communist seizure of power in November 1917. He was leader of Russia until his death in 1924.

Ferdinand Foch (1851–1929)
French soldier and Chief of the General Staff in 1917. In 1918 he was put in overall command of the Allied armies on the Western Front.

Why was the victory at Château-Thierry important?

involved the in Second World War, of the need for government control of the economy. However, it was late summer before there were significant numbers of US soldiers ready to fight, by which time they were needed to help defend Paris.

In October 1917, Lenin's Bolsheviks had carried out the second Russian Revolution. The world's first communist government was set up and it immediately condemned the War and announced its intention to back out, which it did in March 1918. This freed up a million German soldiers from the Eastern Front. General Ludendorff launched a spring offensive, hoping to take Paris before the Americans arrived in force. The gamble almost succeeded and the Germans got to within 40 miles of the French capital.

American forces were under the command of General John J. Pershing, a veteran of the Cuban and Mexican wars. As an 'Associate' power rather than an Allied power, American forces were not integrated into the Allied army under General Ferdinand Foch, but they formed an important part of his counter-offensive launched in the summer. Pershing's men halted the German advance at Château-Thierry and at Bellau Wood. By September, American soldiers were arriving in large numbers. More important, was the psychological effect they were having on both sides. Their youth, enthusiasm and the resources on which they would eventually be able to call breathed new life into the Allied cause. As for the Germans, they knew that if Ludendorff's gamble failed they had lost the War. In September, Foch launched the Argonnes Offensive. The French and Americans defeated the German army at St Mihiel, and the Germans were pushed back. The Ludendorff Offensive had failed and Paris was saved. In October, a new German government was set up under Prince Max von Baden and they asked for an armistice. The War ended on 11 November.

The Americans also contributed to the victory in other ways. When they joined the War in April 1917, Allied shipping losses for that year were

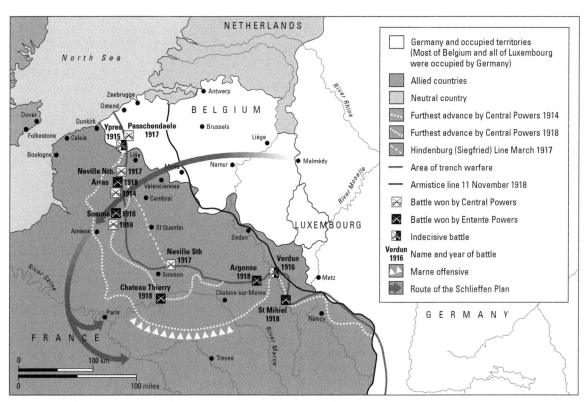

The Western Front

already two million tons. With the American navy joining the campaign against German U-boats, Allied losses fell by two-thirds by the end of the year. In addition, American shipyards embarked on a building programme which meant that they could replace any ship the Germans sank, and more. By the start of 1918, the war at sea had been won. The strength of the American economy was vital. Altogether, they had spent around $35 billion on the war, and their supplies and loans to the Europeans between 1914 and 1917 had been crucial in enabling the Allies to maintain the fight. The Americans may only have been in the First World War for 19 months and their losses may have been low, compared to those of the other powers, but their contribution to victory was as important as that of any of the Allies.

Peacemaking and the Treaty of Versailles

When the Germans asked for peace it was to the Americans that they went, not the British or French. They believed that the Americans would be more lenient. This belief was partly due to the fact that the Americans had not been fighting for so long nor on their own territory, as the French had. They also understood that Wilson's Fourteen Points (see opposite) would form the basis of the peace treaty. In all, there were five treaties with each of the Central Powers which made up the Versailles Settlement of 1919, but by far the most important was the Treaty of Versailles itself with the Germans. The Treaty is generally considered to have been a failure, given that war broke out again between its signatories just 20 years later. Woodrow Wilson is given much of the blame for this failure.

President Wilson was an academic, a history professor who moved into politics in his 40s. He was very bright and, like many presidents, had a great interest in foreign policy, as it is one area of American Government over which the Administration had undoubted control. Wilson believed in America's role as an influence for good in the world. Its power would spread the ideals of liberalism, democracy and capitalism. He was a deeply religious man and is frequently referred to as an idealist. He was an idealist in that he believed in the good in people and had a desire to improve the world, but he was not a fool and he was not weak. His willingness to send troops into Mexico, as well as his support for the Allies in the first three years of the War, showed an understanding of the necessity of force in politics. Like Roosevelt, he used the power of his office to full effect.

Even before US entry into the War, Wilson had a desire to influence the peace. For example, his insistence that American citizens be allowed to travel freely in spite of the dangers from German submarines illustrates one of his foreign policy goals, freedom of the seas for all. As the War was coming to a close in 1918, he outlined his aims for the post-war peace, in common with other leaders. These aims were most clearly laid out in a speech to the Senate on 8 January and became known as the 'Fourteen Points'.

The causes of the First World War are complex and widely debated, but Wilson believed that if one identified the causes of the war and removed them, this would guarantee peace for the future. For example, he believed the network of secret treaties and the arms build-up in the years preceding 1914 had created an atmosphere of mistrust, which was sparked into war by the assassination in Sarajevo. Hence, points 1 and 2 would prevent a recurrence. Likewise, the clauses on **self-determination** would address the issue of Serbian nationalism. Self-determination also embodied Wilson's own belief in democracy and in the American anti-imperialist tradition. By giving as many people as possible a say in their own future, Wilson hoped the causes of conflict would be removed.

Self-determination: The right of people to decide their own future.

In this sense, Wilson was too idealistic. The clauses on Poland illustrate the difficulty of putting things into practice. The peacemakers had to balance the ideals of self-determination with the practical issues of security and economics. Without access to the sea, Poland would be severely weakened, but giving it access meant putting a large area of German territory under Polish rule. However, the practicalities of re-drawing the map of Europe were the least of Wilson's problems. It was the ambitions and desires of the other powers that drove him to distraction and even illness.

When Wilson arrived in Paris, he was greeted as a saviour. European people were grateful for the American contribution to ending the War and believed the ideals Wilson spoke of would, as he said, 'make the world safe for democracy'. But France had fought Germany twice in the previous 40 years, and the First World War had cost them 1.4 million lives. Britain had been bankrupted by the War and had lost 900,000 men. They wanted to make Germany pay. The arguments between the 'Big Four' – Wilson, Britain's Prime Minister Lloyd George, France's Premier Georges Clemenceau and Italy's Prime Minster Orlando – were fierce. The Europeans were determined to have their territorial and reparation demands met. Some were valid and easy to accomplish, such as the return to France of Alsace-Lorraine, which had been taken by the Germans in 1871. Others, such as Italy's claims in the Adriatic, were considered too extravagant. Arguments over the issue had Orlando in tears. Compromises had to be made. Wilson could never have hoped to gain all that he set out to achieve. Whether the claims of the other Allies were just or not, the fact remains that they did have claims. Having fought the War for four years, the Allies would not let Wilson and America dictate terms to them.

However, Wilson did make many mistakes in his handling of the negotiations. He was dead set against imposing reparations on Germany, believing that this would cause resentment and future conflict. But France and Belgium insisted on reparations in order to rebuild the devastated towns and villages of the Western Front. Wilson was forced to give in and accept these demands. Had the Americans not insisted on repayment of the money they had loaned to Europe, the European nations may

---

Summary of Wilson's 'Fourteen Points'

1. Open covenants openly arrived at
2. Freedom of the seas
3. Free trade
4. Disarmament
5. Impartial adjustments of all colonial claims
6. Evacuation of Russia by the Germans and self-determination for the Russian people
7. Evacuation and restoration of Belgium
8. Return of Alsace-Lorraine to France
9. Re-adjustment of Italian frontiers based on nationality
10. Self-determination for the people of Austria-Hungary
11. Evacuation and restoration of Romania, Serbia and Montenegro
12. Self-determination for the peoples of the Turkish Empire
13. Establishment of an independent Poland with access to the sea
14. Establishment of a League of Nations (see next page) with mutual guarantees of independence and security.

Points 1 and 4 were an attempt to address the European causes of the War, and for the Americans it was Point 2. Wilson's belief in free trade was emphasised in both Points 2 and 3. Points 5–13 show how important the idea of self-determination was to the President. He felt that if the principle could be applied as widely as possible, then the causes of much conflict would be reduced. Point 14 was an attempt to bring about peace through cooperation.

How far did these men share common goals?

The 'Big Four' at Versailles – Lloyd George, Orlando, Clemenceau and Woodrow Wilson

League of Nations: Association of self-governing states created as part of 1919 Peace Treaty 'to promote international cooperation and to achieve international peace and security'. The USA did not join, and the association's failure to deal effectively with outbreaks in Japan, Italy and Germany in the 1930s meant that it had lost its relevance by the outbreak of the Second World War. It was subsequently replaced by the United Nations (see opposite).

'Round-robin': A letter signed by several people indicating agreement. No single person is seen as the author.

have been more willing to listen to him. As it was, the Reparations Commission in 1921 saddled Germany with a debt of $33 billion, which they were to pay to the Allies who in turn would use part of it to repay the Americans. The economist John Maynard Keynes resigned from the Conference in protest at the reparations issue and called Wilson 'incompetent'. Given the economic costs of the First World War, it was unlikely the Europeans would ever have agreed to a peace without some form of financial settlement.

Another mistake was Wilson's insistence on having the **League of Nations** as part of the Treaty. Building on an idea that had originated in Britain during the War, Wilson proposed an organisation of nations at which issues and problems could be talked through, instead of resorting to war. The members would also promise to protect each other in the event of an attack, thus making war less likely. This concept was known as 'collective security'. This was so important to Wilson that instead of having a separate agreement, he wanted it written into all five of the treaties. It was written into all five treaties, but it allowed the other powers to use it as a bargaining chip to have their demands met. It was also to cause problems at home.

It was in the domestic arena that Wilson made his most serious errors with regard to Versailles. Firstly, in the mid-term elections of November 1918 he made the forthcoming peace conference a party issue, hoping to give himself a strong Democratic Congress. The plan completely backfired and the Republicans gained control of both Houses. Wilson also made no real attempt to work with the Republicans to gain their support.

When he returned from Paris to present the Treaty to Congress, 39 Senators signed a letter – a **'round-robin'** – refusing to accept the Treaty as it stood. There were some objections to the Treaty itself, but the main objection was to the League of Nations and Article Ten of the Covenant (the clause on collective security). For many Americans this would involve their being dragged into Europe's wars, which were really none of their concern. Wilson made some changes but Article Ten continued to be the sticking point. In an effort to raise support in the country for the Treaty and the League, Wilson went on a speaking tour. Already ill from the stress

Ratification: Vote in the Senate giving legal recognition to a treaty. The vote must have a two-thirds majority to pass.

United Nations: Organisation formed after the Second World War. It tries to encourage international peace, cooperation and friendship.

of the Conference itself, the tour proved too much and Wilson suffered a severe stroke, which was to leave him infirm for the rest of his life. The Treaty was amended in the Foreign Relations Committee, so when it went to the Senate to be voted on Wilson insisted that the Democrats vote against it. He would not accept the Treaty with the amendments. The Treaty failed to get the necessary two-thirds majority vote for **ratification**. A peace was signed with Germany, but for all Wilson's efforts and insistence that the League of Nations be written into the treaties, the United States never joined.

Had Wilson handled the Republicans better, or been more willing to compromise, he might have got the League of Nations accepted. Undoubtedly, the absence of the United States was fatal to the League, but America's presence would no more have been a guarantee against war than its presence in the **United Nations** has been. The Treaty of Versailles had many faults:

● Self-determination set up the weak 'successor states' in Eastern Europe which would fall to the Nazis in the 1930s.

● The 'mandates' allowed powers like Britain to maintain imperialist control of areas like the Middle East, but under a different name.

● The treaty overall created a fierce resentment in Germany and a determination among all political parties to see it destroyed.

However, Wilson did achieve many of the Fourteen Points. The Treaty of Versailles was, of necessity, a compromise between the conflicting demands of the victorious powers. Most historians agree it was a bad treaty: harsh enough to create resentment but not harsh enough to prevent a resurgence of German power. Yet Wilson is not wholly to blame for this. He made mistakes, but so did Lloyd George, Clemenceau and Orlando. The collapse of the settlement was as much an outcome of the events of the 1920s as of the Treaty itself.

The Wars of Intervention

One result of the First World War had been two revolutions in Russia. November 1917 had seen the Bolsheviks take control and pull Russia out of the War. But rather than returning to peace, Russia was plunged into civil war between the Bolsheviks and their enemies. British and French troops were sent to Russia, partly to reclaim supplies they had sent to an ally who had now pulled out of the fight, but also because they supported the anti-Bolshevik cause. The Japanese also sent troops to Vladivostok. In March 1918, Wilson sent 7,000 American troops to Russia, from where they were not finally removed until 1920. They had little effect on the civil war, so why did Wilson send them?

One reason was to support his Allies. The British and French had felt betrayed by Russia's withdrawal and wanted to help defeat the Bolsheviks and possibly bring Russia back into the War. Wilson was showing his support for them by backing their efforts. There was also concern that the Japanese might use the 'Wars of Intervention' to gain territory in the East and Wilson wanted to prevent this. It may also have been, as Lenin had suggested, that the capitalist nations wished to crush Communism at birth. Whatever Wilson's motives, it led to many hundreds of American casualties for no perceptible gain to the USA. More damagingly, it left the Russians with a mistrust of the Americans that was to continue right through to the Cold War.

1. In what ways did the USA contribute to the Allied victory in the First World War?

2. How far did President Wilson achieve his aims at the Paris Peace Conference?

Source-based questions: President Wilson and the First World War

SOURCE A

The people of the United States are drawn from many nations, and chiefly from the nations now at war. It is natural and inevitable that there should be the utmost variety of sympathy and desire among them with regard to the issues and circumstances of the conflict. Some will wish one nation, others another, to succeed in the momentous struggle. It will be easy to excite passion and difficult to allay it. Those responsible for exciting it will assume a heavy responsibility, responsibility for no less a thing than that the people of the United States, whose love of their country and whose loyalty to its government should unite them as Americans all, bound in honour and affection to think first of her and her interests, may be divided in camps of hostile opinion, hot against each other, involved in the war itself in impulse and opinion if not in action. Such divisions amongst us would be fatal to our peace of mind and might seriously stand in the way of the proper performance of our duty as the one great nation at peace, the one people holding itself ready to play a part of impartial mediation and speak the counsels of peace and accommodation, not as a partisan, but as a friend.

President Wilson's Declaration of Neutrality, 19 August 1914

SOURCE B

Unless the Imperial Government should now immediately declare and effect an abandonment of its present methods of submarine warfare against passenger and freight-carrying vessels, the Government of the United States can have no choice but to sever diplomatic relations with the German Empire altogether.

President Woodrow Wilson to the German government, 19 April 1916

SOURCE C

On the first of February we intend to begin submarine warfare unrestricted. In spite of this, it is our intention to endeavour to keep neutral the United States of America.
If this attempt is not successful, we propose an alliance on the following basis with Mexico: That we shall make war together and together make peace. We shall give general financial support, and it is understood that Mexico is to re-conquer the lost territory in New Mexico, Texas and Arizona. The details are left to you for settlement.

Note from the German Foreign Minister, Zimmermann, to the German Minister to Mexico, 19 January 1917

SOURCE D

We have loaned many hundreds of millions of dollars to the Allies in this controversy. While such action was legal and countenanced by international law, there is no doubt in my mind but the enormous amount of money loaned to the Allies in this country has been instrumental in bringing about a public sentiment in favour of our country taking a course that would make every bond worth a hundred cents on the dollar and making the payment of every debt certain and sure. Through this instrumentality and also through the instrumentality of others who have not only made millions out of the war in the manufacture of munitions, etc., and who would expect to make millions more if our country can be drawn into the catastrophe, a large number of the great newspapers and news agencies of the country have been controlled and enlisted in the greatest propaganda that the world has ever known to manufacture sentiment in favour of war.

Speech by Senator George W. Norris in opposition to Wilson's War Message, 1917

SOURCE E

The committee finds, further, that the constant availability of munitions companies with competitive bribes ready in outstretched hands does not create a situation where the officials involved can, in the nature of things, be as much interested in peace and measures to secure peace as they are in increased armaments.
While the evidence before this committee does not show that wars have been started solely because of the activities of munitions makers and their agents, it is also true that wars rarely have one single cause, and the committee finds it to be against the peace of the world for selfishly interested organisations to be left free to goad* and frighten nations into military activity.

Report of the Special Committee on Investigation of the Munitions Industry (The Nye Report), 24 February 1936

*goad = provoke

Source-based questions: President Wilson and the First World War

---

1. Read Source A. What reasons does President Wilson give for the need for Americans to remain neutral in the War?

2. Read Source B. What had led President Wilson to issue this warning to Germany?

3. Read Sources D and E. What support is there in Source D for the view of the Nye Commission on the role of the arms industry in the outbreak of war?

4. How valuable are Sources D and E to a historian studying the causes of the First World War?

5. Using all the sources and your own knowledge, assess the extent to which submarine warfare led to American entry into the First World War.

Further Reading

Texts designed for AS Level students

The Enduring Vision by Paul Boyer and others
    (D.C. Heath and Co., 1993) – easy to read and well-illustrated narrative.
The USA and the World, 1917–1945 by Peter Brett (Hodder and Stoughton, 1997)
    – clear narrative with practice exercises and note-making guide.
A History of the United States of America by Hugh Brogan (Longman, Second
    edition 1999) – good introductory text.
The Limits of Liberty by Maldwyn Jones (Oxford University Press, 1995) – clear
    narrative account.

Texts for A2 and advanced study

The Unfinished Nation by Alan Brinkley (McGraw Hill, 1993) – easy to read and
    scholarly, with good maps.
The War of 1898 by Louis Perez (Chapel Hill, 1998) – a study which provides
    different historical interpretations.
US Foreign Policy in World History by David Ryan (Routledge, 2000) – analysis of
    motives behind US foreign policy.
Manifest Destiny by Anders Stephanson (Hill and Wang, 1995) – study of
    American expansion.

Useful websites

HTTP://WWW.HISTORYOFCUBA.COM – useful information and lots of documents on
    the Spanish–American War.
HTTP://WWW.THEODOREROOSEVELT.ORG – contains documents, speeches etc. as well
    as biographical detail on Theodore Roosevelt.
HTTP://WWW.AMERICANPRESIDENT.ORG – based on PBS television series; covers the
    US Presidents and US foreign policy.
HTTP://TLC.AI.ORG – contains lots of links to other sites on US foreign policy.

Index

Glossary terms

MAIN INDEX